THE POETRY OF
SAMUEL TAYLOR COLERIDGE

GARLAND REFERENCE LIBRARY
OF THE HUMANITIES
(VOL. 247)

THE POETRY OF
SAMUEL TAYLOR COLERIDGE
An Annotated Bibliography
of Criticism, 1935–1970

Mary Lee Taylor Milton

GARLAND PUBLISHING, INC. • NEW YORK & LONDON
1981

Library of Congress Cataloging in Publication Data

Milton, Mary Lee Taylor.
  The poetry of Samuel Taylor Coleridge.

  (Garland reference library of the humanities ;
v. 247)
  Includes index.
  1. Coleridge, Samuel Taylor, 1772–1834—
Bibliography.   I. Title.
Z8182.M54 [PR4483]   016.821′7   80-83650
ISBN 0-8240-9451-4

Printed on acid-free, 250-year-life paper
Manufactured in the United States of America

CONTENTS

ACKNOWLEDGMENTS

Several people and institutions have contributed to the making of this bibliography. I want them to know, once again, that I am grateful. To Jack Stillinger I am most directly indebted. He pointed out the need for a Coleridge bibliography, offered consistent, knowledgeable advice on matters of procedure, and read my work with meticulous care. Charles Shattuck and Alan Holaday also read the manuscript and suggested improvements. The University of Illinois granted me two summer fellowships. The Library's Reference Department borrowed or secured photocopies of any items not already available in the Illinois collection; and Eva Faye Benton, former head of the English Library, cheerfully volunteered information that made the mechanics of the project pleasanter and less time-consuming. Eleanor Gornto proofread my typing of the revised manuscript, and Lawrence Davidow at Garland helped me prepare it for publication.

Two owners of copyrights have given their permission to quote from copyrighted articles: the University of Iowa Press for Thomas M. Raysor's "Coleridge's Comment on the Moral of *The Ancient Mariner*," *PQ*, 31 (1952), 88–91, and the University of North Carolina Press for B.R. McElderry, Jr.'s "Coleridge's Plan for Completing *Christabel*," *SP*, 33 (1936), 437–455.

Other people have contributed indirectly, especially the inspiring teacher James W. Culp, now at Texas Technological University, who introduced me to the value of literary criticism, and my parents, Harry and Catherine Taylor, whose belief in education and in me has always lent immeasurable support.

PREFACE

The most recent list of twentieth-century Coleridge studies is that included in the bibliography compiled by Virginia Kennedy and Mary Neill Barton, published in 1935. It mentions the influential criticism of such scholars as George McLean Harper,[1] John Livingston Lowes,[2] Ada L.F. Snell,[3] Newton P. Stallknecht,[4] B.R. McElderry, Jr.,[5] and Elizabeth Nitchie.[6] But numerous discussions of Coleridge's poetry have appeared since 1935 for which no bibliographical guide is now available.

The present study makes a contribution toward the need for such a work by providing a fully annotated list of the more recent criticism. Because the quantity of Coleridge criticism is sizable and because the annotations are intended to be as detailed as possible, the list has been restricted to the period from 1935 through 1970 and to the criticism on the poetry. The 449 items are arranged chronologically, and alphabetically within each year. They have been compiled mainly from the annual bibliographies in *PMLA*, *PQ* (1935–64) and *ELN* (1965–   ), *Year's Work in English Studies*, and the Modern Humanities Research Association's *Annual Bibliography of English Language and Literature*. Inspection of the card catalogue at the University of Illinois Library and the footnotes, indexes, and bibliographies in verified items provided additional entries.

Regardless of merit, every item mentioned in these sources is included in the list, with the exception of unpublished dissertations, reviews, and studies not written in English. Essays appearing in textbooks of English literature, surveys of English Romanticism, and collections of Coleridge's poems are omitted unless they have been used or cited in the scholarly literature. Items admitted to the list include reprints with cross-references to indicate the original publication, articles or discussions in books and essays not limited to Coleridge's poetry, and studies of his influence that offer specific comments on his poetry. Thus, the bibliography includes Earl R. Wasserman's essay on the Romantics' epistemologies (item 325) and Richard Harter Fogle's book on Coleridge's criticism (item 281) because they provide explications of "This Lime-Tree Bower"; Fogle also devotes a chapter to "Christabel." Books on Coleridge's thought which do not treat the poetry specifically, such as James D. Boulger's *Coleridge as Religious Thinker*, J.A. Appleyard's *Coleridge's Philosophy of Literature*, or Thomas McFarland's *Coleridge and the Pantheist Tradition*, are beyond the scope of this study.

The annotations of the items included are meant to be as concise and informative as possible. They avoid value judgments, and the amount of space given to a particular item is not necessarily proportionate to its length or worth. Instead, the details extracted to develop its argument are intended to be pertinent, accurate, and full enough to indicate the ways in which it might suit a scholarly purpose.

To further enhance the usefulness of the bibliography, several reference tools are included. The Key to Abbreviations gives the full titles of all periodicals which appear more than once in the bibliographical list and are thus abbreviated in the citations. One index arranges the items by author, and the other by titles of poems (e.g., "Dejection: An Ode") and by groups of poems (e.g., the Conversation Poems). For poems discussed by more than ten critics, the title entries are subdivided to indicate both the main concerns dealt with in each item and the appearance of comment on major controversial issues.

Another source of subjects is the introductory essay. Referring to the entries by their numbers, it catalogues all items dealing with certain disputed points in the interpretation of "The Ancient Mariner," "Kubla Khan," and "Christabel." Its usefulness, however, extends beyond that of an index. In its analysis of the main controversies in the criticism of these poems, it is a guide to the arguments and conclusions of many of the major critics. It points out the questions that have been raised, the answers that have been proposed, and, by implication, some of the work that remains to be done.

NOTES

[1] George McLean Harper, "Gems of Purest Ray," in *Coleridge: Studies by Several Hands on the Hundredth Anniversary of His Death*, ed. Edmund Blunden and Earl Leslie Griggs (London, 1934), pp. 131–147.

[2] John Livingston Lowes, *The Road to Xanadu: A Study in the Ways of the Imagination* (Boston, 1927; rev. ed., 1930).

[3] Ada L.F. Snell, "The Meter of 'Christabel,'" in *The Fred Newton Scott Anniversary Papers, Contributed by Former Students and Colleagues* (Chicago, 1929), pp. 93–115.

[4] Newton P. Stallknecht, "The Moral of 'The Ancient Mariner,'" *PMLA*, 47 (1932), 559–569.

[5] B.R. McElderry, Jr., "Coleridge's Revision of 'The Ancient Mariner,'" *SP*, 29 (1932), 68–94.

[6] Elizabeth Nitchie, "The Moral of 'The Ancient Mariner' Reconsidered," *PMLA*, 48 (1933), 867–876.

KEY TO ABBREVIATIONS

AI	*American Imago*
BNYPL	*Bulletin of The New York Public Library*
BuR	*Bucknell Review*
CE	*College English*
CJ	*Classical Journal*
CLAJ	*College Language Association Journal*
CQ	*Critical Quarterly*
DR	*Dalhousie Review*
EIC	*Essays in Criticism*
EJ	*English Journal*
ELH	*A Journal of English Literary History*
EM	*English Miscellany*
EngR	*English Record*
ES	*English Studies*
Expl	*Explicator*
HTR	*Harvard Theological Review*
IJES	*Indian Journal of English Studies*
IJP-A	*International Journal of Psycho-Analysis*
JAAC	*Journal of Aesthetics and Art Criticism*
JEGP	*Journal of English and Germanic Philology*
JHI	*Journal of the History of Ideas*
KR	*Kenyon Review*
L&P	*Literature and Psychology*
LC	*Literary Criterion*
MLN	*Modern Language Notes*
MLQ	*Modern Language Quarterly*
MP	*Modern Philology*
N&Q	*Notes and Queries*
Person	*Personalist*
PLL	*Papers on Language and Literature*
PMLA	*Publications of the Modern Language Association of America*
PQ	*Philological Quarterly*
PTRSC	*Proceedings & Transactions Royal Society of Canada*
REL	*A Review of English Literature*

RES	*Review of English Studies*
RSSCW	*Research Studies of the State College of Washington*
SB	*Studies in Bibliography: Papers of the Bibliographical Society of the University of Virginia*
SEL	*Studies in English Literature, 1500–1900*
SIR	*Studies in Romanticism*
SoRA	*Southern Review: An Australian Journal of Literary Studies*
SP	*Studies in Philology*
SR	*Sewanee Review*
SRL	*Saturday Review of Literature*
TLS	*Times Literary Supplement*
TSE	*Tulane Studies in English*
UR	*University Review*
UTQ	*University of Toronto Quarterly*
VQR	*Virginia Quarterly Review*

Introduction:
Major Issues in Coleridge Criticism

INTRODUCTION:
MAJOR ISSUES IN COLERIDGE CRITICISM

A. "THE ANCIENT MARINER"

Modern interpretations of "The Ancient Mariner" begin with the same question as that reportedly raised by Mrs. Barbauld in 1830 when in a conversation with Coleridge she objected to the poem's lack of "moral" or symbolic significance.[1] Although most critics disagree with her observation, Newell F. Ford (item 157) and Elmer Edgar Stoll (item 108) do not. They read the poem on a literal level only, regarding symbolic analyses as inappropriate to the poem's ballad genre and as inharmonious with the absence of symbolism or allegory in the gloss and in contemporary interpretations. They point, further, to *Biographia Literaria*, in which Coleridge states precisely his single intention of making the supernatural believable, and to his reply to Mrs. Barbauld, in which he found fault with the moralizing of lines 612-617[2] but refused the opportunity to explain the symbolic meaning of the whole poem.

Other critics, however, cite most of these same sources as evidence that Coleridge had in mind something more than a believable tale of the supernatural. Mainly on the basis of his reply to Mrs. Barbauld, his critical theory, his use of the ballad form, and his addition of the gloss, they argue that he intended the poem to have an underlying moral significance with symbolic implications. Regarding the statement to Mrs. Barbauld, they point out that Coleridge objected to the obtrusion of the moral, not to its existence. They explain that although it lacks logical connections between events (items 33, 99) and that its immediate object is pleasure (item 195), the story in *The Arabian Nights* is not meaningless but is obviously dependent on unstated moral issues (item 151) which for Robert Penn Warren (item 94a) and Marshall Suther (item 349) closely resemble those in "The Ancient Mariner." Examining Coleridge's use of the phrase "pure imagination," Warren and others emphasize the union of head and heart (item 151) and the control of the will and understanding (item 233) involved in Coleridge's theory of the imaginative process.

3

In harmony with his indication to De Quincey that the idea preceded the story,[3] this interpretation of Coleridge's one main comment on the poem belongs to the general trend of recent criticism to regard him as a conscious, deliberate artist (especially items 306, 33), quite capable of conveying symbolic meaning within the ballad form.[4] This point is developed in several full discussions of the genre of the poem and of the function of the gloss. Coleman Parsons argues that the poem does have a moral meaning, for one reason because the literary genres to which it belongs combine moral content with other elements. Both Scott's "The Wild Huntsman" and Longueville's "The Hermit," examples respectively of a Gothic ballad and an imaginary voyage, are possible sources for the presence of moral values in "The Ancient Mariner" (item 124). Critics commonly praise its simplicity and naturalness of style (item 306), as well as Coleridge's modification of various other ballad conventions for the purposes of realism (items 130, 392) or thematic design (items 151, 195). For Karl Kroeber, Coleridge's modification and arrangement of traditional ballad elements result in a symbolic pattern so aesthetically sophisticated that he classifies the poem as a kind of epic (items 197, 245). His observation that its symbolic and universal aspects are emphasized in the revisions agrees with the conclusions of others that the gloss adds to the moral tone (items 85, 306) and sharpens the symbolic or spiritual meaning which Coleridge had come to associate with the poem (items 102, 376).

To the cumulative evidence of such studies, J.B. Beer adds a direct reply to anti-symbolist critics, saying in part that the symbolism of Coleridge's major poems is likely to be more subtle and concentrated than that which he normally used and that whether his contemporaries discovered it is not important. What matters is Coleridge's intention. And Clement Carlyon's account of Coleridge's conversation in Germany during his stay there from 1798 to 1799 suggests not only that he intended symbolic meanings when he wrote "The Ancient Mariner" and "Christabel" but also that he was fond of "metaphysical elucidations" of these poems (item 261a, p. 140).[5]

Although the metaphysical meaning of "The Ancient Mariner" remained mysterious for Carlyon, more recent readers have proposed four main themes: the sacramental vision of the "one Life"; the nightmare of a grim, unpredictable world; the imagination; and epistemological error.[6] The theme of the sacramental vision received its most influential analysis in 1946 by Warren. In his extensive essay "'The Ancient Mariner': A Poem of Pure Imagination" he considered the sacramental theme to be "primary," "at the threshold of the poem," and the most obvious outcome of the story of crime, punishment, and reconciliation (item 94a, the 1958 reprint, p. 214). It became

standard for later studies to build upon the assumptions that
the world of the poem is one of benevolent order and law and
that its underlying notion is the natural and spiritual oneness of the universe (item 306),[7] the permeating presence of
the divine in nature (items 216a, 202).[8] Accepting the sacramental context defined by Warren, some interpretations focus
on the movement from crime and punishment to redemption (items
203, 366, 233, 331, 292, 73), from natural depravity to prevenient grace (item 394), from destruction to rebirth (item
333), or from failure to recovery (item 397). Others concentrate on more specific themes such as prayer (items 252, 124);
love (items 207, 364, 398); isolation (items 256, 392); and
the mental adventure (item 109), or discovery of self (items
422, 322, 277) and of the moral and spiritual nature of the
universe (items 402, 212, 407, 398, 255).

A significant number of critics, however, are opposed to
the basic premise that the poem embodies a sacramental view
of the universe. They argue that the Mariner's world is not
one of benevolence, order, and harmony but one of fear, caprice,
and arbitrariness (items 318, 376, 278, 313) in which his
guilt is uncaused (item 315) or, by rational standards, is
certainly out of proportion to his crime (items 49, 299). Instead of the popular assumption that the poem is "an allegory
in favor of redemption by torment," a plan which the Unitarian
Coleridge disapproved of, William Empson regards the poem as a
"parody of the Christian struggle for atonement" (item 315,
pp. 298, 316). Humphry House and Edward Bostetter criticize
Warren in particular for maintaining the sacramental theme too
rigidly and consistently. He has to force such miscellaneous
details as the sinking of the ship into congruence with the
moon-bird-mist-wind image cluster (item 151) and to ignore
the dice game, both of which imply the arbitrary exhibition of
supernatural power (item 278).

This strain in the rigidly logical allegorical readings of
Warren and others comes about because of the presence in the
poem of both lyric and balladic elements which do not always
harmonize (item 306). Many of the lyric and descriptive
passages, as well as the gloss with its moral tone, were added
in 1817, after Coleridge's voyage to Malta when the poem began
to take on a personal spiritual meaning (items 102, 376, 398).
As a result, images such as the moon (item 397) and the albatross (item 303) are not consistently symbolic but at times
function on a purely literal level; and the presence of the
Wedding-Guest serves only a structural purpose (item 306).

Critics like Warren who view the poem primarily as a symbolic presentation of the sacramental world are impressed by
the lyric and descriptive details, the Christian references,
and the prose commentary. Others like Bostetter who see the

poem as a grim balladic nightmare draw support mainly from
the narrative events. This difference in the source of evidence shows up particularly in the degree of emphasis placed
upon the Mariner's passivity, in the interpretation of his
crime and punishment, and in the consideration of the extent
of his recovery.

Establishment of the sacramental theme, for instance, requires the assumption that the Mariner has freedom of will.
Thus, before discussing the symbolism of the crime, Warren
argues against Wordsworth's observation that the Mariner does
not act but is continually acted upon. He explains that since
Coleridge's doctrine of original sin included no previous determination of the will, any comment on the Mariner's lack of
adequate motivation or passivity is irrelevant (item 94a; see
also 22). Influenced by Warren, Hoxie N. Fairchild agrees
that "For the sake of the story the sailor must be granted
sufficient free will for the commission of a sin," but, at
the same time, defines the atmosphere of the poem as "necessi-
tarian" and the Mariner himself as "mainly a passive character" (item 112, p. 293). For W.H. Gardner, however, the
Mariner is "the symbol of an *active* principle," and his shooting the albatross and biting his arm are decisive acts (item
212, p. 115). In addition to these specific acts, Kroeber
lists the Mariner's commands to the Wedding-Guest and the
Hermit and his seizing the oars of the Pilot's boat as evidence
of the power of his will (item 197).

This view of the Mariner as an active, responsible par-
ticipant is not the conclusion of other, more detailed analyses of his actions, especially those which deny the sacramental
theme. They characterize the Mariner as a passive observer and
victim of fate (items 255, 355) whose actions are not morally
responsible (items 371, 278) because they are not willed but
uncontrolled and impulsive, irrational, and instinctive (items
293, 318, 313).

Not one of his actions is meaningful. He wants to tell
his story, but no hint is given that the Hermit is willing to
shrive him (item 313). And though his anguish has compelled
him to repeat the tale many times, his oversimplified moral is
evidence that he still does not understand his experience
(items 313, 402, 322, 334, 255, 284, 266, 113). Again, he
acts when he shoots the albatross, but he did not intend or
choose to do it (items 313, 422). He had no idea of the consequences (item 318). In his appearance as well as his use of
the sudden, unexplained, and stark phrase (item 151), he shows
his horror and bewilderment (item 313). Even though he describes the coming of the albatross with affection and rever-
ence, and looks forward to its visits, he impulsively kills
it (item 293). In his one deliberate act, with tremendous

effort he bites his arm, sucks the blood, and cries out, "A
sail! a sail!" (1. 161). But his hope is immediately shat-
tered. His action leads ironically to the death of the crew.[9]
He blesses the water-snakes, but he is surprised that the
saving act has been performed (item 315). By repeating the
word "unaware" (11. 285, 287) and by retrospectively attribu-
ting his undeliberate blessing to a supernatural influence on
him, he emphasizes that he did not really know what he was
doing.[10] He pulls on a rope alongside his nephew, but their
silent, pointless routine only dramatizes the ruin of the
merry community and the loss of intimacy in a fearful universe
where action is meaningless.[11] Finally, he moves his lips to
talk and picks up the oars of the Pilot's boat, but his action
and appearance frighten his rescuers (items 313, 151).

The Mariner's passivity is indicated not only in the impulsive, ineffective quality of his occasional actions but
also in the language chosen to describe him and the ship.
His "glittering eye" (1. 3 and "bright" in 1. 618), according
to Beer, emphasizes his passiveness (item 216a). Other critics
find fault with E.M.W. Tillyard's characterization of the
Mariner as "an unusually inquiring spirit" (item 109, p. 71)
because it does not take into account the fact that he is
driven by the storm (item 222) and dwarfed by the icebergs
(item 318). He and his shipmates apparently undertake their
voyage without a definite goal and, as suggested by the lack
of specific terms in the poem, remain ignorant of their exact
location. They did not "discover" the South Pole or the
Pacific Ocean; instead, the ice, snow, and mist "came" (11. 51,
53) upon them, and they "burst" (1. 105) into the silent sea.
They did not "arrive" but "drifted" (1. 468) into the harbor,
where shadowy shapes "came" (1. 483) to the Mariner's view
and, after being "Stunned" (1. 550) by a loud sound, he "found"
(1. 554) himself in the Pilot's boat (item 322).

The question of the Mariner's moral freedom and accounta-
bility bears directly on the central, most controversial
issue in the poem--the nature of his crime and the justice
of its consequences. Critics who believe that his world is
one of benevolent order generally reason that his moral freedom and responsibility and the symbolic nature of his crime
justify his terrible physical and mental suffering. They
assume or establish directly the point that the crime is not
trivial because it is symbolic (items 109, 148). Its enormity
lies not in itself but in its indication of the corruption and
latent evil within the Mariner's will (items 94a, 22, 394, 34).
It is analogous to the fall of Adam (items 94a, 216a, 51, 233,
389),[12] the crucifixion of Christ (items 287, 212, 318, 118,
366, 202, 51, 333),[13] the rebellion of Satan (items 109, 255,
318), and the acts of Cain and the Wandering Jew (items 318,
292).

Like these archetypal sins, the Mariner's act is unmotivated. It is a desperate assertion of self (items 109, 255);
and amidst the moonlight, gay fellowship, and hospitality, it
appears shockingly perverse (items 171, 322, 94a). Because
Coleridge intended the deed to be symbolic and motiveless, he
accepted Wordsworth's suggestion of the shooting of an albatross. The murder of a human being would have distracted
from the symbolic significance and, unless the Mariner were
to be a monster, would have required motivation sufficiently
developed to make the act probable (items 402, 94a). In his
relatively short poem Coleridge has appropriately given little
detail to the shooting. Furthermore, he has emphasized its
motiveless character by separating it from the preceding narrative with the question-answer device: the Mariner tells of
his crime during a break in the story in answer to a question
from the Wedding-Guest (item 233).

Even though the Mariner's account of the episode is brief
and though he does not or cannot explain his motives, the
description of the bird and the interpretative comments of the
gloss make clear that his killing it is a violation of the
sacred order of the universe on the animal, human, and divine
levels (item 151). Appearing in the midst of the crystalline
waste, the albatross represents the blessedness of natural
life and the universal bond of love inherent in the concept
of the "one Life" (items 333, 124, 322, 207, 389, 398, 364).
Its human and divine associations appear in the fact that it
is "hailed" as a "Christian soul" "in God's name" (11. 65-66),
flies in circles symbolic of holiness, and receives the crew's
extension of hospitality by answering their call, eating their
food, and playing with them (items 151, 333). Both the gloss
and the Argument of 1800 refer to the Mariner's act as a
selfish betrayal of the trust and affection implied in the
guest-host relationship (items 49, 299, 306). The gloss calls
the albatross "the pious bird of good omen" (at 11. 79-82);
and when it is shot with a "cross-bow," it is placed around
the Mariner's neck "Instead of the cross" (11. 81, 141) to
indicate the violation of the values represented by the cross
(item 398) or to suggest a symbolic transference from Christ,
the slain son of God, to the dead creature of God (item 94a).

Such Christian associations are not so important to the
critics who oppose the idea that the Mariner's world is one
of benevolence and order. Though Empson dismisses the phrase
"pious bird" as a "mild parsonical joke" (item 315, p. 302),
probably more typical of the arguments for the nightmare
world is Adair's observation that the Christian imagery makes
the Mariner's act appear more heinous (item 376). She and
others concentrate less on the description of the bird than
on the significance of the Mariner's suddenly killing it.

They consider his idle, unpremeditated act symbolic of the inexplicable, primeval impulse to hurt. It is part of the unpredictable pattern of action in his capricious arbitrary world (items 376, 278, 293, 322, 318).[14]

Because he does not will the crime and because the game of dice makes his punishment depend on chance (items 278, 408, 376, 313), he does not deserve his severe sufferings. His sense of guilt and worthlessness is out of all proportion to the crime (items 49, 299, 315). Empson postulates that the "wicked whisper" (1. 246) that keeps him from praying is "God is unjust to me" (item 315, pp. 303-304). Bostetter reasons that, by the moral principles of a sacramental universe, "the punishment of the Mariner should have been unthinkable. The God who loved man as well as bird should have been merciful and forgiving" (item 278, p. 247).

Whether the Mariner's punishment is considered just or unjust depends partly on one's attitude toward the continuation of his suffering, toward the fact that even after the blessing of the water-snakes he never fully recovers from the effects of his crime. Readers who consistently maintain a sacramental view of the poem acknowledge the incompleteness of his recovery. But they emphasize its mitigating circumstances. The Mariner has, after all, been redeemed; like Lazarus and the Prodigal Son, by the end of the voyage he has been reborn into a completely new life (item 233). In keeping with the medieval background of the poem, his lifelong penance marks him as one of the elect of the Heavenly City (items 89, 212). His pilgrim life of penitential prayer, Christian fellowship, and selfless teaching constitutes the means whereby he ensures the remission of his sins (item 394). Other indications of his redemption include his intense desire for life (11. 470-471), his shriving by the Hermit (items 414, 333), and the convergence toward the end of the poem of all the familiar images of goodness. In the dawn singing scene and in the pastoral vision of lines 367-372 occur the images of the seraphs, the circle, music, the sun, living nature, water, and sleep. And in the harbor scene merge the good moonlight, a silence which is neither frightening nor sterile, a steady wind, and the reds which now appear as beautiful crimson shadows playing on the white light of the bay. The series of Christian images recalls the description in the Book of Revelation of the New Jerusalem (item 333). The gloss for lines 464-467 of the harbor scene refers to the Mariner's "native country," a term which, according to Beer, has a particular significance in Neoplatonic thought as the world which the soul leaves when it descends into generation and to which it is constantly trying to return. Commenting on "The moonlight steeped in silentness / The steady weathercock" (11. 478-479),

he points to the possibility of a resolution of symbolism:
since the cock is a common symbol for the sun, Coleridge may
have intended to suggest that "the Mariner is not granted a
permanent vision of the Sun but is afforded the calm which
results from having it established now in his imagination as
an abiding, if latent, truth" (item 216a, pp. 166–167).

Besides the assurance of salvation, the Mariner is rescued
and allowed to return to his own country where he participates
in communal worship and, rewarded with the courage of the
mental adventurer, teaches those who have had no such redemptive experience (items 22, 284, 109). Thus, a kind of companionship replaces the lonely sea journey away from the church;
and communication, though compulsive, reverses the previous
silence (items 333, 256). He is homeless; but his wandering
is appropriate for the universality of his message (item 94a)
and, together with his "strange power of speech" (1. 587), is
reminiscent of the missionary wanderings and gift of tongues
of Christ's apostles. He wanders "like night" (1. 586) because
his preaching is symbolically like the apostles' in being almost a subversive activity in a materialistic world (item 212).

If he is set apart from ordinary men, it is because through
suffering he has acquired an understanding of and keen sensitivity to both good and evil, a unique consciousness of the
full heights and depths of human experience (items 202, 398,
216a, 442). He now sees with a double vision (item 216a).
The wedding, for instance, he perceives as a symbol both of
the normal noisy world of human companionship (11. 591–592)
and of the hushed realm of mystic communion (11. 593–594)
(item 333).

From the perspective of the critics who view the poem as
a nightmare, however, none of these circumstances quite can-
cels out the injustice of the Mariner's punishment and incomplete recovery. The term "rebirth" is not really very helpful
in describing the theme of the poem because its final emphasis
is not on renovation but on destruction (items 49, 299, 109,
408). "Instead of the 'One Life,'" says Bostetter, "we are
confronted at the end of the poem by the eternally alienated
Mariner alienating in his turn the Wedding-Guest" (item 278,
pp. 246–247). Because he has never found peace or freedom
from sin and guilt, the Mariner is not a saved person. His
shipmates' public condemnation is finally expiated, but he
can never forgive himself. He is repeatedly forced to relive
the voyage and to re-experience his horror and guilt (items
376, 255, 49, 299). The crimson shadows in the harbor do not
suggest his redemption but the evil that has returned with
him. And the familiar landmarks of his native country serve
only to remind him of his former innocence and of the cheerful
company of living men who had set out on the voyage (items
376, 371).

Though he is returning to his own country, he probably does not expect anybody to be waiting for him. He is over-joyed to see living people and to hear their voices (item 103); but the Pilot, the Pilot's boy, the Hermit, and the Wedding-Guest all respond to him with fear and doubt (items 376, 313). He is never really a part of the human community, not even when he walks to the church among Christian company and worships alongside them, for the relationship he describes in lines 601–609 is abstract and impersonal: "There are loving friends," comments George Whalley, "but they do not seem to be his; the old men are not his brothers or his father, the youths and maidens gay are not his children" (item 102, pp. 387–388). He has learned the value of human companionship but must be forever leaving human company (item 313). He wanders from land to land "like night" (1. 586) because he is never fully accepted or recognized (item 392). His story does convey universal truth, but his telling it suggests not so much his sense of mission as his continual seeking of relief through confession and his desire for understanding from his fearful, doubtful listeners (items 318, 255, 392).

His final state is one of irreparable damage (item 322). His extraordinary perception and sensitivity have isolated him from everyday experience (item 216a). And though he has gained wisdom, he has paid too dearly for it. Ironically, the experience through which he acquired wisdom has rendered him unable to enter into normal social life (items 422, 216).

The ambiguity of the Mariner's recovery and especially the problem of justifying his punishment make it difficult for some critics to view the poem as either a sacramental vision or a grim nightmare. Incorporating parts of both themes, they analyze the poem as a dramatic monologue. They point to Coleridge's stated intention in *Biographia Literaria* and to his interest in portraying psychological processes as external evidence for believing that his main concern was the Mariner and that the most satisfying critical approach is by way of point of view (items 113, 124).[15]

To the extent possible,[16] reading the poem as a dramatic monologue requires the separation of events as they really occurred from the coloring given them by the mentality and prejudices of the Mariner (item 113). Unlike his creator, the Mariner is a simple medieval sailor whose remoteness and superstition Coleridge emphasized by casting the whole poem into medieval language and spelling and later, after modernizing the style, adding the gloss and specifically identifying Death's companion as Life-in-Death (items 245, 113, 124, 266, 371). When storms and calms drive the ship hopelessly off its course, what really happens is that the crew gradually die of exposure and starvation, while the sole surviving Mariner sinks deeper into delirium and does not recover his power to

distinguish between reality and hallucinations until after
his rescue. From inner compulsion, he tries to account for
what would otherwise seem a cruel whim of fate by evolving
what is to him a logical sequence of events (item 113).

Thus, it is the Mariner, not Coleridge, who superimposes
upon his experience the structure of crime and punishment
(item 284), who comes to believe that his trivial act of
shooting the albatross caused his suffering and the tormented
death of the whole crew (item 113). "There is disproportion
between the deed and its enormous consequences," says William
Marshall, "but this is the Mariner's reasoning, not Coleridge's" (item 266, p. 527). It is more the Mariner himself,
argues Bate, than it is his simple act which "makes us feel
that it was so fearful and guilty a deed" (item 402, p. 58).[17]
At first it seemed inconsequential, neither good nor bad, but
the crew persuade him eventually that it was evil (item 266).
Accepting the blame and magnifying the episode in his delirium
(item 113), he comes to attach supernatural significance to
the albatross (item 371) and to relate its body to the cross
as a symbol of his guilt (item 266). It is he, not Coleridge,
who uses a language reminiscent of Christian devotional
literature (item 371) and who finds sacramental symbolism in
such events as his sleeping after physical and psychological
strain or the dropping away of the dead bird from his neck
because of the natural processes of decay and gravitation
(items 266, 113).

Convinced that he was more acted upon than acting (items
151, 284) and unable otherwise to explain such incidents as
his blessing the water-snakes, the reanimation of the crew,
and the sinking of the ship, the Mariner believes in the doctrine of redemption through divine intercession (item 266).
He feels forever set apart as a man of apocalyptic vision,
compelled by an evangelical sense of mission to save others
with the story of his miraculous conversion (item 113).

Whether the poem is read as a dramatic study of the Mariner
or as a symbolic presentation of either the sacramental or the
nightmare world, many critics find that the rich texture of
the poem and certain otherwise unexplained supernatural details require the addition of what Warren calls the "secondary
theme of the imagination" (item 94a).[18] It is developed mainly
by the image of moonlight and its associated images of the
bird, the wind, the mist, the polar spirit, and the spring or
fountain (items 94a, 216a).

Concerned with the context of values in which the Mariner's
story takes place, the epistemological theme stresses the
superiority of imaginative insight over rationality in providing the best clue to life's spiritual mysteries (item 398).
The mariners find themselves in a world with an indistinct

boundary between dreams and things where their clearest insights into the nature of their experience occur in dreams,
trances, swoons, or spells—moments when the consciousness is
suspended and the intuitive power takes over. Their judgments
based on the categories of time, space, and causality prove
inadequate. The rescuers fail in their attempts to give
rational explanations of the Mariner and his ship. And, sig-
nificantly, by the end of the tale the Wedding-Guest departs
"like one that hath been stunned, / And is of sense forlorn"
(11. 622-623). He, as well as the Mariner and the crew, relied too much on what Coleridge, in a 1797 letter to Poole,
had referred to as "the constant testimony of their senses"
(item 398, p. 169).

At this level of meaning, then, the Mariner's sin is
related to that of Cain, who suffered, says Coleridge in his
Prefatory Note to "The Wanderings of Cain," because "he
neglected to make a proper use of his senses" (item 151, pp.
84-85, 98, and elsewhere). Like him, the Mariner abuses
reason by failing to subordinate sense-inferences to the
beneficent powers of the imagination (items 89, 112, 195,
94a, 216a, 376). In shooting the albatross and despising the
water-snakes, he shows a probable influence of the didactic
message of "Lines Left upon a Seat in a Yew-Tree," which
Wordsworth recited to him in June, 1797: "he who feels contempt / For any living thing, hath faculties / Which he has
never used" (item 171, p. 13, and elsewhere). Later in spontaneously blessing the water-snakes the Mariner discovers his
imaginative faculty and uses it to perceive the true spiritual
nature of the universe (item 171).

Some critics, however, feel that the Mariner's imagination does not continue to be the ruling faculty, that his
total experience is not typified by the accord, evident in
the blessing, between mode of perception and object perceived
and by the harmony of all levels of being in the dawn singing
scene (item 334). Instead, they describe the secondary epistemological theme as one of error and frustration (item 151).
Chayes, who has analyzed this theme most extensively, emphasizes the philosophical idea of the limitations of human
knowledge as the purpose of the epigraph, the first-person
narrator point of view, and the tale itself. Speaking of the
Mariner, she claims that "it is as an embodiment of the potentialities of error by the human mind that he becomes a genuinely memorable figure, comparable less to a Cain or *Poète maudit*
than to Melville's Captain Ahab, Kafka's Joseph K., or, especially, Swift's Lemuel Gulliver" (item 334, p. 87).

The Mariner's most obvious error is of course his shooting
of the albatross. It is an epistemological as well as moral
error because it represents his attempt to comprehend the

spirit world by means of the senses (items 334, 349), his
failure to reach the truth about the nature of the universe
(items 151, 202, 398, 171, 222, 389). Coleridge probably recalled the Mariner's thoughtlessness, or idleness of mind and
conscience (item 402), years later when, during the voyage to
Malta, sailors tried to shoot a hawk that had attempted to
land on the ship: "Poor Hawk!" observed Coleridge in his notebook, "O Strange Lust of Murder in Man!--It is not cruelty /
it is mere non-feeling from non-thinking" (item 33, p. 6, and
elsewhere). The Mariner's potentiality for error, evident in
the shooting, is further suggested by the image of mist, the
feeling of wonder and discovery in lines 105-106, the blunder-
ing, innocent nature of the voyage, and the crew's ignorance
of the double character of the tropic sun (items 216a, 334,
151).

Incomprehensibility and frustration continue to characterize the Mariner's experience even after he has blessed the
water-snakes. He greets his rescuers as friends and deliver-
ers but succeeds only in frightening them as later he terrifies
the Wedding-Guest. And he misinterprets the Hermit's startled
exclamation, "What manner of man art thou?" (l. 577) as a command to explain himself in terms of his experience. He then
tells what seem to him the facts of his past; and whenever the
spell of "woful agony" (l. 579) recurs, he mechanically repeats them, without interpretation or discrimination. His
compulsion never results in a new work of art governed by the
imagination (items 334, 422, 402).

In addition to the general problems of symbolic significance and thematic complexity, criticism of "The Ancient
Mariner" has dealt with its genre, sources, and revisions and
with the structural and thematic function of the supernatural,
the gloss, and the Wedding-Guest. Among these more specific
considerations, the most controversial are the sun and moon
imagery, the Mariner's preference for organized worship over
wedding feasts, and his explicit moralizing in lines 612-617.

One explanation of the sun and moon is that they function
only on a literal level to indicate the weather, to reveal the
direction of the ship, or to make vivid the setting (item 157).
Little noticed on land, they are impressive and important in
their own right at sea, particularly during the Mariner's
solitary monotonous voyage over unknown, empty waters
(item 108).

On a symbolic level the sun has reminded critics of the
heart (item 216a), consciousness (item 118), the paternal
principle (items 118, 232), the divine image in human reason,
and God himself, who appears to the diseased imagination of
fallen man as heat or wrath (items 216a, 212, 241) and whose
part in the crew's death is similar to the Hebraic idea that

death results from seeing Yahweh's face (item 368). In its
complimentary role, the moon symbolizes the head (item 216a),
unconsciousness (item 118), the maternal principle (items
118, 232, 127), mutable nature (item 241), God's reflection
(item 216a), and Christ (item 212).

Probably the most extensive and influential explanation
is Warren's. He demonstrates that the moon is associated
with the imagination and with the good, redemptive events,
while the sun is connected with the understanding and with
the bad, punitive events. He explains that the moonlight
death of the crew does not present an inconsistency in the
symbolic pattern but that it suggests the ambiguity of the
imagination, the principle that, if violated and despised,
the imagination persists and exacts vengeance. Similarly,
the sun's good association in the dawn singing scene indicates
the temporary redemption of the understanding when it assumes
its proper role and partakes of the general blessedness
(item 94a).

For other critics, however, these events do present inconsistencies for which Warren's explanations are unconvincing.
They prefer to accept the actions of the sun and moon as both
benevolent and malevolent rather than to designate precise
equivalents for them (items 376, 349, 306, 322, 379, 278,
151).[19] Besides objecting to drawing the equivalents from
Coleridge's later terminology, House finds that, in his other
writings before and after the time of "The Ancient Mariner,"
Coleridge associated moonlight and other half-lights not only
with general creativeness and poetic imagination (item 94a)
but also with delicate emotions, fruitful virtues, subtle processes of the mind, and especially the mysteries and uncer-
tainties of mental life. It is with this area of experience
and with Coleridge's exploration of it that House places the
image of the moon. And with respect to Warren's sun symbolism,
House reminds us that for Coleridge the understanding was
never altogether unnecessary in the whole scheme of the mind's
action but was needed for the proper workings of the reason
and the imagination (item 151).

Less controversial but still a problem to which many
critics give attention is the seemingly paradoxical situation
within the frame story in which the Mariner's message of love
turns the Wedding-Guest away from the marriage feast, an expression of love in the everyday world (items 216a, 284).
The most common explanation of the Wedding-Guest's decision
and the Mariner's own preference for church services is that
both of them have been made sadder and wiser by the Mariner's
experience. Having learned through suffering the value of
universal love, they now understand marriage in a larger context and find it less significant than participation in the

undivided life embracing nature, man, and God (items 398, 94a,
284, 342). They now define themselves in terms of their relationship to God and the universe rather than to society and
consider the pageantry of the marriage feast insubstantial
(item 422). This otherworldliness is considered a mark of
election, of a new spiritual existence (items 394, 371).
Daniel McDonald, however, regards it as a sign of the Mariner's
lack of recovery. He reads lines 597-609 as the Mariner's
preference for religious conventions and social ceremonies
over the disturbing physical and supernatural realities which
he wishes to ignore but cannot. He implies that the social
experience is superficial, though sweeter than the individual
experience (item 318).

Unrelated to either of these interpretations is the view
held by Suther and Yarlott that on a more personal level of
meaning the Mariner's preference represents the conflict run-
ning throughout Coleridge's poetry between marriage and domestic contentment and the deeper concerns of religious devotion
and poetic vision (items 349, 398).

Just after stating his preference for communal worship,
the Mariner bids farewell to the Wedding-Guest with two stanzas
of explicit moralizing. These lines have been criticized as
trite, inappropriate, and inadequately related to the rest of
the poem (items 216a, 392, 308). Coleridge himself was probably referring to them in his famous admission to Mrs. Barbauld
that the moral was too obtrusive. But he did not remove or
modify them, evidently because he felt that they serve an important purpose. Some critics have suggested that he intended
them to represent the central idea of the poem, since the
Mariner's stated sympathy with his fellow creatures has grown
out of his past sin and suffering (items 392, 366, 256, 89,
212). His statement is considered not trite but, like all
great spiritual truths, deceptively simple and childlike
(item 392). House, on the other hand, finds it didactic, epi-
grammatic "almanac art" when detached from its context, but,
coming "after the richness and terror of the poem, it is no
more a banal moral apothegm, but a moral which has its meaning
because it has been lived" (item 151, p. 92; see also items
171, 378).

Other critics justify the moral not because it summarizes
the ethical content of the poem but because it is appropriate
to the medieval spirit and the ballad genre (items 108, 331)
or because it functions structurally or dramatically. On a
structural level the moral does more than round off the narrative and bring the Mariner back to everyday reality (items
392, 308). The repetition indicates personal discovery and
conviction of the universal truth which he had only intuited
when he hailed the albatross "in God's name" "As if it had

been a Christian soul" (11. 65-66). Spoken just after he
hears the vesper bell and tells of his joy in ceremonial
prayer, it evidences his recognition of the superior value of
the prayer that is lived: "He prayeth best, who lovest best ..."
(1. 614) (item 392). Furthermore, by its inclusion of prayer
it adds to the completeness of the poem's moral structure,
which is built on the contrast of self-will, manifested in
the act of shooting the albatross, and love, seen in the selfless act of prayer (item 124; for justification of the inclusion of prayer in the moral see also item 252.)[20]
    In its dramatic function the moral helps to characterize
the Wedding-Guest and the Mariner. Brief, plain, intimate,
appropriately restrained, it is clearly designed for the
Wedding-Guest alone and is in keeping with his level of understanding and spiritual development and with his previous need
for reassurance from the Mariner that he too did not die
(items 301, 394). Both the Wedding-Guest and the moral spoken
to him belong to the comic framework, which is deliberately
incongruous with the tone and content of the central narrative
in order to set off its high seriousness and to intensify
feelings arising from it (item 308). A more frequently suggested possibility, however, is that the moral characterizes
the Mariner, reflecting mainly his limited understanding and
inadequate language (items 284, 333, 322, 255, 233, 303). It
is, after all, the Wedding-Guest who is made sadder and wiser
(item 334). The Mariner is now an old man, free at the moment
of the agony which forces him to relive his experience and
content with the conventional world to which he has returned
(item 308). Simple and unsophisticated, in his effort to
account for his sense of religious dedication to universal
love and brotherhood he has arrived at a *non sequitur* conclusion lacking the support of his experience (items 266, 334,
212, 113, 394, 376). And it is his experience, not his conventional moralizing, that affects the Wedding-Guest (items
371, 402, 422).
    In summary, then, the most popular view of the moral is
that the statement of lines 612-617 represents not the meaning
of the poem but the Mariner's ironic interpretation of what
has happened to him (items 293, 334, 376).[21] The moral is
the Mariner's, not Coleridge's (especially items 113, 371).

B. "KUBLA KHAN"

    While "Kubla Khan" does not present such problems as that
of the significance of the moral tag in "The Ancient Mariner,"

it does require consideration of whether its meaning is relevant to the human situation, whether it is symbolic or literal,
and whether the tone is one of negation or affirmation. And
with "Kubla Khan" discussion of meaning is complicated by the
Preface. In its published form, the Preface tells how Coleridge
composed the poem during an opium dream but, because he was
interrupted by a Porlock businessman, could remember only part
of it. Considered by Alan C. Purves as "one of the major
cruxes in Coleridge criticism" (item 286, p. 187), the head-
note has always accompanied the standard published text and,
in raising the possibilities of its fragmentary nature and
dream composition, has greatly influenced the way the poem is
understood (items 353, 128, 204, 272, 397, 364, 67).

Several critics, for instance, discuss the poem as a fragment. Carl R. Woodring deplores the assumption of recent
criticism that "any poetic work from which we derive high
pleasure must be complete," and proposes that "Kubla Khan" be
considered a fragment with literary value (item 230, pp. 361-
362). Elisabeth Schneider develops this hypothesis more fully
with biographical and internal evidence. She argues that
Coleridge treated the poem as a fragment, not publishing it
for about sixteen years after its composition,[22] and that to
abdicate responsibility for the piece he called it a fragment,
entitling the 1816 Preface "Of the Fragment of Kubla Khan"
and later combining this phrase with the subtitle, "A Vision
in a Dream. A Fragment" (items 155, 353).

Schneider reads the poem as "a fragment with a postscript
added": a description of Kubla's gardens followed by an explanation, written at a later sitting, of why the speaker could
not recreate the vision or finish the poem (item 155, p. 247).
This two-part structure, as well as the disproportionate simile
involving the wailing woman (1. 16) and the image of the ancestral voices (1. 30), is poetically unsatisfactory if the
poem is regarded as a whole. (See also items 245, 298.)
With the impressive but unassimilated image of the ancestral
voices, the time, place, and speaker suddenly change, leaving
the action unresolved. (See also item 397.) And though the
postscript is skillfully linked to the rest of the poem by
the recurrence of the images of the dome and the caves of ice,
the last eighteen lines terminate but do not fulfill the
first part (item 155).

Accepting the poem as a fragment, Schneider then speculates
on why Coleridge did not finish it. She suggests that his
lack of self-trust underlies both the misdating of his poems
and his failure to complete many of them. (For a similar
psychological explanation, see item 111.) From an artistic
standpoint, she notes that, as the opening for a narrative,
the beginning is too rich and concentrated and the movement

too swift to be sustained. As for the form of the poem, she
assumes that Coleridge probably did have in mind a two-part
division. But it is also conceivable that he had planned a
one-directional development but could not continue after the
interrupting comment on the inadequacy of his inspiration (see
also item 67) or that he had intended a three-part structure
with a climactic return to the garden theme but could not
transcend what he had already written. On the other hand, he
might have had no plan at all, beginning the piece as a kind
of doodling, or daydreaming, which might or might not develop
shape and purpose (item 155).

Regardless of Coleridge's intentions or lack of them, most
critics consider the poem as it stands a complete whole. They
praise its unity (items 151, 152), its logical organization
(items 272, 371, 216a), and economy (item 244). They concede
only that if it is read as a narrative, it seems unfinished
(items 133, 375, 306). Deriving aesthetic satisfaction inconsistent with a fragmentary state (item 152), they inevitably
conclude with House that "if Coleridge had never published
his Preface, who would have thought of 'Kubla Khan' as a fragment? Who would have guessed at a dream? ... Who would have
thought it nothing but a 'psychological curiosity'?" (item
151, p. 114).

Specifically, Suther evaluates the biographical reasons
for arguing that the poem is a fragment and finds them strong
but inconclusive. In the first place, Coleridge did not treat
the poem exactly like other fragments. He worked on it extensively, revising and polishing, and eventually he did publish
it. In the second place, his use of the term "fragment" does
not exclude the possibility of aesthetic completeness. He
applied it to both unpublished and published works, including
the finished poem on "The Pains of Sleep," and apparently
meant it in the sense of a group of verses composed deliberately but susceptible of further development. The need for
expansion is in fact implied by Suther's suggestion that the
poem lacks sufficient rhetorical reinforcement of the logical
connection between the first and second parts (items 204, 349).

Other critics too have assumed that Coleridge intended to
continue the first part since he had collected notes on Kubla
and the Tartars and had planned an epic on the subject of
Eastern civilization (items 298, 216a, 376). Chayes points
out that although among the Romantic poets the term "fragment"
sometimes had almost a generic meaning which did not exclude
aesthetic unity, Coleridge probably did regard the poem as in
some way unfinished, since he also called it a "fragment" in
the note attached to the Crewe manuscript (item 353). His
attitude was inevitable, according to Eli Marcovitz, because
the poem itself expresses feelings of incompleteness and loss

(item 317). Still another suggestion is Bernard R. Breyer's
idea that the epithet functions as a Gothic device (item 128).
But whether they regard it as a particular stylistic feature,
a reinforcement of theme, or an indication of Coleridge's
intention to expand the poem, these critics would agree with
Suther that "the decision as to whether a work is a fragment
in the aesthetic sense must in every case be based on *what
is there*" (item 204, p. 7).

Most critics find the internal evidence that the poem is
a fragment unconvincing. In contrast to Schneider, they speculate that Coleridge did not follow through with his promise
to finish the poem because it turned out to be aesthetically
complete (items 349, 204). Any expansion would have destroyed
its balance and unity (items 216a, 286). Thematically, too,
it needed no continuation: it says all it has to say about
poetic composition (items 320, 272, 371) and definitely resolves the Kubla-Cybele contrast (item 298).

It reads like a complete lyric made up of the dreamer's
description of his fragmentary vision (ll. 1-36) followed
logically by his comment on its significance (ll. 37-54)
(items 59, 306, 349, 244). This two-part structure is poetically satisfactory, contributing to the poem's unity and completeness (items 151, 376).[23] The time, place, and speaker
do change; but this shift in point of view is not a persuasive
argument for the poem's fragmentary character (items 343, 349)
for two reasons. (1) It functions thematically, according to
a Jungian reading, to stress the disruption of the creation
by which Kubla hoped to integrate the disparate elements of
his personality (item 244). And (2) it is prepared for by
stylistic indications that the dream is fading. To make the
dream vivid, the first part is told mainly from Kubla's point
of view; but well before lines 37-38, where he is first named,
the speaker slips into the poem. Unobtrusively, he enters
into the excited description of the chasm in line 12, the
point at which the style of the poem becomes both more personal and more conventionally literary, with exclamations and
similes, and thus hints of the half-awakened, responsive mind
on the borders of the dream (items 353, 306). Then as he begins to emerge from his trance in lines 31-36, the dome fades
into a "shadow" (l. 31), and the ocean is reduced to generalized
"waves" (l. 32) (items 378, 316, 376, 353). This indistinct
view of Xanadu helps prepare for the shift of the focal point
of the poem away from Kubla to the poet-speaker of the second
part (item 286).

In addition to stylistic foreshadowing and logical sequence,
the two parts are held together by repeated sound patterns,
mythical references, and images. The "almost innumerable
linkings of sound," analyzed by Schneider, recur in the second

part (item 155, p. 275). Double rhyme, for example, which she points out in lines 2 and 4, is used again in lines 42 and 44 ("within me" and "win me"). The dominant *a* sounds continue, most notably in the proper nouns "Abyssinian" (1. 39) and "Abora" (1. 41). And in "damsel with a dulcimer" (1. 37), "symphony and song" (1. 43), "loud and long" (1. 45), "Beware! Beware!" (1. 49), "flashing eyes, his floating hair!" (1. 50) is repeated the device—seen in lines 3, 4, 8, 12, 17, 25, 26, 27, 29, 33—of foreshadowing the terminal rhyme by a preceding echo of assonance or alliteration (item 155).

In another discussion of the poem's prosody Purves divides the poem into seven sections on the basis of line length and rhyme scheme. He points out that the two sections in the second part (11. 37-41 and 42-54) present variations of the first (11. 1-5) and third (11. 12-24) sections, thus emphasizing the similarities and differences between Kubla and the poet. Furthermore, in rhyme and metrical pattern the last line of the second part echoes the last line of the first part: "A sunny pleasure-dome with caves of ice!" (1. 36) and "And drunk the milk of Paradise" (1. 54) (item 286).[24]

In both parts of the poem occur references to the conventional dream of the Happy Garden (item 341), to the ancient tradition of sun-worship (item 216a), and to the myths of Cybele (items 298, 338), Adonis (items 385, 341), Oberon (item 292), and Isis (item 216a). Less obscure are the images which recur with more than mechanical significance. The dome and caves of ice (11. 46-47), noticed by Schneider (item 155), help provide the transition necessary for the reinforcement of the poem's unity (item 151). The second part is not just an afterthought but, by means of other repeated images, stands in a climactic relationship to the first part. Whereas Kubla could only "decree" (1. 2) a pleasure dome where a "mingled measure" (1. 33) could be heard, the speaker plans to "build" (1. 46) his poetic counterpart with "music loud and long" (1. 45). His vision of Xanadu is the first in a series of progressively heightened visions, including those of the Abyssinian maid, also in the past, and of the frenzied poet. The maid herself refines the "woman wailing for her demon-lover" (1. 16) (item 306); and Mount Abora, the subject of her song, refers to another Eastern paradise (item 376), higher than the pleasure ground of Xanadu but less than the true "Paradise" (1. 54) of the poet in his ecstasy (item 306). As a human embodiment of poetic power he replaces the "mighty fountain" (1. 19). His larger audience supersedes the memory of the dreamer in the first part as he becomes greater than the will-less, ego-less dreamer or the deliberate seeker of inspiration at the beginning of the second part (item 353). Finally, in the speaker's portrait

of him reappear the holiness and enchantment connected with
the chasm and the demon-lover (item 306).

More than the repetition of images associated with a
creator and his paradise, the images of the wailing woman and
the ancestral voices are difficult to explain. Critics who
argue for the poem's aesthetic completeness do not regard
these images as detracting from the poem's unity, although
they do not agree on the images' exact identity and relevance.
The wailing woman, for example, is generally seen as a means
of characterizing the savage landscape of the chasm (items
349, 244, 133), but how she does it is a debatable point.
Suther suggests that, along with the ancestral voices and
weavers of circles, she provides a touchstone from the ordinary world, which contrasts with her lover's realm of heightened
beauty and terror (item 349). Other critics, however, see her
and her lover as part of the same haunted scene. She is
variously interpreted as a daemon (item 317), a witch about
to meet and copulate with the devil (item 341), and a phallic
mother (item 379); she is associated with cults of wailing
women which often had a place in sun-worship (item 216a) and
the women who followed Bacchus (item 376), as well as with
Cybele (items 341, 298, 338), Titania (item 216a), Queen Aso,
Isis, Psyche (item 216a), and Mary Evans (item 398). On a
thematic level she may function to identify Xanadu as a fallen
paradise (item 216a) or to suggest the wrath of God within the
redemptive process (item 152), the power of the unconscious
(items 244, 376), and the struggle experienced by the creative
imagination (item 398).

The image of the "ancestral voices prophesying war" (l. 30)
is thought by some critics to have personal implications outside the poem, referring to Coleridge's fear of an actual invasion (items 244, 341) or, on a psychological level, to his
awareness of personal shortcomings (item 244), his oedipal
struggle, and his failure to accomplish successfully the transition to manhood (item 317). Within the poem the threat of
war may apply specifically to Kubla's paradise or more generally to the speaker and mankind. Anticipated by the violence
of the fountain (item 379), the war image could point directly
to the garden, making explicit its fallen nature (item 216a),
its lack of harmony with natural and supernatural forces
(item 230), and its inevitable destruction (item 133). On
the other hand, if the voices "heard from far" (l. 29) origi-
nate outside the vision within the mind of the speaker, they
represent everyday distractions such as those which Coleridge
tried to avoid by going to the farmhouse between Porlock and
Linton (item 244); or, of more concern, they suggest the instinctive fears (item 370) and other intrusive sensations
which are "ancestral" because they are stored up from the

past in the dreamer's unconscious mind and which prophesy
"war" because they threaten to invade and destroy the vision
and the dream that frames it (item 353). Extended beyond
Kubla and the dreamer, the voices suggest the disruptive forces
that have always plagued man and his attempt to create the
ideal life (items 51, 369, 366, 402, 349, 151). The evil they
represent may be explained by several concepts--original sin
with its constant conflict between the senses and the spirit,
the conscious and the unconscious (items 244, 316, 378); the
war between the generations (item 379); and the psychological
explosion caused by the ego trying to regulate too rigidly
the forces of the id (items 316, 378). The ancestors may be
identified as Adam and Eve (items 244, 316, 378), Chaos and
Old Night (item 341), or the conservers of tradition and
morality (item 398).

Because most critics do regard the images and structure
of the poem as contributing to its aesthetic completeness,
they do not believe that it was composed in a dream. (For
exceptions, see items 317, 100, 111.) In the 1816 Preface
Coleridge claims that the images rose up before him without
conscious effort. "But," responds Adair, "the poem is too
intricately ordered and lucidly controlled to be so entirely
a product of the unconscious as Coleridge makes out" (item
376, p. 7). Watson praises "Kubla Khan" as "one of the best
organized of all Coleridge's works" (item 371, p. 121, and
elsewhere), and S.K. Heninger discusses the poem's "neat
units," rationally presented rather than loosely developed
as in an actual dream (item 244, p. 367).

Schneider argues most thoroughly the case against the
poem's dream composition. Although she does see it as a fragment, she points to several reasons, other than structure, for
believing that the composition was conscious and deliberate.
These include the logical meaning of the poem, its complex
pattern of sounds, Coleridge's revisions of it (see also item
298), and his use of Milton as well as contemporary sources
in the pseudo-oriental tradition. In addition to this positive evidence, she relates medical and biographical facts
which suggest the absence of a real dream. Studies of the
psychological and physiological effects of opium show that
in itself the drug does not cause dreaming. Opium-induced
or not, the dream is not mentioned in any of Coleridge's notebooks, letters, or recorded conversations; and it is unlikely
that he would have kept silent for sixteen years about such
an unusual experience. In fact, the experience is not really
so unusual in the account of it given in the earlier Crewe
manuscript, which omits the sleep, the dream, and the auto-
matic composition, saying only that the poem was written "in
a sort of Reverie" (item 155, p. 26).

The idea that the poem originated in a reverie, or day-
dream, seems to be the most acceptable explanation of
Coleridge's account of its composition (items 224, 376, 292,
385, 341, 298, 216a, 155, 112). For one thing, this interpretation of his statement harmonizes with the most popular
reading of "Kubla Khan" as a dream poem in the sense of relating the experience of a fictional dream (items 306, 353)
and deliberately exhibiting dreamlike characteristics such
as the shiftings of time and place (items 155, 317, 298, 306,
216a) and the "floating effect" created by the softening influence of assonance (item 155, p. 276).[25] (For listings of
other dreamlike characteristics see items 317, 385, 216a, 306.)
    Critics disagree on the question of whether the style of
the description in lines 1-36 should be regarded as another
dreamlike quality. Watson characterizes the tone of these
lines as "matter-of-fact, informative, even slightly technical"
(item 371, p. 121). And House discusses their "precision and
clarity," pointing to the order, or geographical consistency,
of the landscape and emphasizing the element of "plain clear
statement" (item 151, pp. 116-117). (See also items 343,
152, 230.) In opposition to this view is the response of
critics like Yarlott, who contrasts the detailed particulari-
zation of the descriptions in "Frost at Midnight" and "Fears
in Solitude" with the general terms in "Kubla Khan"--"there,"
"gardens," "many an incense-bearing tree," "here," and "spots
of greenery" (ll. 8-11) (item 398). Such lack of geographical
exactness is considered appropriate to an imaginary dream
landscape (items 155, 349, 369) and is explained by Schneider
as Coleridge's deliberate attempt, under the influence of
Lessing, to write a new kind of description whereby the de-
sired effect is produced with the "charm of words" rather
than a clearly painted picture (item 155, p. 278).
    As Coleridge said of Milton's Paradise scene, the descrip-
tion is "musical" rather than "picturesque." The spatial relationships of the dome, the river, the caves, the chasm, and
the gardens remain unmapped (item 155, p. 280; item 298).
The phrase "twice five miles" (l. 6), for instance, is offered
by several critics as an example of geometric precision (items
272, 371, 343, 398), but Woodring points out that it conveys
only the "air of poetic concreteness," since exactly what is
being measured--the two sides, the area, the circumference--
is not clear (item 230, p. 362). Similarly, the geographic
ambiguities in the description of the dome and the river give
rise to critical debates on whether the dome of lines 31-36
is the same one decreed by Kubla (items 216a, 369, 349),
whether the river flows only through the gardens (item 349),
whether it returns to its source (items 298, 216a, 341, 244,
152), and whether its "mazy" "meandering" (l. 25) indicates

uncertainty and purposelessness (items 51, 398, 366) or a
pleasant sense of leisure and freedom (items 349, 152, 232).
That it erupts "momently" (ll. 19, 24) could mean for a moment
only (items 255, 371) or at every moment and at any moment
(items 353, 385), as well as with impetus, momentum, swift-
ness, and suddenness (item 385). Its reflection of the dome
"midway on the waves" (l. 32) may indicate no particular
location (item 155), a point halfway across the river, or a
midposition between the fountain and the caves, or caverns
(items 349, 51, 255, 369).

If "Kubla Khan" is regarded not as an actual dream but as
an aesthetic whole with indefinite topographical outlines and
other dreamlike effects, some difficult questions arise: Why
did Coleridge introduce it as a "psychological curiosity"?
What is the function of the elaborate story of its dream composition? Most critics now reject the literal truth of the
Preface. (Exceptions are items 317, 111, 100.) For Schneider
and others it is not a valid autobiographical document and
therefore unreliable as a key to interpretation (items 155,
59, 293, 17, 402, 151, 178, 315, 112). Coleridge added it
mainly to evade responsibility for what he considered the
poem's incompleteness. Deprecating his achievement and at
the same time implying its uniqueness, he drew attention to
the marvelous origin and the Porlock businessman as a means
of discouraging close analysis (items 155, 293, 17, 379).
He might also have felt uncomfortable with the daemonic implications of the theory of poetry suggested by the amoral,
sensual paradise of Xanadu (item 128) and with the comparison
of the poet and the tyrannical Khan (item 315). And in 1816,
especially, he would have wanted to disclaim the credo as an
expression of his own hope (items 402, 315).

A few critics, however, take exception to this recent
tendency to downgrade the Preface. Chayes considers this
attitude likely to be as erroneous as the earlier one of
unquestioning acceptance. She and Suther view the Preface as
a guide not to the poem's composition but to its content
(items 353, 349). One of the chief revisions in the poem between the time of the Crewe manuscript and eventual publication, the expanded Preface is like Coleridge's other notes
and prefaces in being valuable for its relationship to the
poem. Specifically, it functions as a paraphrase of the
poem's content and as an argument or gloss (item 353). An
allegory of the poetic process and its difficulties (item 128),
the purported story emphasizes the importance of the uncon
scious (items 376, 317, 224), constitutes a general structural
parallel with the poem (item 353), and anticipates the theme
of intrusion in the image of the ancestral voices and the
feeling of having lost the greater part of the poem in the

vision of the Abyssinian maid and her song (item 317). The
published Preface no longer follows but precedes the text,
like an epigraph or argument. As such, it becomes an indis-
pensable part of the poem, making clear to the reader that the
events in the first two stanzas occurred in a vision while the
speaker was dreaming (items 353, 349). Possibly, then,
Coleridge added the Preface not so much out of modesty (item
151) or embarrassment as in response to the need for an even
more fundamental revision (item 353).

Whatever his reasons for writing the Preface and however
he composed the poem, most critics regard it as much more than
a "psychological curiosity." Only a few readers still find
it meaningless (items 112, 245) or consider its statement as
insubstantial (item 293) or unimportant (item 155). Among
these, the most prominent is Schneider. According to her
analysis, "so far as it 'says' anything at all, [it] says
nothing of the least importance to us" (item 155, p. 20). Its
significance lies in the interlacings of form and meaning,
not in the theme itself or in its symbolism. Believing that
symbolic interpretations have originated from considerations
extraneous to the poem, she argues that it was Coleridge's
practice to have explicit rather than hidden meanings, that
his poetic theory demanded "translucence," and that he had no
taste for symbolic poetry, such as Blake's, in which meaning
is implied rather than expressed (item 155, p. 258).

This position is contrary to the assumptions underlying
most interpretations, and critics such as Suther and Beer
have chosen to attack it directly. Believing that symbolic
interpretations grew out of the need to explain the initial
impact of the poem, Suther presents evidence indicating that,
though Coleridge did write some poetry with explicit meaning,
in theory he did not recommend it and in practice usually
composed "symbolic" poetry, or poetry which characteristically
delivers its meaning by implication, for poetry which operates
otherwise is not another style but another form of discourse.
Coleridge's refusal to expound the symbolic meanings in "Kubla
Khan" does not imply their absence (item 349).

Beer objects to Schneider's method of drawing conclusions
about the major poems from the minor ones (item 216a), although
Suther, Bostetter, and Yarlott use it to some extent when they
hope to illuminate the symbolic meanings of the images in
"Kubla Khan" by studying them as they appear in other poems
where their meaning is stated outright (items 349, 293, 398).
Still others, relying in this respect on the text alone,
choose to read the poem symbolically because of its unusual
arrangement of imagery, its disregard for normal discursive
order (items 232, 422). They would no doubt agree with
Suther, though, as he reverses Schneider's position: "We

should have exceptionally good reason before we suppose that
the poems in which he seems most nearly to have practiced
what he preached, *The Ancient Mariner*, *Christabel*, and 'Kubla
Khan,' have no symbolical depth susceptible of relevant and
fruitful interpretation" (item 349, p. 11).

Statements of symbolic meaning usually focus on the theme
of human creativity. At the ethical and practical levels,
this idea constitutes the human interest of the poem, conveying as it does the impossibility of man's complete and permanent control over primitive and irrational forces within
himself and in nature. Kubla has enclosed and cultivated a
portion of the wilderness, but his imposed paradise of order,
security, and pleasure is threatened by untamed forces which
still exist--the violent, uncontrollable fountain, the meandering river which empties into measureless caverns, the ancient
forests, and the "woman wailing for her demon-lover" (1. 16).
Within the walls Kubla hears the tumult of the river's origin
and end and, more ominously, the "Ancestral voices prophesying
war" (1. 30). His dome, precariously constructed partly of
ice, leaves no impression on the river other than a shadow
(items 402, 369, 398, 255, 293, 216a, 316, 378, 133).

As the last eighteen lines make clear (items 349, 371),
on the imaginative level the theme of creativity applies
specifically to the poet and the poetic experience.[26] Symbolic
of what it describes (items 128, 353, 349, 341, 364), the poem
moves from dream to poem to poet in a process involving the
faculties of memory, fancy, primary and secondary imagination,
and will. Except for lines 3-5 the dream vision of the first
stanza is dependent for its materials on memories of Purchas
and is a paraphrase and elaboration by the fancy of the passage quoted in the Preface. The stylistic change in the second
stanza suggests not only the presence of the dreamer but also
the influence of the imagination, represented in its secondary
aspect by the river and in its primary function by the fountain and in the third stanza by the experience of music and
delight. Will and consciousness assume full importance in
the third stanza with the definite first-person point of view
and the speaker's expression of purpose concerning his poem.
Unlike Kubla, who could only command that the pleasure dome
be constructed by someone else, the poet-speaker would more
directly "build" (1. 46) his poetic counterpart of it, expressing his will as a conscious action of his own (item 353). He
seeks not merely to emulate the mightiest of human material
power but to surpass it. Unrelated to measurement and destruction, his finer, more lasting dome would be created with music
"loud and long" (1. 45), would reach an audience wider than
his own memory, and would provide a continual source of pleasure both as a vision, which could be summoned again and
again, and as a poem (items 353, 286, 402, 255, 306).

On both levels the theme of creativity is developed by
the pattern of opposites. Discordant qualities characterize
Kubla's human paradise as well as the imaginative poem which
would describe it. Xanadu is described in terms of contraries
--heat and cold (items 305, 343, 364, 286), light and dark
(items 305, 224, 155, 306, 230), solids and liquids (item
343), the round and the angular (item 306), height and depth
(items 152, 151, 349, 230, 398), the hard and the soft (item
151), quiet and noise (item 364), the near and the far-off
(item 152), fertility and sterility (items 152, 349), life
and death (items 306, 255, 305, 51), beginning and ending
(items 305, 306, 286), production and destruction (items 255,
349), the bounded and the boundless (items 349, 306, 343, 230,
338, 316, 378), the orderly and the chaotic (items 293, 316,
378, 349, 305, 364), peace and violence (items 305, 152, 306,
343), stasis and motion (items 343, 305, 316, 378, 385, 341),
the royal and the plebeian (item 343), the human and the
daemonic (items 343, 349).

These contrasting descriptions are sometimes discussed
as stemming from a central opposition, variously identified
as the conscious and the unconscious aspect of the mind
(items 376, 353, 293, 244); the rationalistic understanding
and the romantic imagination or Gothic love of horrible sublimity, unrestrained energies, and powerful destruction
(items 398, 371, 216a, 230, 364); the world of the sun and
the moon (item 244) or of Kubla and Cybele (items 298, 338);
male and female (items 338, 152, 379, 232, 317, 51); pleasure
and pain (items 366, 338, 224); profane pleasure and sacredness or solemnity (items 303, 398, 414, 151, 133, 316, 378,
369, 230, 155); affirmation and negation (item 155) or manic
and depressive elements (item 317); Paradise and Hell (items
155, 353); the finite and the infinite (items 230, 349); art
and nature (items 293, 338, 398); the natural and the supernatural (item 128); the mechanical or artificial and the
organic or natural (items 230, 371, 303, 316, 378).[27]

More important than identifying the opposites is the
problem of assessing their function in the poem. Especially
in light of Coleridge's later theory most critics assume
that the opposites are reconciled at least temporarily by
Kubla and permanently by the poet. (See mainly items 224,
305, 133, 349, 353, 152, 385, 298, 151.) They see the dome
and garden as a visual illustration of the reconciliation of
opposites and thus as an emblem of imaginative poetry. They
point out numerous examples of mediation: the incense-bearing
trees and the dome, both of which suggest a blend of the
sensual and the religious (items 133, 349); the ancient
forests "Enfolding sunny spots of greenery" (1. 11) (items
349, 224); the slanting chasm and the partially subterranean

river (items 133, 353, 152); the presence of daemonic love
within holy precincts (item 152); the fountain described in
imagery of production and destruction ("chaffy grain," "hail,"
and "thresher's flail," ll. 21-22), stasis and motion (the
"dancing rocks," l. 23, the cascade of bouncing hailstones,
and the arc of flying chaff) (items 385, 255); and the tumult
of the river's descent into the sea crossing the distance of
the whole landscape and reaching the hearing of Kubla (item
353). In the afterglow of the river's reconciling circuit
occur more obvious instances of unification: the shadow of
the dome floating on the waves; the "mingled measure" (l. 33)
which combines and regularizes the fountain's "turmoil" (l. 17)
and the caves' "tumult" (l. 28); the miracle of a design, or
"device," which appears spontaneous (l. 35); and "A sunny
pleasure-dome with caves of ice" (l. 36). The crowning image
of reconciliation, the dome with its icy caves, brings together
nearly all of the various opposites implicit in the description
of Xanadu (items 353, 224, 305, 349, 317, 298, 341, 51, 216a,
398, 152). Corresponding to it on a higher level, the vision
of the poet brings the whole poem to resolution, representing
a reconciliation of the "mighty fountain" and Kubla's successor
the poet, imagination and will, creation and perception, experience private and communicated, dream and art (items 353,
370).

   Not all readers, however, can accept these instances of
reconciliation without qualification. Heninger, for one,
writes that in lines 25-26 the conscious and the unconscious
contact each other and intermingle but do not interfuse. The
river returns to its habitual place in the sunless "lifeless
ocean" (l. 28), carrying with it the remains of the fallen
dome. This means that "the attempted integration of conscious
and unconscious has failed" (item 244, p. 364). Similarly,
Beverly Fields and Schneider warn that Coleridge's idea of
the reconciliation of opposites is often used to justify confusion and that, although it is a convenient way of describing
the special quality of "Kubla Khan," it is overworked and not
quite accurate. What actually occurs is not reconciliation
but extreme tension or oscillation (items 379, 155). For
Schneider the poem's deepest meaning is probably ambivalence,
or oscillation, "between giving and taking away, bright affirmation and sunless negation, light flowing music that nevertheless stands still" (item 155, p. 287).

   The question of whether the opposites are reconciled bears
directly upon the interpretation of the major images in the
poem--Kubla Khan, his dome, the surrounding garden, and the
poet-speaker. The ambivalence in these images has given rise
to widely divergent opinions about whether the poem's total
effect is one of fulfillment or frustration and failure and

whether Kubla and his paradise are genuine or false.[28] Reconciled, or balanced, the opposites emphasize the favorable view
of Kubla and his accomplishment and define the success of the
poet. Unreconciled, they function ironically to establish
the unfavorable attitude toward Kubla and his creation and to
suggest the failure of the poet.

The negative interpretation of Kubla stresses his tyrannical pride, exclusiveness, and impercipience. A "barbarous
fop" (item 371, p. 126), he is connected with the wicked,
cruel king of the Tartars, a people whom Coleridge would have
associated with Ham's descendants, sun-worship, violence, and
the Satanic (items 216a, 315, 303, 402), Since Coleridge
hated tyranny, luxury, and political ambition, he would have
condemned Kubla's despotism (items 230, 275, 371). He would
have disapproved of Kubla's haughty withdrawal from the in-
fluxes of nature and from normal human relationships. Within
the massive walls and towers, Kubla hears only the ghostly
voices of the past and possibly the wailing woman. As indicated by the passive voice in lines 6-11, his dealings with
the slave force which enacted his decree are utterly impersonal
(items 398, 191, 133). His "commanding genius" is comparable
to that of Napoleon, a manifestation of daemonic powers (item
216a, p. 226). He is presumptuous and impercipient in locating
the garden above the chasm, the tumult, and the prophecies of
war and in attempting to appropriate the sacred river for his
own trivial pleasure (items 230, 371). His limited understanding never grasps the significance of the river or the
mysterious eternities represented by the measureless caverns
and the ancient forests (items 216a, 398). A remorseless
despot, separated from nature and from the larger spiritual
life of the universe, he certainly does not qualify as a model
of the poet whose "heart and intellect should be *combined*,
intimately combined and *unified* with the great appearances
of nature" (item 398, p. 133; item 230).

His enclosed garden is a lost, or fallen, paradise
(items 216a, 230, 292, 398, 232), and his pleasure dome
represents "a mistaken ideal," fallen man's desire to re-
create the paradisal garden and to regain his lost knowledge
(item 216a, p. 224). In contrast to the true synthesis, indicated by the dome of lines 31-36, is the disjunction of pleasure and sacredness suggested by the dome ordered by Kubla
and the differentiation within his garden (items 216a, 398).
Although walls and towers geographically encircle the forests,
the chasm, and the river, these rugged features evidently remain unassimilated into the general texture of Kubla's "fussy
little paradise" (item 398, p. 134). The river only appears
amenable to his facile ingenuity, for tumult and bewilderment
prevail, and nothing really comes of its creative energy

(items 398, 244, 402). Without it, however, the description of the garden is not particularly attractive or appealing. Its heavy stresses and abrupt masculine rhymes create a slow, ponderous rhythm which has a hammerlike quality; and its generality is emphasized by the contrast with what Coleridge considered a true paradise in "The Garden of Boccaccio" (item 398).

Unlike that garden, Kubla's creation is distinguished mainly by its artificiality and sensuality. These qualities are heightened within the poem by juxtaposition with savagery and holiness (items 316, 378, 371) and outside the poem by Coleridge's sources and parallel usages (items 216a, 398). He chooses the word "dome," for example, instead of Purchas' "house" or the Preface's "palace"; and this modification, as well as the natural dome images in other poems, indicates the dome's lack of practical function, its removal from an integral relationship with nature (items 216a, 398). Coleridge describes the dome and its surroundings as "stately" (l. 2) and "bright" (l. 8)--epithets which he typically used in distinguishing art from nature. For Purchas' "pleasant Springs, delightfull Streames," Coleridge substitutes the metallic phrase "gardens bright with sinuous rills," which has sinister, almost reptilian, associations. Furthermore, he excludes from Kubla's garden Purchas' live creatures (item 398, p. 134).

With respect to sensuality, however, Coleridge did not change the coloring of the details suggested by his sources-- Purchas' description of Cublai Can's estate and of Aloadine's Mohammedan Paradise (items 398, 376); Milton's conception of Pandemonium in *Paradise Lost*, I, 710-713 (items 385, 216a),[29] and inclusion among the false paradises of IV, 268-284, the Abyssinian Paradise on Mount Amara (items 216a, 376); Wieland's account of Oberon's pleasure palace (item 292); and the pleasure dome best known in his own day, the Russian ice palace belonging to the sensual despot Catherine. Since he abhorred this "foul Woman of the North" and referred to her mock palace as "glittering, cold and transitory," it may have influenced Kubla's "sunny pleasure-dome with caves of ice" (l. 36) (item 275, p. 51, and elsewhere; items 303, 230). In other poems Coleridge used the dome image to suggest material values, moral laxity, and purposeless or excessive sensuality. And in "Kubla Khan" he links it with "pleasure" (ll. 2, 31, 36)-- a concept which he distinguished from joy and usually represented in pejorative terms. Thus, his hyphenating of "pleasure-dome" probably implies moral disapproval (items 398, 298, 230).[30]

His poem "To Nature" and the detail of the blossoming "incense-bearing" trees (l. 9) further indicate the fallen nature of Kubla's paradise. Associated with sun-worship

(item 216a), incense suggests a manufactured perfume rather
than a natural fragrance; and in light of its significance in
other poems, the blossom image probably connotes unethical
sensuality. In contrast are the incense and dome images, as
well as the emphasis on "wild" and "I," in "To Nature":

> So will I build my altar in the fields,
> And the blue sky my fretted dome shall be,
> And the sweet fragrance that the *wild* flower yields
> Shall be the incense *I* will yield to thee.
>
> > (item 398, p. 137)

Similarly, the speaker in "Kubla Khan" would build his
dome "in air" (1. 46), would compose an ideal poem which unified art and nature, pleasure and sacredness (items 349, 398,
230, 51, 371, 152).[31] But, in the negative view of the poem,
he cannot. In contrast to the regenerated poet in "The
Garden of Boccaccio," he is aroused only to wishful desire.
The deep delight of joy is as much beyond his reach as it is
Kubla's--a situation for which he seems to blame the loss of
his past relationship with the maid and, consequently, his
inner psychological harmony (item 398).

His failure hinges mainly upon a heavy emphasis of the
words "once" (1. 38) and "Could" (1. 42). "Once" means only
once, for the influence of the maid is now lost (items 151,
232). And the conditional statement "Could I revive within
me" carries the sense of "If only I could, but I can't" (items
151, 375, 293, 244, 155, 59, 224, 341, 398, 343, 232, 379,
306).

These implications signify the speaker's cry of frustration and the imaginary context of his ecstasy (items 293, 398).
Ushered modestly and indirectly into the poem, through the
vignette of the Abyssinian maid, the last eighteen lines are
despondent, gloomy, despairing, bitter, and--with respect to
the possibility of the poet's communicating his insights to
others--even cynical (items 402, 155, 232, 343, 244).

If, on the other hand, the total effect of the poem is
considered positive, then the speaker's tone is hopeful,
prospective, joyous, exalted, ecstatic (items 292, 376, 320).
Kubla may be regarded as admirable, and his paradise as genuine
and ethical. Such an interpretation characterizes him as
representative man (items 133, 151, 402, 349), godlike in his
power, detachment, and creativity. Adapted from Purchas, his
name connects him with the Tartar conqueror, distinguished
for his breadth of mind, religious tolerance, and generosity
toward men of letters (items 151, 155). Several notebook
entries indicate that Coleridge thought of him as a powerful
king who concerned himself with increasing the knowledge of
his people. This evidence coincides with Coleridge's practice

in the matter of titles and his use of monarchy in other
poems: Kubla is not a villain but a creator associated with
poetry and the absolute. His decree, like that of any creator, is presumptuous but necessary to the realization of his
fullest potential as a man (item 349). It images man's power
over the disparate elements of his environment and his ability
to make his paradise himself, to give substance to his dreams
(items 286, 151, 402, 317, 293). The reality of Xanadu is
possible, in fact, because of Kubla's practical wisdom in
locating it in the chasm neighborhood near the only source of
water (item 349). Because he depends on the river for irri-
gation, he is not completely cut off from life outside the
walls and towers (items 152, 128). He lives in splendid isolation—aloof, but within hearing distance of the tumult and
the mingled measure (items 293, 17). In this position, whether
an emblem of God or mankind, he functions mainly to prepare
for the similar but greater role of the poet (items 353, 286,
341, 385, 317, 51, 316, 378, 402).

His creation represents human life at its best, ideally
balanced between pleasure and sacredness, the rational and
the irrational (items 357, 306, 349, 286, 133, 224, 402, 152).
"Acceptance of the Paradise, in sympathy," says House, "is
the normal response, from childhood and unsophistication to
criticism: to most people rejection would mean a ruinous and
purposeless wrench" (item 151, p. 120; item 349). It is
fallen only in the sense that everything is. Since it is
built and defended by man, it is impermanent and continually
vulnerable to the forces of evil. Precariousness, the risk
that it may be lost, constitutes its chief import, not artificiality or sensuality (items 354, 224, 152, 286, 349, 151,
306, 369, 402, 303, 133, 293).

Although Xanadu is a "rare device" (1. 35), it is not artificial in any unfavorable way. Coleridge did not think of
the artificial, or constructed, as undesirable. In characterizing literary composition as "artificial," he used the term
as one of praise, evidently in the sense of "artistic, highly
skilled" (item 385, p. 151). And in his poetry, images of
mountains and man-made domes are roughly interchangeable, both
spurring imaginative creation (item 349).

Thus, the fact that Kubla's dome and garden are constructed
does not automatically make them opposed to nature. The dome
has a simpler shape than the forms of nature, but it blends
with them (item 133). It is "stately" (1. 2) in the sense of
having connections with the state and of combining dignity
and pleasing simplicity with the awesome, the massive, and
the majestic (items 316, 378, 349). Only in comparison to
its creator's original idea can it be called cold or lifeless
(item 369), the word "dome" being chosen perhaps for its

fullness of sound (item 155). Similarly, the garden surrounding the dome is above and beyond nature yet continuous with
it. Set apart and protected yet in contact with nature and
the everyday world, Xanadu is both a faraway place and every
wood and dale (items 133, 349, 152, 128).

It cannot be absolutely equated with any of the various
paradises from which Coleridge drew his imagery--neither the
false paradises nor Milton's Eden (item 317), the Promised
Land of Canaan, Elysium, the Garden of the Hesperides (item
376), Spenser's Garden of Adonis, or Dante's earthly paradise
(items 51, 341, 151). The pseudo paradise of Abyssinia indicates the impermanence of Xanadu as an imitation of God's
eternal creativity (item 369) and relegates it to a compara-
tively low position among the three paradises mentioned in
the poem (item 353). But, House warns, "because the Abassin
kings and Mount Amara belong with one false paradise it does
not follow that the Abyssinian maid and Mount Abora belong
with another" (item 151, pp. 119-120). In fact, Coleridge
marked out "Amora" in the Crewe manuscript to avoid the suggestion that he was drawing inspiration from an admittedly
false paradise (item 402).[32]

Kubla's garden, then, is neither false nor specifically
religious or sacramental (items 151, 402, 255, 306). But the
evidence that it is intended to convey moral disapproval is
unconvincing. The image of the blossoming, incense-bearing
trees, for example, is cited by Breyer as an instance of the
lack of sensuality in Xanadu, where pleasures are mainly
visual rather than appetitive. He notes the absence of fruit
trees and, along with other scholars, defines the pleasure
linked with the dome as the aesthetic pleasure which Coleridge
associated with poetry (items 128, 224, 349). Certainly the
pleasure is controlled (items 293, 316, 378) and modified by
the dome's stateliness, or seriousness (item 244).

While the dome does not convey excessive sensuality, it
does suggest the pleasant sensations of roundness, smoothness,
and fullness (items 133, 151, 152). It images unity and
completeness (items 369, 224), satisfaction and fulfillment,
with words like "fertile" (1. 6), "girdled" (1. 7), and "Enfolding" (1. 11) reinforcing its connotation of security,
shelter, or refuge (items 349, 151, 402, 133). These associations make it a symbol not only of a great civilization,
shaped from the wilderness by the creative spirit of man, but
also of the ideal poem (items 151, 422, 349, 224, 369, 376).[33]

Given sufficient inspiration, the speaker of "Kubla Khan"
will create such a poem, or, indeed, may have already done so.[34]
His achievement is not lessened by the use of "once" (1. 38),
a lightly accented word indicating delight, surprise and the
sense of unique privilege, or by the conditional form of the

statement in lines 42-47, which again should be read with
only a slight emphasis on "Could" (l. 42). The condition is
then an "'open' condition," explains House, "like 'Could you
make it Wednesday instead of Thursday, it would be easier for
me'" (item 151, p. 115; items 320, 316, 378, 178, 303, 376).
If this analogy "pushes things too far," as it does for
Suther,[35] the lines may be read as a simple cause-effect
statement: "could I do one thing the result would be such
that I would do something else." In either case, however,
"but I cannot is nowhere implied in the poem" (item 349, pp.
178, 275; item 353). And the conditional statement becomes a
prophecy of poetic triumph (item 353).[36]

This positive reading of "once" and "Could" is supported
by biographical circumstances as well as rhythmical development and the referent of "that dome" (l. 46). Instead of bemoaning the loss of his creative power, in 1797-98 Coleridge
was just discovering its strength (items 151, 349). In response to his feeling about that discovery, the last paragraph
of "Kubla Khan" moves easily from delight and surprise, through
enthusiasm, to ecstasy. The light and fast meter creates a
lilting rhythm which asserts rather than denies the ecstasy
and conveys assurance and power rather than frustration
(items 151, 366, 376). And such confidence seems justified
in light of the reference of "that dome" to the beautifully
complete and final description of Xanadu (item 151). The
poem is not an apology for failure but a powerful, triumphant
affirmation of the potentialities of poetry (items 151, 353).

While Yarlott disagrees with this interpretation of the
poem, he no doubt represents the feelings of critics on both
sides of the question when he introduces his discussion of
"Kubla Khan" with the following observation: "We may question
without end *what* it means, but few of us question if the poem
is worth the trouble, or whether the meaning is worth the
having" (item 398, p. 127).

C. "CHRISTABEL"

Unlike "The Ancient Mariner" and "Kubla Khan," "Christabel"
is undeniably a fragment (item 151). Although Coleridge
claimed to have written more of it (items 376, 65, 30, 28),
the known manuscripts and published versions contain only
two of its intended five parts. Consequently, it has not
attracted the serious attention given to the other major
poems (item 398). Studies of "Christabel" are necessarily
limited mainly to considerations of whether Coleridge had a

plan for the whole, the extent to which he unified the first
two parts, and the reasons why he did not finish the poem.

B.R. McElderry, Jr., begins his article on the criticism
of "Christabel" with this comment: "Few poets have bequeathed
to posterity so many puzzling questions as the artist-philo-
sopher Coleridge. And among these questions none is more
insistent than this: what shall we make of *Christabel*?" (item
52, p. 206). Like the early reviewers, some recent critics
are unable to make anything of it. They read the poem
literally as a supernatural tale depicting the seduction of
the innocent mortal Christabel by the witch Geraldine. To
support this interpretation they point to Coleridge's interest
in witchcraft, his dreams of strange ladies vaguely reminiscent
of Geraldine, and his heavy debt to popular ballads and Gothic
romances (items 213, 270, 319, 30, 52, 371, 303, 23). Donald R.
Tuttle, for example, concludes that Percy's *Reliques* and the
Gothic novels influenced the atmosphere, the characterizations,
and almost every important episode. Among the borrowed details he lists the heroine's name; the wrenched accent of
words like "countrée" (1. 225); and such standard Gothic devices as the setting in a still, moonlit forest at midnight,
the crowing cock, the owl, the mastiff bitch, the huge oak
tree with a touch of green, the confusion of the wind with
moaning, and the description of the castle with its bells,
dying fire, armor on the wall, hanging lamp, clock, and iron
gate. He cites parallels for Geraldine's corpse-like appearance, her abduction by the five ruffians, her fainting on
entering the rescuer's bedroom, her bewitchment of Leoline's
beautiful daughter, and her feelings of apprehension and
refreshment, and also for Christabel's leaving her room at
midnight, returning through the courtyard and castle halls,
trimming her lamp, lighting up Geraldine's eye and Leoline's
shield, relaxing from her trance, being unable to tell of
her experience, sleeping with tears shining on her eyelashes,
and begging a request of her father (item 23; see also items
319, 270). As the heroine of a Gothic romance, Christabel is
expected to wander, suffer, and at last be rescued. It is
inappropriate to attach moral significance to her suffering
(item 23).

On the other hand, Coleridge criticized the Gothic novel
for its lack of moral truth and human interest (items 52, 30,
376) and in *Biographia Literaria* says he planned to include
such truth and interest in his own supernatural tales (item
11). He referred to the idea of "Christabel" as "extremely
subtle and difficult" (item 11, pp. 443-444, and elsewhere).
His son Derwent believed that "the sufferings of Christabel
were to have been represented as vicarious, endured for 'her
lover far away.'" And his friend and biographer James Gillman

explained that "the story of Christabel is partly founded on
the notion, that the virtuous of this world save the wicked.
The pious and good Christabel suffers and prays for 'The weal
of her lover that is far away'" (item 11, pp. 438, 444, and
elsewhere).

These statements constitute the external evidence from
which most critics conclude that Coleridge did intend a moral
or thematic significance. Along with the skillful, sensitive
description of the setting and the complexity of the characters,
it is this moral or metaphysical dimension which distinguishes
Coleridge's poem from the standard Gothic tale (items 398,
306, 293, 319, 30, 52). "For all its Gothic-looking materials,"
says Kathleen Coburn, "Christabel" is not a Gothic romance,
"but rather makes use of the medium to project an inner experience" (item 164, pp. 127-128). It describes the usual
conflict of innocence and evil, but with the moral purpose of
showing the way evil works upon and transforms innocence
(item 185). It explores more deeply the serious psychological
areas only touched in the elementary story of Gothic horror
(item 151).

These areas have been identified in various terms, the
oldest and most frequently offered being those of religion and
sex. Both Derwent Coleridge and Gillman agree that the main
theme of the poem is based on the religious doctrine of vicarious suffering (items 11, 151, 376, 30). Because this
idea is a part of the traditional conception of martyrdom,
their view is supported by Coleridge's statement to Thomas
Allsop: quoting the second stanza of Crashaw's "Hymn" to the
martyred Saint Theresa, Coleridge commented that "these verses
were ever present to my mind whilst writing the second part of
Christabel; if, indeed by some subtle process of mind they
did not suggest the first thought of the whole poem" (item 30,
p. 208, and elsewhere).

Evidently Coleridge intended the idea of vicarious atonement to establish the poem's moral justification and to give
the semblance of truth to its supernatural events (items 30,
11). The efficacy of Christabel's suffering is the connection
between the first episode of her leaving the castle to pray
and the final event according to Gillman of her lover's safe
return (item 11). Through her encounter with the preternatural
being Geraldine, Christabel takes the daemonic evil into herself and eventually will transform it into good (items 30,
216a). In some way her Christlike suffering is intended to
redeem her lover (items 216a, 30), Geraldine (item 65), or
Leoline and Langdale Hall (item 81). In this redemptive function she, like Saint Theresa, is a "youthful hermitess"
(1. 320) loved by all "who live in the upper sky" (1. 227)
(items 376, 30);[37] as a type of martyr, she knows but cannot
speak of Geraldine's identity (item 366).

As with Crashaw's Saint Theresa, however, Christabel's
martyrdom is not altogether religious. The early reviews and
continuations recognized the sexual nature of her enchantment
and accused the poem of obscenity. Coleridge never denied
the charge; and, probably because of the poem's obvious sexual
theme, he seemed nervous about publishing it (items 30, 65,
270, 398). Recent critics have found Christabel's experience
too complex to be explained simply as vicarious suffering.
For House both the "Hymn to Saint Teresa" and "Christabel"
concern "the psychological borderland where matters of religion overlap with matters of sex" (item 151, p. 130; see also
item 347, p. 63). Within this borderland Thomas R. Preston
places the emphasis on religion: as in the writings of Crashaw
and other mystics, the sexual embrace is a metaphor for
Christabel's mystical union with the Divine (item 81). Roy P.
Basler, on the other hand, speculates that Coleridge planned
to use the religious idea only to develop the aesthetic pattern
of the story, the central motivation of which is sexual.
Christabel's romantic love for her knight and desire for a
test of her love parallels Saint Theresa's spiritual love of
Christ and wish for martyrdom for his sake. In spite of her
mother's influence in the two parts completed, Christabel's
love is thwarted by Geraldine's seduction of her body and soul
(item 65).

Though it is a mental recapitulation as well, the enchantment is obviously sexual (items 319, 135, 378). This is made
explicit by the physical action of Geraldine's lying down in
"appropriately medieval nudity" and taking the equally naked
Christabel in her arms to work the "spell" (1. 267) (item 65,
p. 83). It is indicated further by the psychological realism
in the descriptions of Geraldine's desire (11. 256-278) and
Christabel's trance (11. 292-297) and "after-rest" (11. 312-
318); the narrator's "specifically vague" apostrophe to her
shame and sorrow (11. 296-297) and his broken reference to
the nature of her dream (1. 295); the phrase spoken of
Geraldine, "Thou'st had thy will" (1. 306); and the detail of
her "heaving breasts" (11. 379-380), which indicates the
transforming power of her embrace (item 65, p. 84; item 81)[38]
or her sensual behavior as she sets out to captivate Leoline
(item 398).[39] These suggestions are underlined by the erotic
language in which Bracy tells of his dream. At midnight, the
same time that Christabel met Geraldine, he saw the dove named
Christabel alone in the forest, fluttering and moaning, with
a snake coiled around it: "And with the dove it heaves and
stirs, / Swelling its neck as she swelled hers" (11. 553-554)
(items 398, 81, 135).

In light of the sexual nature of the enchantment, Geraldine's peculiar faintness at the oak tree and the references

to marriage become thematically significant. Geraldine's repeated request for Christabel to "stretch forth" her hand
(11. 75, 102) indicates a desire for physical contact and begins a series of advances which culminate in the embrace and
enchantment (item 65). In the context of the first scene,
however, Geraldine appears to be a tired, distressed lady.
It is only after Christabel leads her through the forest to
the castle gate that she acts suspiciously. There she faints,
and Christabel carries her over the threshold. This act is
only partially explained as a renewal of physical contact and
as a portent of evil based on the popular superstition that
an evil or preternatural spirit could not enter a home which
had been properly blessed without the assistance of the inhabitants. Christabel could have invited Geraldine to enter
the castle in numerous ways, even by the guiding touch of her
hand. Carrying her over the threshold imitates the familiar
action of bridegroom and bride, suggesting the idea of a marriage. The reversal of positions need not be significant;
but if taken literally, it stresses the unnaturalness of the
bridal which is about to follow (items 378, 135, 65; for
another interpretation of the threshold scene, see item 117).

   Another preparation for the ironic marriage is Christabel's
seemingly irrelevant remark that on her deathbed her mother
had predicted that she should be awakened by the castle bell
striking twelve on her daughter's wedding day (11. 198-201).
In a sense, this is what happens. At the beginning of the
poem the clock has struck twelve (1. 1), and the Baron's old
watchdog has answered it and perhaps has seen the mother's
shroud (11. 9-13). Later Geraldine thinks she has heard the
castle bell (11. 100-101), and in the bedroom the mother's
ghost actually appears. Knowing the power of her prophecy
and eager for its fulfillment, Geraldine welcomes her and then
with an "altered," "hollow" voice orders, "Off, woman, off!
this hour is mine" (11. 204, 210-211) (items 81, 135, 378,
347).

   In addition to the mother's prophesied appearance, the
midnight wedding bells, and the threshold scene, there are
several suggestions of a marriage ceremony. Geraldine is
dressed in a "silken robe of white" (11. 59; see also 11.
250, 364) with "jems entangled in her hair" (1. 65). The
flaming brands in the castle hall and the hanging lamp in
Christabel's room resemble the altar candles and sanctuary
lamp in medieval churches (item 347). Geraldine renews her
strength with a "wild-flower wine" (1. 220) reminiscent of
the communion wine drunk before the marriage ceremony. And
as she takes the "maiden" (11. 259, 262, 263, 299) into her
arms, she pronounces a curse which will be "lord" of Christabel's utterance (1. 268). With the "seal" (1. 270) of her

shame and sorrow she binds Christabel to her as much as if
she had encircled her finger with a wedding ring (item 135).
The implication seems clear that Christabel has consummated
her marriage (item 81).

The religious-sexual embrace takes on another dimension
in "The Conclusion to Part I" where it is related to the
parent-child motif: Geraldine sleeps with Christabel "As a
mother with her child" (1. 301), and Christabel smiles "As
infants at a sudden light" (1. 318), comforted during her
"after-rest" (1. 465) by a sweet vision of her guardian
mother (11. 326-328). Christabel introduces the theme when
she offers Geraldine the cordial wine made by the mother
(1. 193) and tells her of the mother's prophecy and death
(11. 197-201). It is picked up at the beginning of Part II
by Leoline, who in continued mourning of his wife's death has
established the custom of daily funeral obsequies whereby
the morning bell is to be a reminder to everyone of mortality
(11. 332-344). Again at the end of Part II Christabel in-
vokes the long-cherished memory of her mother as she pleads
with her father to send Geraldine away (11. 616-617). Re-
iterating her plea, the narrator recalls Leoline's love for
his wife and child before reporting that in confusion and
rage he turned his back upon Christabel. In abandoning his
only child Leoline destroys the most meaningful human relationship left to him. His mixed feelings of love and hatred are
universalized in "The Conclusion to Part II" (items 398,
261, 376).

As this passage indicates to many critics, the significance of the parent-child relationship is its ambivalence.
Especially after Leoline embraces Geraldine, his behavior
toward his daughter is ambivalent. His own pride and self-
centeredness override his concern for her feelings when,
assuming that she is bent on insulting his baronial hospitality, he turns away in anger (items 319, 398). His reaction
is parallel on a personal level to Coleridge's ambivalent
feelings toward his sons Hartley and Derwent (items 65, 398).[40]
On a thematic level it is related to Leoline's unconscious
identification of the loss of his wife with the birth of his
child. The association in Christabel's birth of love and
life with death is also the source of ambivalence in her relationship with her mother. Literally, of course, she owes
her life to her mother. Symbolically, she participates in
the cyclical process of nature wherein life springs from
death (items 347, 65).

The ambivalence which distinguishes the parent-child relationship is present for some critics in the sexual and religious themes as well. The problem in reading "Christabel,"
argues Enscoe, is not to point out its obvious concern with

sexual passion but to discover the significance of the theme, to determine how the reader is to respond to the enchantment. Enscoe finds that Coleridge's attitude toward the enchantment and the sexual force in general is one of ambivalence. The destruction of Christabel's innocence is regrettable but inevitable and necessary for life in this world. By the end of Part II she is helpless and isolated in an almost daemonic state, but for this high price she is now awake to life and reality, having been saved from the mechanical, deathlike existence within the castle (item 378).

In Arthur Wormhoudt's psychoanalytic reading the poem is concerned more with conflict and hate than with sexual or religious love. The idea of Christabel's vicarious suffering has little or no textual support, and the concept of martyrdom in Coleridge's reference to Saint Theresa should be understood in the psychological sense of masochism, not in the religious sense (item 117). Aware of the same ambiguity, Adair nevertheless accepts at face value Coleridge's comment and the interpretations of Derwent Coleridge and Gillman. She explains that especially in Part I Coleridge must have intended the theme of vicarious suffering but by the time he started Part II he had discovered that evil was deeply rooted within even the innocent sufferers and was therefore not redeemable by human power. At the end of Part II Christabel's will has been so corrupted that evil is indistinguishable from good. And in his only direct remark on how he would continue the poem, Coleridge referred to composing "the third part of *Christabel* or the song of her desolation" (item 164, p. 127, and elsewhere). Neither in this notebook entry nor in the conclusion of the poem is there any suggestion of redemption (item 376). For Bostetter the theme of Christabel's vicarious suffering is a source of irony. The view of Geraldine as an instrument for divine purposes, an emissary of those who live in the upper sky and who love Christabel, is perhaps "the most terrifying twist of all" (item 192, p. 183).

Whether or not they find ambivalence in these specific themes,[41] most critics agree that the general concern of the poem is the ambiguity of evil--its shifting nature, its ability to escape definition by assuming almost any shape, its dependence on virtue (items 319, 402, 311, 216a, 292, 376, 245, 366, 373, 364). Geraldine has evil intentions; yet she appears graceful and beautiful. Introduced in a context of prayer, she accomplishes what Henry Nelson Coleridge called her "witchery by daylight" through Christabel's openheartedness and Leoline's impulse for forgiveness (item 311, p. 400, and elsewhere; items 255, 376, 366, 402). In the world of the poem good and evil are inseparable: the love of Leoline and his wife results in death as well as life, the innocent

Christabel lies in the arms of an evil enchantress, her vision
afterward is both sweet and fearful, parasitical mistletoe
entwines the dormant oak, and the snake coils around the dove
(items 366, 311, 309, 347). When virtue is rewarded with an
evil enchantment and charity leads to the alienation of family
ties, when the matinal bell signals death and the sacristan's
"warning knell" (1. 342) is mockingly echoed by the devil's
"merry peal" (1. 358)--the moral universe has gone awry. Good
and evil are inverted (items 311, 398).

Consideration of whether Coleridge had a plan for the
whole includes not only his thematic purpose but also the
problem of the ending. Whether he really had a concrete
plan for finishing his story is much argued. In 1838 appeared
Gillman's lengthy summary of the remaining action--Bracy's
exposure of Geraldine's deceit, her disappearance and reappearance as Christabel's absent lover, and the return of her true
lover, followed by the happy marriage and reconciliation
(items 30, 151, 11). But for various reasons critics have
doubted the validity of this account. In the first place,
Wordsworth claimed to know of no "definite plan," only
"embryos."[42] And his skepticism appears justified in light
of Coleridge's many attempts to complete the poem and the
implications of uncertainty in his statements to Allsop. In
1820 he said that he would try to finish "if a genial recurrence of the ray divine should occur for a few weeks." Without specifying any details, he now planned to introduce "new
characters ... and incidents," for when he began the poem
more than twenty years ago, he had in mind only "the whole of
the two cantos" (item 11, p. 443, and elsewhere). In 1821 he
remarked that while writing Part II he was thinking of
Crashaw's lines on Saint Theresa; then, as an afterthought,
he added the possibility that "by some subtle process of the
mind" they might have influenced the design of the whole
(item 30, p. 26).

As for the plan itself, critics have speculated that
Coleridge was teasing Gillman with a simple, prosaic account
of an ending suitable only for a ghost story or a trivial
Gothic novel (items 402, 30, 151, 293). They further object
that it contributes nothing to the reader's understanding of
Geraldine's character (items 293, 262, 30, 216a), the symbolic
structure (item 216a), or the theme (items 402, 216a). It is
inconsistent with the triumph of evil at the end of Part II
(items 400, 311, 293), and for Enscoe's particular reading
the lover's return contradicts the tone of the first two parts
where Christabel is already symbolically rescued by Geraldine
(item 378).

Other critics, especially McElderry, argue that the plan
as reported by Gillman is genuine and poetically sound. The

strongest external evidence to the contrary is Wordsworth's statement to Coleridge's nephew. Coburn suggests that one reason for Wordsworth's doubt is the lack of any one whole story on which "Christabel" depends (item 164). And McElderry questions an unqualified acceptance of Wordsworth's statement because, for one thing, it was made in 1836, two years before the appearance of Gillman's summary and so many years after the poem's composition and the poets' quarrel that it is unlikely to be very reliable. Furthermore, it does admit the "embryos" of plans which Coleridge must have had when he wrote Parts I and II. For these reasons it does not sufficiently controvert the previously mentioned opinions of Derwent Coleridge and Gillman and Coleridge's own assertions of the wholeness of his plan (item 11, p. 441).

Probably the best known of these statements, the 1816 Preface, contains this reference to his plan for the poem as a whole and his intention of finishing it: "as, in my very first conception of the tale, I had the whole present to my mind, with the wholeness, no less than the liveliness of a vision; I trust that I shall be able to embody in verse the three parts yet to come, in the course of the present year" (item 11, p. 437, and elsewhere).[43] Coleridge's letter to Byron on October 22, 1815, anticipates the Preface: "I should say that the plan of the whole poem was formed and the first Book and half the second were finished" in 1797 (item 11, p. 442, and elsewhere). His reference to "the whole of the two cantos" in the 1820 comment to Allsop is balanced by the entry in Table Talk for July 6, 1833, in which he reiterates his contention of the Preface: "The reason of my not finishing *Christabel* is not that I don't know how to do it--for I have, as I always had, the whole plan entire from beginning to end in my mind" (item 11, pp. 443-444, and elsewhere). Partially corroborating these assertions, Carlyon shows no surprise when, recalling Coleridge's "metaphysical elucidations" of his poems in Germany, he says that "what he [Coleridge] told us fellow travellers respecting *Christabel*, he has since repeated in print"--that is, in the Preface of 1816, in *Table Talk*, and in *Allsop's Letters, Conversations, and Recollections* (item 11, p. 442). It is in this context that Coleridge made the many arrangements for publishing the completed poem and that Gillman introduced the plan as if it were commonly known. Finally, it is a verification of Gillman's accuracy that none of Coleridge's contemporaries objected to the summary (items 11, 261, 30).

Considering the plan itself, McElderry and others find it reasonably consistent with the rest of the poem. While it is not imaginative, it is no more prosaic than summaries of Parts I and II would be (items 216a, 11). It does not allow

Geraldine much opportunity to continue her vampirism, but
probably Coleridge would not have developed this trait much
further anyway. The grisly horrors of vampire legends would
not have given the subtle effect he wanted (item 52).

More characteristic of Coleridge's poems during the period
of "Christabel" is Geraldine's reappearance as Christabel's
lover, the symmetrical narrative structure, the moral pattern,
and the optimistic tone revealed by the projected action.
The central episode in the plan, Geraldine's disguise as the
absent lover is a logical development of her character and
serves to refocus attention on Christabel. This second impersonation would probably form the substance of Part IV and
would thus parallel Part II, exceeding it in intensity and
climactic effect. Part V would then center on the disruption
of Geraldine's scheme by the return of the true lover, an
event which completes the moral pattern of the poem by sub-
stantiating the efficacy of Christabel's vicarious suffering
and gives purpose to her leaving the castle to pray for his
safety. Foreshadowed in Part I, the lover's return and marriage to Christabel is a fitting conclusion to the indications
that good will triumph (items 11, 52, 50, 51, 292, 27, 65).[44]

Even critics who do not read the poem with such moral optimism have accepted Gillman's summary as an outline of
Coleridge's plan for the conclusion. Virginia L. Radley
points out that it continues the theme of ambiguity in love
relationships through Christabel's ambivalent feelings toward
her false lover Geraldine (item 319). And Coburn views it as
a sort of fantasy, in harmony with Christabel's inner experience of loneliness and fear (item 164).

The poetic soundness of Gillman's account, however, is
less important in the criticism of the poem than the unity
within the two completed parts. This is the most obvious
evidence that Coleridge had at least an embryo of a plan. In
McElderry's argument, "the very perfection and fullness of
the detail, the sureness with which the unique atmosphere is
created and maintained, the consecutiveness of the action in
Parts I and II--all suggest a confident grasp of the narrative
material, rather than an aimless sketching of pretty episodes
in the Micawberish hope that eventually 'something might turn
up'" (item 11, p. 441). It is not within the scope of his
essay to develop this point, but other critics have analyzed
the extent to which Coleridge unified the two parts in terms
of the function of "The Conclusion to Part II" and the consistent treatment of setting, imagery, and main characters.

Of these subjects, one of the most controversial is "The
Conclusion to Part II." It is well known that the lines about
the "limber elf" (656 ff.) exist in manuscript form only in
the letter to Southey of May 6, 1801, where they refer to the

child Hartley (items 261, 65, 192, 191, 376, 398). Consequently, they are sometimes criticized for not being composed
as part of the poem and for being unrelated to it (items 261,
65, 371, 292). In contrast to the dramatic propriety of the
last scene in which sickness and evil move off together as
Leoline leads forth the Lady Geraldine, the tacked-on lines
of the Conclusion stick out uncomfortably (items 402, 185).
They add nothing to help solve the mystery of Geraldine
(item 30). They contribute only paternal sentiment, which
fulfills Coleridge's satiric requirement that Gothic romances
use "some pathetic moralizing on old times, or anything else,
for the head and tail pieces" (item 213, p. 475).

More often, however, critics defend these lines as belonging to the poem and as relevant to its structure and theme.
Although originally they might have been intended for the end
of the poem (item 366) or for Part III (item 28), they were
probably composed as a part of the poem (item 376). The fact
that they were inspired by Hartley presents no inconsistency,
since he is a direct source of other lines as well and a background influence on the whole poem (items 261, 216a). Furthermore, during the months before he included them in the letter
to Southey, Coleridge was busy planning to finish and publish
the poem and had it on his mind constantly. It is unlikely
that he would have written twenty-two lines so pertinent to
his story except as a part of it (item 261).

Structurally, they function like "The Conclusion to Part
I," to summarize and interpret the preceding action (items
261, 65). Placed just after Leoline leaves the castle with
Geraldine, they represent his increasingly somber reflections
during the walk and reveal an insight into human nature which
provides a more penetrating explanation of his anger than
his earlier excuse of insulted hospitality (items 261, 65,
192). In addition, the narrator's description of the child
with red cheeks, "Singing, dancing to itself" (ll. 657-658),
recalls the image in Part I of the dancing red leaf (ll. 49-
52) (items 309, 117). And his parenthetical lament "O sorrow
and shame should this be true" (l. 674) repeats his earlier
horrified comment on Christabel's dreams as she sleeps in the
arms of Geraldine (l. 296) and echoes Geraldine's reference
to her own physical deformity (l. 270) (item 192).

Thematically, the lines of the Conclusion provide a key
to the whole poem (item 376), for they indicate the scope of
its "subtle and difficult" idea (item 192). They point to the
ambiguity of evil evident in a kind of natural perversity
within the human heart in which love and hate are mixed
(items 402, 65, 293, 213, 398, 255, 216a, 373, 347). Because
of these "uneasy and unpredictable contrasts," Bate offers
this explanation of the father's "words of unmeant bitterness"

(1. 665): "In the excess of devotion we may begin to recoil,
as if in some instinctive need for balance, and to rebuke,
perhaps even to profane, what we most cherish" (item 402, pp.
73, 74). The dependence of evil on good raises the possibility
that love and pity may come "seldom save from rage and pain"
(1. 676) (items 192, 255). This ambiguous relationship applies most obviously to Leoline's quarrels with Lord Roland
and Christabel (items 398, 261, 319, 376, 347),[45] but its
implications link the Conclusion to the religious and sexual
themes as well. Though not a martyr, the child suffers
through no fault of his own (item 347), and in such a world
of sin his innocence will inevitably be corrupted (item 378).

In addition to their structural and thematic function,
the lines of the Conclusion indicate Coleridge's personal in-
volvement with the meaning of the poem. The ambiguous relationship of good and evil is a truth he knew from his own
experience. In their original context the lines clearly
apply to his mixed feelings toward Hartley--an attitude
which in the poem links him not only to Leoline but also to
Geraldine and Christabel by means of the phrase "O sorrow
and shame" (1. 674) (items 65, 293, 379, 216a). Thus, instead
of being tacked on to pad out the poem, the last lines were
intended generally to emphasize the real human feeling in
the whole poem and particularly to confirm the psychological
probability of the last scene (items 261, 376, 398).

Less defensible for most critics is the shift from a non-
specific medieval setting to the detailed geography of the
Lake District. The mysterious events of Part I take place
during a spring night in a dimly lit castle and nearby wood-
land.[46] But in the daylight of Part II this romantic strangeness gives way to the local legends and realistic landmarks
of Cumberland--Bratha Head, Wyndermere, Langdale Pike, Witches
Lair, Dungeonghyll, Borodale. These specific place names
seem out of keeping with the anonymous details of Part I;
and Florence Marsh points out how well they harmonize with
Coleridge's satiric first requirement for poems like Scott's
"Lady of the Lake": "The first Business," said Coleridge,
"must be a vast string of Patronymics, and names of mountains,
rivers, etc." (item 213, p. 475; items 306, 156, 135, 398,
151, 292). Extending Marsh's observation, some critics consider this verisimilitude part of the general falling-off of
terseness and imaginative power that makes Part II seem like
a separate poem (items 306, 151, 255, 371, 117).

Woodring, however, maintains that the setting of the poem
has an "adequate continuity" (item 373, p. 45). He believes
that the action of both parts occurs in medieval Cumberland
but that the exact locale is withheld in order to increase
the dreadfulness. He stresses the fact that the scenic details

of Part I as well as Part II are drawn from the real world, noting that images such as the "thin gray cloud" (1. 16) and the "one red leaf" (1. 49) have parallels in Dorothy Wordsworth's Alfoxden journal while the phrases "tairn and rill" (1. 306) and "wood and fell" (1. 310) from "The Conclusion to Part I" describe the Lake District. Although he does not find in Part II the kind of scene painting done by William Gilpin and Anne Radcliffe, he does mention the contemporary appeal of such realistic details as the grandeur of Borrowdale and the unusual echoes (item 373).

As a measure of the poem's unity, however, the locale is less important than the imagery used to describe it, and the source of such details as the cloudy sky is less significant than their function in the poem. For House, "the experience of reading the First Part of 'Christabel' is more an acquaintance with an atmosphere than the apprehension of a poetic unity" (item 151, p. 123). The imagery heightens the poem's mystery by skillful suggestions of contrast, surprise, or slight distortion in behavior; but because the mystery is both clueless and incomplete, the imagery is finally unsatisfying and fragmentary. He and others note the limited function of a number of images including the sky and the moon partially hidden by the cloud, the castle clock striking twelve midnight, the owl's weird cry and the mastiff's groan, the dying brands lying in white ashes, and the strange oak tree supporting green moss and mistletoe and one red leaf at the top (items 151, 67, 366). To increase the suspense of these ominous signs, the narrator frequently uses the Gothic device of a series of unanswered questions (item 371).

In opposition to this view, most critics consider the imagery a major contribution to the poem's unity as well as to its mysterious atmosphere. Smith, for example, claims that the "intricate web of thoughtfully devised imagery" functions to give the poem the kind of organic unity Coleridge admired, a unity which "makes the fact that Part II was written three years after Part I artistically irrelevant" (item 309, p. 44). Charles Tomlinson points out that readers like House may feel a certain incompleteness about the poem because it ends in psychological stasis. But, though Christabel's isolation will never be resolved, the poem offers a satisfying completeness concerning what does happen (item 185).

According to Tomlinson, Smith, and others the conclusion is prepared for by thematically functional images. Like the slowly advancing spring, the moon at the beginning of the poem connotes unfulfilled potential. It has achieved its most fruitful phase yet lacks the brightness of a full moon. Its "small and dull" (1. 19) appearance in the cloud-threatened sky provides an emblem of Coleridge's theory of evil as a

distortion of good (item 216a) and, within the poem, suggests
precarious uncertainty, incipient disease, and spiritual isolation. The disappearance of Christabel's spiritual guardian
(ll. 211-213) is accompanied by the silence of the night-
birds' music (l. 305); the stillness of the wind (ll. 45, 48),
which, along with the cloud, is mentioned again in Part II
(l. 360); and by the veiled moon, whose heavenly light is
"dim in the open air" and completely absent from Christabel's
chamber (ll. 175-176). The condition of the sky, covered but
not hidden, reinforces the significance of the diseased moon.
The sky should offer spiritual protection to Christabel:
Geraldine has assured her that the inhabitants of the "upper
sky" (l. 227) love her, and she herself knows "That saints
will aid if men will call: / For the blue sky bends over all"
(ll. 330-331). But during the time of the action the sky is
not blue. Though it can be seen, its influence no longer
operates on the world below (items 185, 309, 398, 366, 232).

Christabel is not only spiritually isolated. As is indicated by the images of Part I and dramatized at the end of
Part II, she is also physically defenseless. Her lover is
absent; her mother is dead; and Bard Bracy, the only one in
the castle who senses her danger, is sent away (items 192,
402). Though her father is tall, he is old and unwell. No
longer the symbol of strength and brightness suggested by the
name "Leoline," he hangs his unused shield "in a murky old
niche in the wall" (l. 163), lives in the past, and thinks
continually of death. Appropriately, his castle is guarded
by a "toothless" (l. 7) mastiff who, like the iron gate, is
completely ineffectual and powerless to keep out the enemy
(items 309, 81, 398; for other interpretations of the importance of the mastiff, see items 379, 216a, 117; for the castle
gate, see item 379).

Of further significance, the image of the mastiff automatically answering the clock contributes to the echo motif
in the poem and to the suggestion of the mechanical, dying
life within the castle. Beginning with the auroral cock
aroused by the owls' hoot, the echo motif includes the narrator's rhetorical questions and, at the beginning of Part II,
the echoes of the castle bell by the devil and the ghosts of
three sinful sextons. The emphasis of these images on distortion and ambiguity provides a fitting background for Christabel's obedient, imitative responses to Geraldine (items 311,
216a; see also item 117 for another explanation of the owls'
hoot). Her loss of innocence seems even more inevitable in
the context of the contrast between the mechanical, decaying
world of the domesticated cock and the toothless mastiff and
the green, fertile world of spring, wild owls, and mistletoe
(item 378; see also items 81, 373, 379, 376, 402, and 366 for

discussions of the ominous sounds and impressions of regular-
ity and confinement indicating that something dire awaits
Christabel).

Together with the oak and the leaf, the mistletoe forms a
larger aggregate image which comprehends most of the other
imagery in the poem. The scene in Part II of Geraldine embracing Leoline reflects the picture of the dormant oak entwined with parasitical mistletoe. Emblematic of the
paradoxical relationship between life and death, the mistletoe owes its vital greenness to the life-sap of the now barren
oak and threatens to take the place of the leaf (items 309,
347). And the single leaf in its precarious position at the
top of the tree emphasizes Christabel's loneliness. Like her,
it is "the last of its clan" (1. 49). Without the wind it
does not "twirl" (1. 48) but dances fitfully on the twig that
"looks up at the sky" (1. 52), just as Christabel without
spiritual support looks in vain toward the blue sky that bends
over all (items 185, 347; for another reading of the significance of the leaf and the mistletoe, see item 117).

In Part II the fitful dance becomes a desperate struggle.
The tree-leaf-mistletoe aggregate is replaced by the image
of the snake coiled around the wings and neck of Leoline's
dove (item 309). This image, says Tomlinson, "is one of the
most startling and suggestive touches in the poem" (item 185,
p. 110). It recalls the scene of Christabel sleeping in the
arms of Geraldine and transfers to the sexual-religious implications of the enchantment the connotations of parasitism
inherent in the life-death theme (items 185, 376, 347).[47]
Discovered beneath the oak, the snake resembles the mistletoe
in color and shape. Furthermore, the traditional picture of
the snake sucking milk from the ewe is suggested by the image
of the mistletoe drinking sap from the tree. This additional
link between the two images reinforces the thematic significance of Geraldine's twice refreshing herself by drinking the
"wild-flower wine" of "virtuous powers" (11. 190-193, 220)
and deriving strength and beauty from her contact with
Christabel. Like the snake that moves in imitation of the
dove, Geraldine covets the identity of Christabel, who in
turn accepts something of Geraldine's evil. In thus giving
succor to the pale lady at the expense of her own vitality,
Christabel reenacts the deaths of her mother for her, of a
bride for her lover, and of Christ for mankind (items 185,
347).

More obviously, the snake-dove image represents the
struggle within Christabel between good and evil (11. 292-
331, 457-469, 589, 614) and the external conflict between her
and Geraldine for the confidence of Leoline (item 347).
Adumbrating the evil which is overcoming Christabel, it is

part of the ophidian imagery used throughout the poem. Its
introduction gives a reflected significance not only to the
mistletoe but to several other images as well--the wildly
glittering gems entangled in Geraldine's hair (ll. 63-64),
reminiscent of the designs of brilliant jewels conventionally
drawn in the heads of serpents; the "tongue of light" (l.
159) that rises from the dying coals as Geraldine passes; the
"reptile souls" (l. 442) of Geraldine's captors; the hissing
sound of Geraldine as she undresses, "drawing in her breath
aloud, / Like one that shuddered" (ll. 247-248); and its echo
in Christabel when she recalls Geraldine's cold, painful
touch: "She shrunk and shuddered ... And drew in her breath
with a hissing sound" (ll. 454, 459) (items 309, 347, 311,
30, 376).

To the snake and dove images following Bracy's dream, the
snake-dove struggle imparts irony. The rejuvenated Leoline
mistakenly calls Geraldine a "beauteous dove" (l. 569) and
promises to "crush the snake" (l. 571). Responding with
"wonder and love" (l. 467) to her "large bright eyes divine"
(ll. 595, 574), he does not see their serpentine qualities
(ll. 583-585) when she "folded her arms across her chest, /
And couched her head upon her breast" (ll. 579-580). He reacts with anger, however, to Christabel's look of hate
(l. 606) and easily hears her shuddering and hissing (l. 591)
(items 30, 309, 51).

For most recent critics Christabel's acceptance of
Geraldine's ophidian traits seems consistent with the moral
ambiguity which she exhibits throughout the poem. But for
some others this development impairs the unity of the poem
because it is out of character with the moral absolute of
goodness which she represents (items 50, 23, 185, 397, 303,
245). Christabel is often seen as completely innocent even
in the criticism based on the assumption of poetic unity.
She is thought of as demure, gentle, loving, pure, trustful,
and benevolent--a "model of medieval piety" (items 402, 232,
366; item 289, p. 24). Unlike the Mariner, she is a child of
nature, attuned to the one Life (items 216a, 398). She smiles
"As infants at a sudden light" (l. 318), prays "Like a youthful hermitess" (l. 320), occupies a room with religious carv-
ings suggestive of intuitive devotion (ll. 179-181), and trims
a lamp attached to the feet of an angel (l. 183) (items 81,
376, 289). In her redemptive function she parallels Saint
Theresa, Isis, and Christ, whose name inspired her own as well
as the pet dove's (items 347, 81, 117, 65, 30, 289, 398,
216a, 255).

She demonstrates this Christlike innocence in specific
actions throughout the poem. Although her leaving the castle
alone at night is typical of Gothic heroines and provides for

a convenient meeting with Geraldine (items 23, 117), her purpose of prayer and her acceptance of a supernatural being
foreshadow the spiritualization of her love (item 81). Furthermore, the repetition of Geraldine's request to "Stretch
forth thy hand" (11. 75, 102) and its echo in Christabel's
response (1. 104) underline the innocence of her assistance
(item 311). Then she charitably opens the castle gate (items
255, 376) and, in a life-giving act, carries Geraldine across
the threshold (item 127). In sharing her bed with her unexpected guest she epitomizes hospitality (item 398) and, since
the enchantment is a metaphor for her union with the Divine,
achieves a spiritual love (item 81). In spite of her sense
of sin afterward she is not responsible for it because she
was hypnotized (items 402, 30, 376, 50, 185). She remains
as spotless as she was before (item 135). Still able to pray,
she experiences no immediate revulsion toward Geraldine and
confidently leads her to the Baron (items 81, 378). Later in
a supreme effort of will she begs him to send Geraldine away,
fighting against succumbing to her spell (item 135). Her
shudders and hisses suggest that she is putting on Christ in
the flesh (item 81), rather than assuming the characteristics
of a literal serpent-woman (item 135). The ophidian imitations do not really affect her inner purity and innocence,
for it is "With forced unconscious sympathy" (1. 609) that
her eyes picture Geraldine's look of hate--"As far as such a
look could be / In eyes so innocent and blue" (11. 611-612)
(items 378, 376).

For most readers, however, Christabel's apparent innocence
is not a simple matter. It is complicated by something that
takes its own steps and makes its own advances, by imprudence,
slyness, and subterfuge (items 402, 262). "We feel for
Christabel," says Woodring, "because she is relatively inno-
cent--remarkably innocent--but also because she is humanly
susceptible to temptation" (item 373, p. 47). The drama and
human interest lie in her vulnerability, her moral ambiguity
(items 349, 402, 379, 270).

Drawn from some of the same popular sources, Christabel's
actions are not altogether separable from Geraldine's (items
23, 245). It is Christabel's help and initiative that allow
Geraldine to reveal her daemonic nature and to progress from
the oak through the forest to the castle gate, the courtyard,
the threshold, the hall, and Christabel's bedroom (item 373).
The enchantment occurs because Christabel thoughtlessly
leaves the safety of her father's castle at midnight (items
402, 373; see item 117 for another explanation of the significance of Christabel's leaving the castle). The connection
between these two events is underlined in "The Conclusion to
Part I" when the narrator contrasts Christabel's praying with

her fearful dreaming after the enchantment and then asks the
rhetorical question, "Can this be she, / The lady, who knelt
at the old oak tree?" (ll. 296-297). To some extent she is
responsible for her sorrow and shame (items 65, 349, 117),
for she went to the oak voluntarily and presumably without
her father's knowledge (items ·65, 349, 402, 373, 398). Her
ostensible purpose was prayer (item 67). But since the shrine
of the Virgin is evidently inside the courtyard, a more likely
explanation is her natural restiveness. Living in confinement
with a father whose mind is obsessed with death would make
her understandably receptive to something different (item 402),
and the fact that she chose to pray beneath an oak entwined
with mistletoe suggests that the devout Christian maiden hopes
to strengthen an especially urgent prayer by participating in
Druidical rites (items 166, 349).

Because she herself is less than innocent, she has ambivalent feelings toward Geraldine. Upon discovering the pale
lady, Christabel is afraid and, like the narrator, asks for
heavenly protection (ll. 54, 69). But she is also sympathetic
and attracted to the stranger's beauty--so much so that she
suspends her fear (item 319), accepts Geraldine's irrational,
unconvincing story (items 402, 376, 347), and extends her hand
(item 373). Then in a "pragmatically seductive" "hyperbole
of courtesy" she bestows her bed on Geraldine and begs a
place in it: "And I beseech your courtesy, / This night, to
share your couch with me" (ll. 121-122) (item 255, p. 213;
item 373, p. 48; items 402, 379).

Leading Geraldine back through the forest, Christabel
neglects the implications of her guest's weakness and lifts
her over the threshold, thus actively introducing evil into
the household (items 373, 262, 117, 402, 379, 245, 255). Even
before they enter the castle, Christabel feels the need to
warn Geraldine that they should walk "as if in stealth"
(l. 120). The "as if," says Bate, is "merely palliative to
her own conscience" (item 402, p. 72). Very much in earnest,
she insures secrecy as they approach Leoline's shield by re-
minding the barefooted Geraldine to tread softly (l. 164) and
by taking off her own shoes before they pass his room (items
373, 402).

Once inside her chamber Christabel unequivocally dispels
the impression that she is an utterly innocent victim. She
revitalizes the faint Geraldine with the wild-flower wine made
by her mother and, though she loves her mother, excuses
Geraldine's ravings against her (ll. 216-217) (items 373, 379,
319). In return Geraldine promises to "requite" (l. 232)
Christabel and commands her hostess to disrobe. Christabel
responds with alacrity amazing enough to require exclamation:
"Quoth Christabel, So let it be! / And as the lady bade, did

she" (11. 235-236). Unlike the innocent maidens in the tales
of terror who would have fallen asleep or remained fearfully
awake, Christabel cannot sleep because of her many thoughts
of "weal and woe" (1. 239). In her restlessness and curiosity
she provokes Geraldine to cast the spell when she props herself up on her elbow to look at her visitor. Commenting on
this scene, Woodring observes that "an absolutely pure
Christabel could not, even through innocence, have been sub-
jected to a view of Geraldine's 'bosom and half her side'"
(1. 252). "The erotic emanations in her chamber ... come to
us because innocence is not the whole of her frailty" (item
373, p. 47; items 255, 349, 117).

     After the enchantment Christabel shows signs of guilt.
During her after-rest she experiences both joy and sadness
(11. 313-318). Confused and troubled by dreams too horrible
to mention, she wakes up and confesses, "Sure I have sinn'd"
(1. 381) (items 373, 349, 378, 255, 319, 311). Later the
sight of her father embracing Geraldine stirs the ambiguous
feelings of jealousy and fear which she expresses in an
ophidian hiss (1. 459). Her imitation of Geraldine's serpentine traits on this and other occasions is an outward symbol
of her inner corruption. Emphasizing her ambiguity and psychological complexity, it occurs simultaneously with a spontaneous look of angelic innocence: the Baron turns in the
direction of the hiss and sees "his own sweet maid / With
eyes upraised, as one that prayed" (11. 461-462) (items 378,
65, 245, 319, 311, 127, 117).

     Though Christabel was no doubt intended to be the main
character, the central, most interesting figure in the poem
is the mysterious Geraldine (items 30, 402, 65)--demon,
witch, snake, vampire, lamia, lesbian, and beautiful woman
(items 30, 255, 65, 192, 319, 364, 135, 270, 373, 311, 309,
156, 262, 209, 52, 289, 86, 27, 255, 231, 398, 117, 371, 349,
402, 306, 216a, 292, 232, 366). Because of her ambiguous
identity, her shame and reluctance, and her vitality, many
readers find it difficult to categorize her as either good or
evil. Others, agreeing with Gillman, regard her more simply
as the embodiment of evil, the moral antithesis of Christabel
(items 303, 192, 185, 50).

     "To say that Geraldine is not a malignant being is non-
sense," argues Bostetter. Not in terms of ultimate motivation
but within the human terms of the poem, "she is as evil as
opium or Coleridge's dreams" (item 192, p. 193, and elsewhere).
She is described in images suggesting the ophidian and is
associated with parasitism and the pallor of death (items 309,
366, 30, 185). Ironically she sleeps with Christabel "As a
mother with her child" (1. 301) (items 185, 379, 232), having
piously aligned herself with the spirits of the upper sky

(ll. 227-230) and hypocritically promised, "Even I in my degree will try, / Fair maiden, to requite you well" (ll. 231-
232) (items 65, 311, 292, 232).

Although she disguises herself as the daughter of Lord
Roland, her sinister nature is made apparent before the enchantment by such ominous details as the midnight hour of her
encounter with Christabel (item 30); her eagerness for physical contact (item 112b); her account of having "crossed the
shade of night" (l. 88) (item 376); her struggle against the
spirit of Christabel's mother (items 65, 185, 50, 262, 135,
86, 117, 151, 292, 232); the silence of the night-birds during
the hour of enchantment (item 292); the narrator's fear for
Christabel's safety and his repetition of the fervent, yet
ironic, plea "Jesu, Maria, shield her well" (ll. 54, 254, 582)
(items 311, 309, 50). Even more obvious are the evil portents
based on popular superstition: Geraldine's faintness at the
threshold (items 65, 50, 30, 262, 86, 27, 117, 376, 135, 402);
her unwillingness to join Christabel in prayer at the shrine
of the Virgin (items 65, 185, 135, 376, 112b); the mastiff's
angry moan as the two women cross the courtyard (items 30,
112b, 65, 292, 376, 185, 50, 135, 86); the flaring of the
brands, lighting up Geraldine's shining eye as they pass down
the castle hall (items 65, 30, 185, 262, 135, 117, 292, 376);
and Geraldine's weakness when she observes the carved angel
in Christabel's chamber (items 30, 112b, 65).

The sense of evil created by these events is heightened
during the enchantment when the narrator calls attention to
Geraldine's disrobing, withholding the nature of her power
while reacting violently to it (ll. 245-254) (items 311, 366).
In Part II she becomes unmistakably evil (item 398). Continuing her deception, she triumphantly witnesses the results of
her previous night's spell and insures its continuation by
enchanting Leoline and leading him to reject Christabel
(item 378).

For most critics, however, Geraldine is never simply an
evil enchantress. In harmony with Coleridge's conception of
supernatural poetry, she is humanly complex, believable, and
partly sympathetic (items 373, 30, 319, 398, 309, 366). Her
struggle with the spirit of Christabel's mother follows her
echo of Christabel's wish for the mother's presence (items 30,
112b, 117). She casts a spell upon Christabel, but its evil
is tempered by her grateful, apparently sincere, apologetic
promise that in her own way she will try to return Christabel's
kindness (items 65, 378, 151, 185, 319, 50, 30, 135, 117).
And in Part II her hateful ophidian glances are accompanied
by dread and grief (items 30, 378, 192, 270). "There is
surely no doubt in any reader's mind," says Douglas Angus,
"that Geraldine is a most ambiguous witch, a most inscrutable,

tantalizing, puzzling miniature of love and sinister evil"
(item 232, p. 662; see also items 378, 402, 364, 255). She
is both pitiable and horrible, attractive and repulsive, passive and aggressive (items 30, 379).

Critics sometimes explain this duality as a reflection of
Coleridge's sources (item 292); his view of evil (items 216a,
402) or God's wrath (item 81); or his ambivalent attitude
toward sex (item 378), his mother (items 117, 232, 127, 379),
or his fellow poet Wordsworth (item 289). But more often they
relate it to his thoughts on the preternatural, metempsychosis,
and the legendary figures of the vampire and the lamia.
Accepting Derwent Coleridge's interpretation of Geraldine as
"no witch or goblin or malignant being of any kind, but a
spirit, executing her appointed task with the best of good
will" (item 30, pp. 37, 206, and elsewhere), Nethercot and
others identify her as a kind of vampire, or lamia (items 30,
65, 293, 373, 156, 262, 52, 371, 402, 306, 366). Because of
some past sin, symbolized by her physical deformity, she is
now the unwilling instrument of Christabel's martyrdom, the
preternatural agent of those who live in the upper sky (items
30, 231, 398, 378). She is especially pitiable because she
bears no responsibility for her vampire-like behavior: vampires
are traditionally innocent people who died after being bitten
in their sleep by another vampire. Furthermore, she regrets
her sin and feels ashamed of its mark. But her hope of eventual transformation depends on the successful accomplishment
of her disagreeable mission (items 30, 112b, 319, 52, 398,
151, 292).

Coleridge's treatment of the enchantment scene emphasizes
Geraldine's sympathetic qualities of shame and reluctance.
She compels Christabel's silence not out of motiveless malig-
nancy but for self-protection (item 373). Shamefully and
sorrowfully aware of her disfigured bosom (1. 270), she takes
no delight in her sinister powers (items 378, 135, 366, 50,
65, 270, 192). She hesitates to undress, slowly rolling
around her eyes and "drawing in her breath" (1. 247). And in
lines 256-262, a passage which Coleridge added in 1828,[48]
she approaches the seduction with extreme reluctance. Her
look is "stricken" as she struggles against that part of herself which is capable of kindness and gentleness. She "eyes
the maid and seeks delay." Then putting aside temptation,
"as one defied," she "collects herself in scorn and pride, /
And lay down by the Maiden's side!" Finally, she pronounces
the words of the spell "with low voice and doleful look"
(1. 265) and even in Part II continues to feel some pity for
her victim when the next morning she "shakes off her dread"
(1. 362), blends "Such sorrow with such grace ... As if she
feared she had offended / Sweet Christabel" (11. 377-379),

looks at her "with somewhat of malice, and more of dread"
(1. 586), and then turns away from the fainting, hissing
Christabel "like a thing, that sought relief, / Full of wonder
and full of grief" (11. 593, 594) (items 30, 112b, 151, 185,
311, 52, 127, 398, 402).

In addition to emphasizing Geraldine's pity and reluctance,
in the published version of the poem Coleridge toned down the
horror of the enchantment scene by blurring the physical details of Geraldine's bosom. Originally he had described it
precisely as "lean and old and foul of hue" (item 378, p. 48).
By substituting the vague line "A sight to dream of, not to
tell" (1. 253), he avoids an image which would establish
Geraldine as a traditional witch-like hag and leave no room
for ambiguity (items 378, 376).

Geraldine is not a simple witch, however, and the consequences of her enchantment are not altogether undesirable.
Apparently she enjoys the "still and mild" (1. 300) sleep of
the innocent (items 311, 255, 51, 127, 81), for she awakens
refreshed and even more beautiful than she appeared under the
oak tree (item 378). The night-birds burst into "jubilant"
(1. 308) rejoicing in celebration of the success of her mission (item 378). And Christabel smiles "As infants at a
sudden light" (1. 318), an image which does not indicate a
scene of alarm or horror but the personal illumination of a
"vision sweet" (1. 326) (item 81). If she seems restless,
"'tis but the blood so free / Comes back and tingles in her
feet" (11. 324-325), an image which suggests not so much an
attack by a vampire (item 30) as the new awareness, the awaken-
ing of one whose eyes were once "more bright than clear"
(1. 290). Released from her deathlike innocence, Christabel
now dreams with "open eyes" (1. 292). And in contact with the
vitality of Geraldine, the Baron rouses from his accustomed
sickness and apathy (item 378).

In keeping with his ambiguous treatment of the enchantment and its effects, Coleridge associates Geraldine with
images of life and beauty. Sleeping with Christabel, she
resembles a "mother with her child" (1. 301) (items 30, 127,
81). Outside the castle in the month of April she appears in
a moonlit forest under a "huge, broad-breasted" oak (1. 42).
The green mistletoe which entwines it suggests fertility and
contributes to establishing her as an embodiment of erotic
forces (items 378, 81, 309). Her external brightness and
glitter fascinate the narrator (11. 58-68). Even after he
views the shriveled, discolored skin of her bosom, he continues to refer to her as "fair Geraldine" (11. 391, 449)
and "so bright a dame" (1. 402) with "large bright eyes divine"
(11. 474, 595). And when Leoline meets her, he deems her
"sure a thing divine" (1. 476) (item 311). Reinforcing the

emphasis of these responses, Bracy dreams of a "bright green"
(1. 54) snake whose struggle with Leoline's dove suggests the
embrace of two lovers engaged in sexual intercourse (items
378, 65, 135). Perhaps even more than her sinister nature,
it is Geraldine's sexual, life-giving quality that accounts
for her being carried like a bride over the threshold, for
her understandable inability to pray to the Virgin, for the
angry growl as she intrudes into the decaying life guarded by
the toothless mastiff, and for the rekindling of the fire's
warmth and heat as she passes (item 378).

Concerned as he was with the ambiguity of good and evil,
Coleridge seems to have treated Geraldine as well as Christabel
with a consistency remarkable enough to convince most critics
that he did indeed have a plan for the whole. But, having
reached this conclusion, they can only speculate about why he
left the poem unfinished. Some suppose that the main problem
lay within his material, while others think that it had more
to do with his personality.

Coleridge himself gave various reasons. When he could not
have the poem ready for the 1800 edition of Southey's *Annual
Anthology*, he explained that he had "scarce poetic enthusiasm
enough" to finish it (item 11, p. 442, and elsewhere). On
October 22, 1815, he wrote to Byron of financial difficulties
which made it necessary for him to devote his time to sermons
and newspaper pieces. Since 1800, he protested, there has
not been "a single half-year, nay, any three months, in which
I possessed the *means* of devoting myself exclusively to any
one of many works, that it would have been my Delight and
hourly pleasure to have executed. So help me God! never one!"
In the Preface of the following year, however, he blamed his
failure to complete the poem on the temporary suspension of
his poetic powers and credited his delay in publishing at
least the fragment to his "own indolence" (item 11, pp. 168-
169). He continued to talk of finishing the poem until the
year before his death. In *Table Talk*, under the date of
July 6, 1833, he maintained:

> I could write as good verses now as ever I did, if I
> were perfectly free from vexations, and were in the
> *ad libitum* hearing of fine music, which has a sensible
> effect in harmonizing my thoughts, and in animating
> and, as it were, lubricating my inventive faculty.
> The reason of my not finishing Christabel is not that
> I don't know how to do it--for I have, as I always had,
> the whole plan entire from beginning to end in my
> mind; but I fear I could not carry on with equal success
> the execution of the idea, an extremely subtle and
> difficult one [item 11, pp. 433-444, and elsewhere].

Accepting this statement, a number of critics believe
that the idea was so subtle and difficult that it proved
aesthetically and morally inappropriate and, for Coleridge,
philosophically untenable. "The whole concept of the poem,"
says Bate, "was too great for the vessel of this quasi-Gothic
tale" with its limited conception of character (item 402,
p. 73; see also items 373, 315, 371). By the end of Part II
"the poem had almost completely disintegrated" (item 402,
p. 74; see also items 135, 117); the story had become separated
from the idea (item 376). As he lost control (items 306, 67),
Coleridge allowed Geraldine to become unambiguously evil
(items 30, 398) and devoted excessive attention to preternatural details (item 67) and Gothic elements such as those
he ridiculed in Scott's "The Lady of the Lake" (item 213).
Aware of his dependence on Gothic romances and of their
notoriously weak endings, he realized the direction the poem
was taking but could not rescue it (items 213, 23, 52).

The sexual overtones of his material presented additional
problems. In 1800 he could not handle such double references
to sex and religion as Christabel's martyrdom without awkward-
ness and risk to his moral respectability (items 151, 315,
65, 398). And certainly a continuation of the martyrdom,
with Geraldine in the guise of the absent lover, would neither
avoid these difficulties nor resolve his confusion toward the
erotic without destroying its ambiguity (items 65, 378).

Furthermore, by this time Coleridge was also having
trouble working out a satisfactory doctrine of redemption.
Although in Part I Christabel believes "That saints will aid
if men will call" (1. 330), by the end of Part II the redemption of evil by means of her vicarious suffering no longer
seems feasible (item 311). Her unconscious assumption of evil
leaves her essentially untouched by it and thus implies that
an innocent virtue is the highest virtue (items 216a, 376).
On the other hand, a conscious acceptance of evil would place
it within and make the redemptive function impossible for her
human power (item 376). Without the efficacy of vicarious
suffering, Coleridge had no answer to the question raised in
the poem: "Why does evil befall the innocent?" (items 311, 398).

In contrast to the month it took him to write Part I,
Coleridge struggled with Part II during the next three years,
a circumstance which Bate uses to support his conclusion that
"there was really nothing to prevent him during these three
years (not to mention the next fifteen) from finishing the
poem--except for the nature of the poem itself.... Our love
of Coleridge--and he was a lovable human being--and our
admiration for the range of his genius should not prevent us
from acknowledging as much" (item 402, p. 74).

Opposing this commonly held opinion, other critics remain equally convinced that Coleridge's loss of momentum as well as his failure to complete the poem is better explained by his acute personal problems. In addition to his loss of contact with the concrete philosophy of Hartley (items 50, 52), his limited spiritual experience (item 81), and his habits of procrastination and indecision (items 292, 164), they point out that during the summer and autumn of 1800 he felt especially depressed. Unhappily married, short of enough money to support his growing family, and feverishly rheumatic, he was becoming seriously addicted to opium, increasingly anxious and self-abasing, and uncomfortable in his relationships with his mother, Lloyd, Lamb, and Wordsworth (items 28, 398, 366, 164, 371). In this state of mind he came to associate the poem with his own life, giving Part II autobiographical significance in its particular setting in Cumberland, its long exposition on the youthful quarrel of the two friends Leoline and Roland, and its conclusion about a father's mixed feelings toward his child (items 398, 376, 192). Less obvious but more important, he began to identify himself with Christabel. He saw her situation as his own and could not bear to face the hopelessness of finding a solution to their desolation and dejection (items 164, 292, 192, 293).

With a poetically sound plan clearly in mind (at least in the beginning), he made many engagements with himself to go on with the story (items 30, 11). One of his last remarks on the subject was, "Of my poetic works I would fain finish the *Christabel*." "His failure to do so," claims McElderry, "was not inherent in the material he chose nor in the plan he adopted, but in himself. That was the tragedy" (item 11, p. 455).

[1]The version of this conversation most often quoted is that recorded by Henry Nelson Coleridge in *Table Talk* (1835), under the date May 31, 1830, in which Coleridge reported the following:

> Mrs. Barbauld once told me that she admired the Ancient Mariner very much, but that there were two faults in it,--it was improbable, and had no moral. As for the probability, I owned that that might admit some question; but as to the want of a moral, I told her that in my own judgment the poem had too much; and that the only, or chief fault, if I might say so, was the obtrusion of the moral sentiment so openly on the reader as a principle or cause of action in a work of such pure imagination. It ought to have had no more moral than the Arabian Nights' tale of the merchant's sitting down to eat dates by the side of a well, and throwing the shells aside, and lo! a genie starts up, and says he *must* kill the aforesaid merchant, *because* one of the date shells had, it seems, put out the eye of the genie's son [item 148, p. 88].

There exists, however, an earlier version of the story in H.N. Coleridge's review of Coleridge's poems in the *Quarterly Review* for August, 1834. Here Coleridge reportedly explained his criticism in a different way:

> In a work of such pure imagination I ought not to have stopped to give reasons for things, or inculcate humanity to beasts. 'The Arabian Nights' might have taught me better. They might--the tale of the merchant's son who puts out the eyes of a genii by flinging his date-shells down a well, and is therefore ordered to prepare for death--might have taught this law of imagination.

According to Thomas M. Raysor, this earlier account is the more credible because in it Coleridge evaded the real issue in Mrs. Barbauld's literal-minded observation and, instead of referring to the underlying moral which gives structure and human feeling to the whole poem, finds fault with the lines of explicit moral at the end of the poem (item 148, p. 88).

[2]Most critics (items 308, 113, 233, 266, 376, 349, 371, 151) agree with Stoll (item 108) and Raysor (item 148) that Coleridge intended to criticize lines 612-617 only. But various other possibilities have been suggested--namely, the epigraph (item 334), the last third or half of the poem (items 306, 402), the whole poem (items 89, 13, 216a, 94a), and the notions of crime and penance in it (item 422).

[3]In his *Literary and Lake Reminiscences*, De Quincey reports Coleridge's remark that "before meeting a fable in which to embody his ideas, he had meditated a poem on delirium, confounding its own dream-scenery with external things, and connected with the imagery of high latitudes" (item 94a, p. 204).

[4]Newton P. Stallknecht is among the critics who find intentional symbolic meaning in the poem but not without qualification. He theorizes that Coleridge began the poem without any didactic intention and realized its philosophical possibilities only by the time he reached the third and fourth parts (item 89). Eugene Marius Bewley thinks that Coleridge wrote the poem with only the dramatic motive in mind; and though he could not help letting the Christian moral show through, he did not develop it (item 34).

[5]Carlyon begins his account of Coleridge's conversation with the following general comment:

> Coleridge was in good spirits, very amusing, and as talkative as ever, throughout this little excursion. He frequently recited his own poetry, and not unfrequently led us rather farther into the labyrinth of his metaphysical elucidations, either of particular passages, or of the original conception of any of his productions, than we were able to follow him [item 216a, p. 140].

[6]In addition, parallels between Coleridge and the Mariner have been discussed by critics interested in biography (items 103, 398, 45) and in psychoanalysis (items 117, 232, 379, 127, 408).

[7]Several earlier studies also proceeded on the assumption that underlying the poem is a sacramental world. H.F. Scott-Thomas read the poem as Coleridge's demonstration "that the whole universe is permeated by a spirit of sympathetic charity that flows from and includes a Supreme Being" (item 22, p. 350). Bewley and Stallknecht emphasized the ideas of supernatural and aesthetic love (items 34, 89), while G. Wilson

Knight found that the "final lesson" in the story of "sin,
loneliness, and purgatorial redemption" is "a total acceptance
of God and his universe through humility, with general love
to man and beast" (item 51, pp. 84, 88).

[8]Beer modifies Warren's statement of the sacramental theme,
saying that "the sacrament is more closely religious than his
article suggests." Beer makes it clear that the "one Life"
"signifies not simply a biological phenomenon.... The bird
has to be seen as a symbol both of physical and transcendental
life" (item 216a, pp. 167-168).

[9]Assuming a quite different view of the Mariner, Alice
Chandler considers him in this action an "inverted redeemer."
She calls attention particularly to the use in the gloss of
the word "ransom" (at 11. 157-161) with its Christlike associations and to the Mariner's sacrifice of his own blood for what
he hoped would bring good fortune (item 333, p. 405).

[10]Noting the passive quality in the Mariner's blessing of
the water-snakes, George Watson finds unconvincing the Christian
interpretation of the Mariner as being saved through an act
of charity. "The point of emphasis," he insists, "is not
that the Mariner sins and repents ... but that both sin and
repentance are visited upon him. The Mariner is simply not
felt to be morally responsible, as he would be in any ordinary
Christian parable" (item 371, p. 97).

[11]Of all the supernatural incidents, the reanimation of
the crew is one of the most difficult to explain. It serves
no practical purpose, since the manipulating of the sails and
ropes is not necessary to make the ship move, and it does not
represent a real resurrection (items 94a, 151, 322). Several
critics agree with House that the behavior of the crew, especially in lines 341-344, dramatizes to the Mariner's consciousness the horror of the deaths, the violation of family
ties, the utter ruin of the merry, unified community which
had set out on the voyage (items 151, 366, 398). Geoffrey
Yarlott adds the comment that on a personal level their silent
work and curses may be a projection of Coleridge's own sense
of insecurity, particularly his bitter memory of broken family
relationships and of rejection by his brothers. "This incom-
munication between blood-relations," he says, "represented an
extreme of punishment for Coleridge, since he made it the
most painful aspect of Christabel's 'martyrdom' also" (item
398, p. 170). J.W. Purser and Stallknecht see the incident
as suggesting the extent of the Mariner's alienation, his
lack of love and understanding, and his need for sympathetic

human contact (items 202, 89). Patricia Adair writes that "it would be a travesty of Christianity to call this resurrection" (item 376, p. 68).

Yet most critics, concentrating more on the action of the angelic troop than on that of the crew, do emphasize such positive meanings as the incarnation and resurrection (items 94a, 34, 51), the coming of the Holy Spirit (item 331), God's forgiveness (item 256), cosmic harmony (items 207, 222), and the Mariner's expression of his own regeneration (items 284, 266). Beer argues that the center of the poem is not the Mariner's blessing of the water-snakes in the moonlight but his vision of communion and universal harmony in the scene of his dead shipmates stopping their work at dawn and gathering around the mast while sweet sounds arise from the angelic spirits to the sun (item 216a). Georg Roppen sees the hymn to the sun as an introduction to the more comprehensive pastoral vision of lines 367-372, as a provision for the Mariner's relief from the horror of his shipmates' deaths, and as a clear hint of spiritual resurrection (item 322).

Walter Jackson Bate accounts for the reanimation of the crew in still another way. He points out that the navigation of the ship by the dead men was suggested by Wordsworth as a practical means of returning the Mariner to human society. He therefore remains skeptical of symbolic interpretations which "strain with too much subtlety and indirection at what we may call the 'machinery of the return.' A return was needed, and Wordsworth provided one" (item 402, p. 64).

[12]Other critics object specifically to importing the myth of the fall to account for the gravity of the Mariner's act. Stuart C. Wilcox points out that besides the facts given in the text, the preparation in the Argument of 1800 makes the act appear criminal (item 274). And Harold Bloom argues that the Mariner is neither disobedient nor changed by the first effects of his deed and that the slaying of an albatross is not at all "an adequate symbol of a lapse that demands expression in the language of theology" (item 255, p. 207).

[13]Critics such as Charles Rowell point to the suggestions of the crucifixion in lines 81, 223, 404-405, 141-142, 512-513 (item 287). W.H. Auden relates the albatross to the Dove of the Holy Spirit and hence to the innocent victim Christ (item 118). Chandler adds the qualification that "the albatross is not Christ, to be sure, but he is certainly the incarnation of the life force, and his slaying has the stature of a crucifixion" (item 333, p. 409). Indicating still less precision, House acknowledges only the hint of a function as a Christian emblem when the bird is hung around the Mariner's neck. He

warns against the incompatible equation of the killing with
both the murder of a human being and the fall (item 151).

[14]Still another interpretation is Empson's practical suggestion that the Mariner shot the albatross for food, since
the victuals that remained after the storm had spoiled (item
315). Parsons, however, asserts that the ship's supplies were
ample at the time and that "the Mariner does not have the excuse of eighteenth-century voyagers who sacrificed albatrosses
to their hunger" (item 124, p. 118).

[15]Max F. Schulz does not intend to develop the idea but
claims that there is much in favor of reading the poem "as a
dramatic study in abnormal psychology" (item 306, p. 55).

[16]Charles Owen adds the qualification that it is impossible
completely to disentangle what is objective reality from what
takes place only in the Mariner's mind. Certain events like
the shooting of the albatross occur in both realms (item 284),
but the appearance of the phantom ship is probably a hallucination produced by the Mariner's delirium (item 124).

[17]Bate then concludes that "we therefore strain needlessly
at the poem when we try to rationalize the horror of the act
(for example, viewing it too literally as equivalent to the
murder of a human being--partly because of the Mariner's own
statement that the albatross had come to them out of the fog
'*As if* it had been a Christian soul')" (item 402, p. 58).

[18]By "imagination," Warren means the poetic, or secondary,
imagination of Coleridge's later critical theory. And he considers the Mariner's ambiguous position at the end of the poem
similar to that of the *poète maudit* of later romanticism
(item 94a).
    Except for Irene H. Chayes (item 334), critics have not
objected to the *poète maudit* analogy. But several discussions
of the imagination theme have disagreed with Warren's precise
reference to the secondary imagination. They believe instead
that the poem deals with the primary imagination or with the
general imaginative process (items 171, 255, 398, 112). They
agree with House, who most specifically states his criticism
of Warren's treatment of the imagination theme: (1) Coleridge
never fully brought into relation his own creative experience
and his critical theories; and (2) since his important critical
work was written much later than his major creative work, we
cannot be sure how much of his critical opinion may be fairly
applied to the poetry of 1797-98 (item 151).

In the notes added to the 1958 reprinting of his essay,
Warren replies to House's objection with the following evidence
that Coleridge's later theory of the imagination represents a
development of his position at the time he wrote the poem:
(1) Coleridge indicates in *Biographia Literaria* that he had
formed his basic conception of the imagination early; (2) he
refers to the shaping power of the mind in certain early
poems; and (3) he carefully revised the poem with no indication that it did not satisfactorily embody his theories of
1817 (item 94a).

[19]The positions of Beer and Roppen bear some qualification.
Beer sees no inconsistency in the death of the crew by the
light of the moon because he thinks it is the star between
its horns that is associated with the dying and cursing. But,
unlike Warren, he does not identify the sun only with retribution, an equation which he claims runs counter to Coleridge's
normal use of the sun as a symbol for benevolence (item 216a).
Roppen agrees with Beer and House that the sun has a double
character but insists that its dual quality is objectively
real and does not derive from the mariners' erratic perception
of it (item 322).

[20]Malcolm Ware points out an obscure reason for including
man in line 613, "Both man and bird and beast": Coleridge has
indicated the consequences of violating the natural bonds of
man to man by referring to a slave ship in the incident of
the spectre-bark (item 271).

[21]The irony lies not only in the relation between the
tale and the moral aphorism (item 334) but also in the Mariner's inability to use whatever wisdom he has gained (item
216). This ironical function, however, was perhaps not intended by Coleridge, since the moral does represent what he
wanted to believe (items 278, 376).

[22]Schneider dates the poem tentatively during 1799–1800.
In its summary and evaluation of the evidence used by other
critics for 1797 and 1798, as well as its detailed presentation of the case for her own new dating, her eighty-four-page
chapter on "The Date" is so thorough that the problem will not
be discussed in this essay. (See item 155.)

[23]Although most critics do think that the structure of the
poem contributes to its unity, they agree only that line 36
is the main dividing point. Otherwise, they recommend a number of different schemes for dividing the poem into stanzas

and main parts. On the basis of the Crewe manuscript, John
Shelton believes Coleridge intended two stanzas, lines 1-36
and 37-54 (item 369), while Hans H. Meier finds twelve--lines
1-5, 6-11, 12-16, 17-22, 23-24, 25-30, 31-34, 35-36, 37-41,
42-47, 48-52, and 53-54 (item 385). The most common stanzaic
division, based on the standard printed text, is three--lines
1-11, 12-36, and 37-54 (items 353, 316, 378, 349, 151, 402,
306, 379). But some scholars make lines 31-36 a separate
stanza, giving four in all (items 341, 298, 216a, 398, 272,
305), and Purves subdivides the poem into seven "sections" on
the basis of rhyme scheme and line length--lines 1-5, 6-11,
12-24, 25-30, 31-36, 37-41, 42-54 (item 286, p. 188).

Most critics discuss the structure of the poem in terms
of two main parts, lines 1-36 and 37-54 (items 272, 305, 353,
286, 349, 375, 341, 385, 316, 378, 155, 244, 402, 151, 306,
376, 379). Others suggest three parts--either lines 1-30,
31-36, and 37-54 (items 51, 59, 224) or lines 1-11, 12-36,
37-54 (items 292, 385). And Richard Gerber recommends a
sonata form of four main parts--lines 1-5, 6-30, 31-36, and
37-54 (item 298).

[24]Purves' omission of the word "pleasure" from his quotation of line 36 makes its length, as well as its meter and
rhyme, exactly the same as that of line 54 (item 286, p. 189).

[25]A prominent exception to this view of the poem is
Watson's opinion that, however it was composed, it "is not in
any formal sense a dream-poem," since it does not claim to
relate the experience of a dream and since it is not dreamlike
in the sense of being vague, shadowy, or mystical (item 371,
p. 120, and elsewhere).

[26]Watson reads the poem only in these specific terms
(item 371). Others insist that it concerns the wider human
situation as well. (See especially items 255, 349, 303, 385,
379.)

[27]Several critics specifically object to the treatment of
the natural and the artificial as an opposition. They argue
that Coleridge did not think of the artificial as evil and
the natural as good (items 385, 349).

[28]For Meier and Gerald Enscoe, Kubla's dome and garden
remain ambivalent. Meier warns that appreciation of "Kubla
Khan" cannot be enhanced by "worrying about Good or Evil in
its symbolism." The ambivalence of the dome contributes to
the poem's mysterious tension which suspends all ethical
curiosity (item 385, p. 152). Enscoe argues that the attitude

of the poem toward the areas of experience represented by
both the dome and the river is one of ambivalence. The dome
is sunny and pleasurable but an artificial escape from reality.
Looking back on his faded vision, the speaker is wistful, almost nostalgic; but he does not accept the dome without reser-
vations. On the outside it was bright and attractive, but it
was cold and dark within (items 316, 378).

Breyer and Suther consider the Abyssinian maid to be
another morally ambiguous image, although she is not often
discussed as such. They point out that she is not completely
wholesome because she produces an effect on the visionary
that requires a ritual of exorcism (items 128, 349).

[29]Coleridge's reference to the "radiant domes of Pandemonium" suggests that he thought of the Satanic Pandemonium
as dome-like and that he probably associated it with Kubla's
dome. Such a connection would facilitate a harmonious relationship between the pleasure-dome and the demon-lover and
would prepare for the note of ominousness beginning with "But
oh" (1. 12) (item 385, p. 149).

[30]It is questionable whether the dome's submerged sexual
implications are relevant to a discussion of its thematic significance. Some critics identify it with the maternal breast
and the *mons veneris* (items 232, 317, 379, 111) and think the
"feminine" adjectives ("fertile" [1. 6], "girdled" [1. 7],
and "Enfolding" [1. 11]) lend a narcissistic tone to the description of the surrounding garden. But Bate considers this
a "desperate" equation unworthy of his attention (item 402,
p. 79). Enscoe acknowledges the possibility of a psychological connection between the dome and Coleridge's feelings about
his mother but views it as "extraneous to the language of the
poem" (item 316, p. 31, and elsewhere).

[31]Enscoe suggests the possibility that "in air" (1. 46)
also conveys the speaker's realization that only in art can
there be complete reconciliation of opposites (items 316, 378).

[32]For suggestions of other reasons why Coleridge changed
"Amara" to "Amora" in the Crewe manuscript and then substituted
"Abora" in the printed text, see items 298, 341, 338, 163,
216a.

[33]The dome is also thought to symbolize true immortality
(items 51, 366) and fullness of life (item 152).

[34]Some critics believe that in lines 1-36 Coleridge has
already built the dome, or poem, before our admiring eyes

(items 151, 303, 178, 128, 293). Others argue that it remains
to be done. Commenting on line 46, Watson makes the point
that "Coleridge has not just done this. The syntax makes it
very clear that the project remains unfulfilled" (item 371,
p. 124). Partly on the evidence of the "music loud and long"
(l. 45), Adair thinks that the future project refers to one
of Coleridge's plans for an epic poem, perhaps "The Conquest
of India by Bacchus in Hexameters" (item 376).

[35]House's reading of "once" and "Could" has also been
criticized by other scholars whose view of the poem is less
positive than Suther's. Woodring argues that because House
and his readers cannot appreciate "Kubla Khan" as a fragment,
they are compelled to misconstrue these words so that they
bear "surprising burdens" (item 209, p. 362). And Yarlott
thinks that House's interpretation of the poem hinges on "a
feat of implausible linguistics" (item 398, p. 147).

[36]Among the critics who view the speaker as successful,
some find within his conditional statement a hint of diffi-
dence or ambivalence. For them it suggests the possibility
of failure (item 152) and maybe a note of longing stemming
from the correspondence of the speaker and the Abyssinian
maid to the wailing woman and her demon-lover. Its tone is
probably best described as somewhere between "methinks I
could" and "if only I could" (item 349, p. 276). Beneath
the seeming cry of disappointment is the addict's unconscious
conviction of a second chance (item 317) or the dreamer's
assuring belief that Xanadu is potentially summonable again
and again (item 306).

[37]Arthur Hobart Nethercot points out, however, that the
comparison of Christabel to a "youthful hermitess" (l. 320)
should not be attributed to Crashaw's portrait of Theresa but
to Coleridge's knowledge and interest in her biography
(item 30).

[38]In the first version of the poem Coleridge had described
Geraldine's bosom as "lean and old and foul of hue." He
later substituted the more abstract line, "A sight to dream
of, not to tell" (l. 253) (item 65, p. 86, and elsewhere).

[39]Showing how Geraldine deliberately entices Leoline with
her courtesan's beauty, Yarlott cites this detail as well as
Geraldine's arraying herself almost like a bride (ll. 363-
365), her prolonging of Leoline's embrace with "joyous look"
(l. 450), and her feigning a modesty she does not really
possess (ll. 573-575) (item 398).

[40]Yarlott points out that Coleridge's affection for Hartley was probably the main impediment to his pursuit of Sara Hutchinson and that the birth of Derwent in September, 1800, was not a welcome event. Coleridge's mixed feelings of love and resentment are reflected in Leoline's abandonment of Christabel, especially since the "limber elf" passage (11. 656 ff.) is a description of Hartley that first appeared in a letter in which Coleridge was contemplating what the loss of the child would mean to him. Preceding the passage, he had written that the loss of Hartley "would exceedingly deaden my affection for any other children I may have" (item 65, p. 89; item 398). To Basler this statement indicates a parallel between Coleridge's speculated behavior toward Derwent should Hartley die and Leoline's unreasonable cruelty toward Christabel because of his love for his dead wife (item 65).

[41]In addition to the specific themes most often discussed, several others have been suggested: the psychic conflict and poetic rivalry between Coleridge and Wordsworth (item 289), appearance versus reality (items 309, 379), the juxtaposition of ordinary understanding and intuitive insight (item 398) or of orthodox and heterodox realms of experience (item 349), the paradise lost motif with emphasis on the fall (items 412, 379, 366, 292, 376) or on redemption (item 216a).

[42]Justice John Taylor Coleridge recorded that Wordsworth

said he had no idea how "Christabel" was to have been finished, and he did not think my uncle had ever conceived, in his own mind, any definite plan for it; that the poem had been composed while they were in habits of daily intercourse, and almost in his presence, and when there was the most unreserved intercourse between them as to all their literary projects and productions, and he had never heard from him any plan for finishing it. Not that he doubted my uncle's sincerity in his subsequent assertions to the contrary; because, he said, schemes of this sort passed rapidly and vividly through his mind, and so impressed him, that he often fancied he had arranged things, which really, and upon trial, proved to be mere embryos. I omitted to ask him, what seems obvious enough now, whether in conversing about it, he had never asked my uncle how it would end. The answer would have settled the question [item 11, p. 440, and elsewhere].

[43]The Preface remained practically unchanged until 1834, when this passage was omitted (item 28).

[44]The following details have been suggested as indicating
the eventual triumph of good over evil: the full moon (item
309), the narrator's hope for Christabel's freedom in "A star
hath set, a star hath risen" (1. 302) (items 86, 65), Geraldine's promise to "requite" Christabel (1. 232), the recurring
mention of the nearness of Christabel's mother, Christabel's
"sweet" vision (1. 326), her knowledge that the "saints will
aid if men will call" (1. 330) (item 50), and her assurance
that "'all will yet be well'" (1. 472) (items 86, 309).

[45]Enscoe, Bloom, and Bostetter, however, take exception
to this opinion. Although they see the Conclusion as a statement of the major theme of the poem, they find it unrelated to
the action of any of the characters. Bostetter explains that
Leoline's anger is provoked by Christabel's look of hate,
whereas the father's "wild" words (1. 671) have no external
motivation (items 192, 378, 255).

[46]Schneider points out some inconsistencies in the description of the setting of Part I: colors ("green" [1. 33] of the
moss and mistletoe and "red" [1. 49] of the leaf) are introduced by the light of a "small," "dull" (1. 19) moon showing
through a thin film of cloud, and the "one red leaf" conveys
autumn rather than the "month before the month of May" (1. 21)
(item 156). To Raymond Smith these visual discrepancies suggest the symbolic rather than naturalistic purpose of the
description (item 309). But to Schneider they indicate the
possibility that the opening scene was not all written at the
same time and thus add weight to her supposition that both
Part I and Part II may have been the product of late 1799-1800
(item 156).

[47]Smith points to other examples of the life-death theme
in the image of the "dying" torches, "amid their own white
ashes lying" (11. 156-157) and in the association of Christabel
with redness and life and Geraldine with whiteness and death
(item 347).

[48]This passage replaced an earlier version of only two
lines: "She took two paces and a stride, / And lay down by
the maiden's side" (item 151, p. 125).

Annotated Bibliography
1935–70

ANNOTATED BIBLIOGRAPHY, 1935-70

1935

1. Canceled.

2. Chambers, E.K. "The Date of Coleridge's 'Kubla Khan,'"
   RES, 11 (1935), 78-80.

   A note, written by Coleridge in 1810, links his retirement to the farmhouse with the failure to finish "Christabel," still in progress in the spring of 1798, and mentions
   a conversation, which probably took place in December of
   1797, between Dorothy Wordsworth and Charles Lloyd. But
   the date of "Kubla Khan" remains uncertain.

3. Evans, B. Ifor. "Coleridge's Copy of 'Fears in Solitude,'"
   TLS, April 18, 1935, p. 255.

   In his copy of the "Fears in Solitude" quarto Coleridge
   made several notes correcting the text of "France: An Ode"
   (11. 46, 79) and clarifying the meaning of its last stanza,
   explaining his omission of the last six lines of "Frost at
   Midnight," and commenting on the prosaic quality of "Fears
   in Solitude" (11. 159-175) and on his present sense of
   loss of peace and creative work. He probably wrote these
   notes at Coleorton in January, 1807, when Wordsworth's
   reading of *The Prelude* prompted his tribute in "To William
   Wordsworth" and focused his attention on the poems he had
   composed during the early years of his friendship with
   Wordsworth.

4. Rochlin, S.A. "Coleridge's 'A Hymn,'" *TLS*, January 17,
   1935, p. 33.

   Coleridge's "A Hymn" was first published in the October,
   1832, issue of the *Cape of Good Hope Literary Gazette*, not,
   as E.H. Coleridge says, in *Poems*, 1852.

5. Smith, Fred Manning. "The Relation of Coleridge's *Ode
    on Dejection* to Wordsworth's *Ode on Intimations of
    Immortality*," *PMLA*, 50 (1935), 224-234.

    Inspired by Wordsworth's "Intimations" ode and by the
    contrast between the two poets' situations, Coleridge's
    "Dejection" resembles in several ways the first 129 lines
    of its companion poem. Both odes treat the difference
    between the past and the present in images of light and
    glory, weight, unseeing eyes, weddings, and funerals.
    Unlike Wordsworth, however, Coleridge can *"see, not feel"*
    (l. 39) the beauties in the sunset sky and can find no
    relief for his grief. Instead of a sign of hope, he sees
    the new moon with the old moon in its arms; instead of a
    happy child (Coleridge's son Hartley) who is a philosopher,
    a prophet, and a comic actor, he tells of a lost, grieving
    girl (Wordsworth's Lucy Gray) and associates the poet and
    the tragic actor with the wind.

6. Warne, F.J. "Prester John in Coleridge's 'Kubla Khan,'"
    MLR, 30 (1935), 55-58.

    The connecting link between Xanadu and Abyssinia is
    Prester John, mentioned in Purchas' *Pilgrimages* as well
    as in the longer *Pilgrimes* as the king of Abyssinia who
    received tribute from the Tartars and was slain by Genghis
    Khan. The priest-king was recalled to Coleridge's mind
    by Purchas' reference to Tartar marriage customs in the
    passage immediately preceding his description of Xamdu.

7. Watson, H.F. "'The Borderers' and 'The Ancient Mariner,'"
    TLS, December 28, 1935, p. 899.

    The calm preceding the marooning episode in "The Border-
    ers" is a likely source of the calm and shortage of drink-
    ing water in "The Ancient Mariner." Both poems treat the
    common theme of the wandering sinner haunted by remorse;
    and both Oswald and the Mariner tell their stories, long
    after the events occurred, as a warning to a younger man
    who interpolates a word or two.

8. Woodbridge, Homer E. "Coleridge and the Nightingale,"
    SRL, September 28, 1935, p. 9.

    The editorial "Debunking the Nightingale" (*SRL*,
    August 3, 1935, p. 8) should have mentioned Coleridge's
    full and truthful description of the bird's cheerful
    song.

1936

9.   Beatty, Arthur. "'The Borderers' and 'The Ancient
      Mariner,'" *TLS*, February 29, 1936, p. 184.

      Since Coleridge checked out of the Bristol Library the
      sixth volume of the *Harleian Miscellany*, he might also
      have read the story of a Dutch sailor in the seventh
      volume and passed it on to Wordsworth, for the story has
      the following elements in common with "The Borderers": a
      desert island, thirst, calm, scarcity of water and search
      for it, and digging for water. Like "The Ancient Mari-
      ner," it includes the quenching of thirst with blood and
      prayers.

10.   Leavis, Frank Raymond. "Coleridge's Beginnings," in
      *Revaluation: Tradition and Development in English
      Poetry* (London: Chatto & Windus, 1936), pp. 142-147.

      With its reminiscences of Gray's "Elegy," Collins' "Ode
      to Evening," and Milton's "L'Allegro" and "On the Morning
      of Christ's Nativity," "Songs of the Pixies" exemplifies
      the poetic climate of the early 1790's.

11.   McElderry, B.R., Jr. "Coleridge's Plan for Completing
      Christabel," *SP*, 33 (1936), 437-455.

      Gillman's account of Coleridge's plan for completing
      "Christabel" is genuine and poetically sound. It har-
      monizes with Derwent Coleridge's note about Christabel's
      vicarious sufferings and verifies the wholeness of vision
      repeatedly claimed by Coleridge and corroborated by
      Carlyon and the many arrangements for publishing the
      finished poem. Evidently, the plan was commonly known
      to Coleridge's friends; and no contemporary specifically
      objected to Gillman's account of it, although two years
      earlier, in 1836, Wordsworth stated that Coleridge had
      only embryos of plans, never anything definite. In con-
      trast to the amateurish sequel by "V," however, Gillman's
      ending provides a reasonable development of action and
      character. The return of Christabel's real lover, for
      instance, is anticipated in the opening scene of Part I,
      and her hesitant consent to marry the false lover con-
      trasts naturally with her quarrel with Leoline at the
      end of Part II. Finally, the plan is typical of Coleridge
      in its use of a symmetrical narrative structure, the de-
      vice of the lover falsely impersonated, and a moral pat-
      tern which makes credible the supernatural events.

12. Van Patten, Nathan. "A Presentation Copy of Coleridge's
     Sibylline Leaves, with Manuscript Notes, Altered Read-
     ings, and Deletions by the Author," *Library*, 17 (1936),
     221-224.

     This article reprints Coleridge's marginalia and other
     notes in his copy of *Sibylline Leaves* formerly owned by
     the Gillman family and now at Stanford University.

13. Waples, Dorothy. "David Hartley in 'The Ancient Mariner,'"
     JEGP, 35 (1936), 337-351.

     The Mariner and, to a lesser extent, the Wedding-Guest
     exemplify the six psychological stages in Hartley's pro-
     cess of education. After his crime the Mariner progresses
     from the stage of imagination, in which he experiences
     fear, to that of ambition, when he feels shamed by the
     crew's evil looks and by their hanging the dead albatross
     around his neck. He then reaches the stage of self-
     interest, expressed by his disgust with the world and
     himself. He moves to sympathy in blessing the water-
     snakes and theopathy in regaining the ability to pray.
     He affirms the moral sense by returning to human society
     and concerning himself with the duty of telling others
     what he has learned.
     That Coleridge intended this associationism is indi-
     cated by his use of it in "Religious Musings," "The
     Destiny of Nations," "Fears in Solitude," "Frost at Mid-
     night," "The Nightingale," and "The Wanderings of Cain,"
     and by Wordsworth's use of it in *Peter Bell* and the Mount
     Snowdon passage at the beginning of Book XIV of *The Pre-
     lude*. By the time of Coleridge's reported conversation
     with Mrs. Barbauld, however, he had rejected Hartleian
     psychology and hence regretted its presence in the poem.

                              1937

14. Coats, R.H. "Kubla Khan," *TLS*, December 18, 1937,
     p. 964.

     Both Coleridge's "Kubla Khan" and Wordsworth's "The
     Solitary Reaper" concern a poet overhearing a maiden
     singing, seeking some imaginative equivalent of her song,
     and rendering it in the poem as a whole.

15. De Selincourt, Ernest. "Coleridge's 'Dejection: An
     Ode,'" *Essays and Studies by Members of the English
     Association*, 22 (1937), 7-25. Reprinted in

Wordsworthian and Other Studies. Oxford: Clarendon Press, 1947.

Even in its original form Coleridge's "Dejection" is an acute, tragic analysis of his own mental and emotional state in contrast with that of his friend Wordsworth. This contrast is apparent not only in the relationship of events in the lives of the two poets at the time of composition but also in the text of the verse letter to Sara Hutchinson, printed here for the first time.

16. Meyerstein, E.H.W. "Chatterton, Coleridge and Bristol: 'The Sacred River,'" *TLS*, August 21, 1937, p. 606.

   For his description of Alph, Coleridge is indebted to Chatterton's three "African Eclogues," John Selden's notes on Drayton's *Polyolbion*, and the actual underground channels at Bristol.

17. ————. "Completeness of Kubla Khan," *TLS*, October 30, 1937, p. 803.

   In spite of Coleridge's Preface, "Kubla Khan" is a complete poem with the usual metrical form of a short Pindaric ode and a climactic structure made up of lines 1-36 describing the dome and its environment and of lines 37-54 considering the ecstasy resulting from successfully recreating it.

18. ————. "Kubla Khan," *TLS*, December 4, 1937, p. 928.

   Chatterton's imagery in "Songe to AElla," drawn from the Avon Gorge, influenced the imagery of "Kubla Khan." The simile of a broken friendship in "Christabel" (ll. 421-423) has parallels in Shiercliff's "The Bristol and Hotwell Guide," Manby's "Fugitive Sketches of Clifton," Chatterton's "Clifton," and Collins' "Ode to Liberty." (Cf. items 16, 17.)

19. Morley, Edith J. "'The Rash Conjurer,'" *TLS*, May 8, 1937, p. 364.

   A passage from Crab Robinson's Diary for August 20, 1812, proves that Coleridge wrote "The Rash Conjurer" several months earlier than the date suggested by Ernest Hartley Coleridge.

20. Sypher, F. Wylie. "Chatterton, Coleridge and Bristol," *TLS*, August 28, 1937, p. 624.

The generally accepted date of "Kubla Khan" is 1798, and in 1797-98 Coleridge could have known at least one cave and underground stream at Cheddar and much of Wookey Hole. (Cf. item 16.)

1938

21. Patton, Lewis. "The Coleridge Canon," *TLS*, September 3, 1938, p. 570.

"To a Primrose" and three of the *Watchman* epigrams attributed to Coleridge are not his but were borrowed from an Irish magazine, *Anthologia Hibernica*. On the other hand, "Lines on the Portrait of a Lady" probably is his, since it was signed "S" and printed in the *Watchman* along with two other poems, signed "T" and "C," which Coleridge did claim.

22. Scott-Thomas, H.F. "The Ethics of 'The Ancient Mariner,'" *DR*, 18 (1938), 348-354.

The moral demonstrated throughout "The Ancient Mariner" and stated explicitly at the end is that the universe is permeated by a spirit of sympathetic charity which flows from and includes a Supreme Being. Sin is a breaking of the affectionate bond and results in isolation. In this context the Mariner's acts of shooting the albatross and of blessing the water-snakes are not trivial and incommensurable with their consequences but are indicative of the moral states of selfishness and generosity. Once the Mariner has reestablished communion with all things, his sanctification takes the form of saving the unredeemed by specific warning and by personal example.

23. Tuttle, Donald Reuel. "*Christabel* Sources in Percy's *Reliques* and the Gothic Romance," *PMLA*, 53 (1938), 445-474.

Influenced by the same popular literature which contributed to "The Ancient Mariner" and "Kubla Khan," the atmosphere, the characters, and most of the important episodes in "Christabel" derive from Percy's *Reliques* and the Gothic romances of Mrs. Radcliffe, "Monk" Lewis, and Mrs. Robinson. The ballads--especially "Sir Cauline," "The Child of Elle," and "The Marriage of Sir Gawaine"-- contributed mainly to the development of the larger details of the plot. In addition, "Sir Cauline" furnished the name of Christabel and phrases which resemble the

descriptions of the leaf as "light" and "high" (1. 51)
and of Geraldine as a "ladye bright" (11. 88-89, 58-59).
Emmaline in "The Child of Elle" and Guinevere in "The
Marriage of Sir Gawaine" each supplied ideas for the actions of both Christabel and Geraldine; the quarrel between their fathers appears in "The Child of Elle."

More important than the ballads, however, are the romances, particularly the lengthy passage quoted by
Coleridge in his review of Mrs. Radcliffe's *The Mysteries
of Udolpho*. From this excerpt came the episode of
Christabel's leaving her room at midnight and returning
through the courtyard and castle halls; incidents such
as the trimming of her lamp, the lighting up of Geraldine's eye and Leoline's shield, and Geraldine's fainting; and the detail of the little door within the iron
gate. Geraldine's story of her capture occurs here as
well as in *The Romance of the Forest* and Mrs. Robinson's
Hubert de Sevrac. Finally, in *The Mysteries of Udolpho*,
immediately following Coleridge's quotation, Emily's
conduct resembles Christabel's relaxing from her trance
and then being unable to tell of her experience.

In the same scene Christabel is pictured, like Ellena
in *The Italian*, sleeping with tears shining on her eyelashes. Lewis' *The Monk* contains nearly every detail
used in the characterization of Geraldine--she is a composite of Antonia, a woman in a religious procession,
and the demon Matilda--and a bedroom scene in which the
roles of the Bleeding Nun and Raymond parallel those of
Geraldine and Christabel. The psychology of Christabel's
relationship with her father probably derives from
Hubert de Sevrac, where Sabina suffers from her promise
to keep silent about the planned murder of her father.

More generally, Mrs. Radcliffe's romances provided a
storehouse of such standard Gothic devices as the midnight setting of moonlight and stillness; the suspenseful
details of the moaning, the strange oak tree, and Christabel's difficulty in going to sleep; and the description
of the castle with its halls, dying fire, hanging lamp,
clock, ringing bell, and iron gate.

1939

24. Beyer, Werner W. "Coleridge, Wieland's *Oberon*, and *The
Ancient Mariner*," *RES*, 15 (1939), 401-411.

Coleridge was translating *Oberon* at the same time he
was writing "The Ancient Mariner" and must have recalled

some of the romantic sections of Wieland's poem—the
storm at sea, the elfin music of Oberon's fairies, and
the hermitage scenes—for his use of the images of the
rising and setting sun (11. 83-86), of the daemonic music
heard by the Mariner (11. 358-372), of the storm and
lightning (11. 318-326), and of the hermit is similar to
Wieland's in phrasing, "melody," and narrative context.

25. Burke, Charles Bell. "Coleridge and Milton," *N&Q*, 176
     (1939), 42.

Coleridge's use of the phrase "genial spirits" in line
39 of "Dejection" is probably a deliberate echo of Milton's *Samson Agonistes*, line 594.

26. ————. "Coleridge and Shelley," *N&Q*, 176 (1939), 98-99.

Although the opening of Shelley's "Alastor" resembles
Coleridge's invocation of the clouds, waves, and woods in
"France: An Ode," Shelley is preoccupied with healing
through the beneficent ministry of nature, whereas
Coleridge is concerned with political freedom.

27. Griggs, Earl Leslie. "An Early Defense of *Christabel*,"
     in *Wordsworth and Coleridge: Studies in Honor of George
     McLean Harper*, ed. Earl L. Griggs (Princeton: Princeton
     University Press, 1939), pp. 173-191.

An unpublished defense of "Christabel" against Hazlitt's
inexplicably malicious attacks has been recently discovered among the papers of A.H. Hallam Murray. Apparently
written by John J. Morgan under the inspiration of his
conversations with Coleridge, the review outlines the
narrative and then discusses the management and arrangement of its events, mentions the consistency of its
characters, illustrates its impressive moral sentiments
(11. 408-415, 416-426) and the poet's descriptive and
imaginative powers (11. 14-17, 20-22, 43-52, 127-128,
220-225, 351-359), and explains the meter and its suitability for conveying Geraldine's mysteriousness (11.
267-278). In conclusion the article denies Hazlitt's
charge of obscenity and points to the introduction of
Christabel's mother and the early reference to Christabel's wedding as preparation for the end of the poem
and thus as evidence for the wholeness of the plan.

28. McElderry, B.R., Jr. "Coleridge's 'Preface' to
     Christabel," in *Wordsworth and Coleridge: Studies in
     Honor of George McLean Harper*, ed. Earl L. Griggs

(Princeton: Princeton University Press, 1939), pp. 166-172.

The 1816 Preface to "Christabel" is anticipated by two of Coleridge's letters. The one of December, 1811, denying that Scott was guilty of plagiarism, contains the images of the spring and the tank and speaks with contempt for the critics who assume that every thought and image is derivative. Like the Preface, the letter to Byron of October 22, 1815, mentions the date of composition and the plan for the poem as a whole which Coleridge had in mind from the beginning; it refutes the charge that "Christabel" was an imitation of other writers and discusses its new concept of meter. But behind the Preface's "indolence" is the fuller explanation in the letter, blaming the failure to finish the poem on the lack of financial security which would have permitted Coleridge to write poetry instead of sermons and newspaper pieces.

29. Milley, Henry J.W. "Some Notes on Coleridge's 'Eolian Harp,'" *MP*, 36 (1939), 359-375.

"The Eolian Harp" occupies an important position in the poetic development of both Coleridge and Wordsworth. It is the first poem to show the improved quality of Coleridge's verse resulting from his firsthand discovery of the English countryside. Especially in the draft for the edition of 1797, it anticipates some of the images, cadences, and ideas expressed in "Kubla Khan." It influenced the philosophy and form of Wordsworth's "Tintern Abbey" and in its method of composition demonstrated Wordsworth's theory of the process of poetic inspiration, for it was written on two separate occasions. On August 20, 1775, Coleridge described the evening scene and then, some time after his marriage on October 4, recalled its tranquility and told of reclining with Sarah on the hillside in the noon sequence.

30. Nethercot, Arthur Hobart. *The Road to Tryermaine: A Study of the History, Background, and Purposes of Coleridge's "Christabel."* Chicago: University of Chicago Press, 1939.

In contrast to other Gothic romances and the early reviews and continuations, Coleridge intended "Christabel" to have a moral purpose. According to his son Derwent and his biographer James Gillman, he based the poem on the idea of vicarious atonement. His choice of

Christabel's name and association of her with Crashaw's
Saint Theresa indicate that she is suffering innocently
for the sake of her absent lover. To bring about her
suffering is the mission imposed upon the preternatural
being Geraldine, who is herself suffering a probationary
trial in expiation of some past sin symbolized by her
physical deformity.

Coleridge's conception of Geraldine must not have been
perfectly clear, for her malignant qualities began to
override her ultimately altruistic purpose, contributing
to the more general lack of control that made it impossible for him to finish the poem. Certain elements in
her character, however, become well-defined when Coleridge's reading during the 1790's is retraced. She resembles a vampire in her weakness, paleness, coldness of
touch, desire for physical contact, renewed vitality,
power to induce imitation within Christabel, extension
of her spell to another member of the family, and lack
of responsibility. Such traits were prominent in the
vampire lore which Coleridge was reading in the scholarly
articles of John Ferriar, Voltaire, and Calmet and in
Southey's *Thalaba* and Goethe's "The Bride of Corinth."
Even more than with the vampire, Geraldine shows an
affiliation with the lamia, a particular kind of pitiable
female vampire with serpent characteristics. Coleridge
knew the story of the transformation of Lamia, queen of
Libya, into a serpent-daemon through Greek and Latin
historians such as Diodorus Siculus, Pierre Bayle, and
some of Ferriar's sources--Wier, Cardan, Calmet, Apol-
lonius, Philostratus, and Burton. His description of
Geraldine's ophidian traits, including her "witch's
mark," or "mark of the beast," and her fascinating
glance, could have been drawn from his reading of Dante's
Inferno, the story of an American farmer bitten by a
copperhead in *The Annual Register* for 1782, an account
of a green snake attacking a bird in volume five of the
abridged *Philosophical Transactions* as well as the discussions of Bartram, Mather, Antonius Mizaldus, Bryan
Edwards, Samuel Hearne, Ferriar, Sennertus, Wier, Del
Rio, Thomas Burnet, and Richard Cumberland. Finally, he
may have derived her strange vascillation between sinister
and kindly impulses from the doctrines of metempsychosis
which he was reading about in articles by Depuis, William
Enfield, Cottle, Purchas, William Jones, J. Marshal, and
Cudworth.

Coleridge's reading and experience also help to clarify
his conception of the guardian spirit and to locate
Christabel's stone angel and the names of characters and

places. Christabel's mother apparently resides in Purgatory, though she combines the functions of the pagan "Lar" and "larva" in being permitted to hasten to her daughter's side when needed. The angel whose feet are attached to Christabel's lamp appears in Coleridge's description in a letter to his wife of the baptismal ritual in the churches of Göttingen. Christabel's name comes from Percy's version of the ballad "Sir Cauline," and Bracy's from Nash's *Worcestershire*. Hutchinson's *Cumberland* furnished the names of Sir Leoline, Geraldine, and Lord Roland de Vaux of Tryermaine as well as the familiar scenery and places in the Lake District and the unfamiliar landmarks of Bracy's journey.

31. Sypher, Wylie. "Coleridge's Somerset: A Byway to Xanadu," *PQ*, 18 (1939), 353-366.

Probably written in the fall of 1797 at Ash Farm in the parish of Culbone, "Kubla Khan" was influenced by what Coleridge read as well as by what he saw. For example, local scenery in Somerset—particularly Cheddar Gorge with its legend of exorcism and the grotto at Wookey Hole—moulded the images of the chasm, the wailing woman, the subterranean river Alph, the pleasure-dome, the caves of ice, and the measureless caverns.

32. T., C.C. "Coleridge and Shelley," *N&Q*, 176 (1939), 159.

A common source for the invocations by Shelley in "Alastor" and by Coleridge in "France: An Ode" may be found in Aeschylus' *Prometheus Bound* (11. 88-90), a play known to both poets. (Cf. item 26.)

1940

33. Bald, R.C. "Coleridge and *The Ancient Mariner*: Addenda to *The Road to Xanadu*," in *Nineteenth-Century Studies*, ed. Herbert Davis, William C. De Vane, R.C. Bald (Ithaca: Cornell University Press, 1940), pp. 1-45.

The later notebooks supplement the Gutch memorandum book available to Lowes in three ways. They elucidate a number of passages in "The Ancient Mariner"; they indicate that Coleridge deliberately planned his reading to store up in his mind materials for use in his poetry; and they suggest that the influence of opium probably furnished impressions which were incorporated into the poem. The Malta notebook constantly recalls significant

words, phrases, and incidents from the poem and records
the firsthand experience partly responsible for such
alterations in the 1817 text as the expansion of four
colorless lines describing a strong tempest to ten lines
personifying the "Storm-blast" (11. 41-50); the temporary
revision of "The furrow followed free" to "The furrow
stream'd off free" (1. 104); the addition of "star /
Within the nether tip" (11. 210-211) and the helmsman;
the substitution in line 212 of "star-dogged Moon" for
"horned Moon"; and the addition of the moon gloss.

Passages from the notebooks and letters indicate that
Coleridge intended to write an epic on the origin of
evil, a theme which he later changed to the destruction
of Jerusalem. With this project in mind, he deliberately
chose the reading chronicled in *The Road to Xanadu* and
was no doubt aware of the complex literary sources of
his poem.

The notebooks also describe the psychological experience
of opium, which influenced both specific passages in the
1817 version of the poem and general characteristics in
the original version. Opium possibly accounts for the
extreme auditory sensibility in lines 201-202, while
recollections of the horrors of opium dreams appear in
the unreasoning sense of fear in lines 193-194, 204-205,
and 45-49. Probably in response to Wordsworth's criticism, Coleridge added the 1800 sub-title "A Poet's
Reverie," thus placing the poem in the category of mental
states which included those produced by opium and in
which events were related by association rather than by
logical connection. Besides this dreamlike quality,
opium contributed to the use of water, vivid colors, and
sounds; to the repetition of imagery; to its appeal to
the emotions of wonder and fear; and to the widened and
sharpened perceptions not evident in the earlier poems.

34. Bewley, Eugene Marius. "Revaluations (XII): The Poetry
     of Coleridge," *Scrutiny*, 8 (1940), 406-420.

"Dejection" is Coleridge's best poem because the mature
feeling of regret is a natural and valid experience controlled by the intellect. "The Ancient Mariner," on the
other hand, is confusingly ambiguous because it uses
supernatural machinery for the trivial dramatic purpose
of creating an air of mystery about the events instead
of for the development of their latent moral significance.
The fragment of "Kubla Khan" is nothing more than an indefinite suggestion of visuality which declines in poetic
intensity after the first verse paragraph.

35. Beyer, Werner W. "Coleridge, Wieland's *Oberon*, and *The Wanderings of Cain*," *RES*, 16 (1940), 274-289.

    Wieland's *Oberon*, which Coleridge was translating by November, 1797, contains settings, atmosphere, charac- ters, and incidents analogous to those in "The Wanderings of Cain." Both Cain and Huon suffer from thirst, hunger, and daemonic persecution as they wander across deserts of shattered rocks and scorching sand and down winding paths through fir-forests. Both heroes cry out to higher powers, sink to earth, and yearn for death before finally meeting the ghost of Abel and the hermit. In both poems these incidents and landscapes are described in visually powerful images.

36. Bonnard, G. "The Invasion of Switzerland and English Public Opinion (January to April, 1798): The Background to S.T. Coleridge's 'France: An Ode,'" *ES*, 22 (1940), 1-26.

    A review of the English press during the early months of 1798, preceding the April 16th publication of "France: An Ode," supports the *Morning Post*'s claim that English- men everywhere shared Coleridge's deep indignation over the French invasion of Switzerland. Although they drew different lessons from it, both Whigs and Tories con- demned the ruthlessness of the French conduct. Having had a genuine and spontaneous interest in Swiss affairs, they sympathized with the brave Swiss soldiers and at first hoped for a successful resistance.

37. Hartman, Herbert. "'The Mad Monk,'" *TLS*, November 2, 1940, p. 555.

    Although the earliest mention of the "Intimations" ode is an entry in Dorothy Wordsworth's *Journal* for March 27, 1802, it is quite possible that with "The Mad Monk" re- cently in his mind Wordsworth began thinking about the ode as early as 1800 or 1801, during which time the young Hartley Coleridge visited the Wordsworths frequently. Coleridge himself echoed "The Mad Monk" in "Dejection" (ll. 76-77, 84-86). (Cf. items 39, 40.)

37a. Lovejoy, Arthur O. "Coleridge and Kant's Two Worlds," *ELH*, 7 (1940), 341-362. Reprinted in *Essays in the History of Ideas*. Baltimore: Johns Hopkins Press, 1948.

    Coleridge's generalization in "Dejection" is not an expression of Kant's transcendental idealism, in which the mind gives form to the objects it perceives, but a

psychological observation that the pleasure he receives
from nature depends on joy, a subjective state beyond
his control.

38. Meyerstein, E.H.W.   "'The Mad Monk,'" *TLS*, November 9,
       1940, p. 567.

     Wordsworth's echo of "The Mad Monk" in the "Intimations"
     ode extends to line 16 of Coleridge's poem. The parallel
     between these two poems and "Dejection" has been discussed
     by Fausset as well as by de Selincourt. (Cf. items 39,
     40, 37.)

39. ―――――.   "'The Mad Monk' and Wordsworth," *TLS*,
       September 7, 1940, p. 447.

     Might the similarity between Coleridge's "The Mad Monk"
     (11. 9-16), first published in 1800, and Wordsworth's
     "Intimations" ode suggest a date as early as 1800 for
     the first stanza of the ode?

40. Muir, Kenneth.   "'The Mad Monk,'" *TLS*, October 12, 1940,
       p. 522.

     There is no evidence that Wordsworth composed the
     "Intimations" ode as early as 1800, but on the night of
     April 4, 1802, Coleridge echoed the first four stanzas
     in the first draft of "Dejection." (Cf. items 39, 37.)

41. Nethercot, Arthur Hobart.   "Christabel's Wild-Flower
       Wine," *MLQ*, 1 (1940), 499-501.

     The recipe for the "wild-flower wine" with which
     Christabel revived Geraldine appears in one of Coleridge's
     memorandum books. Made of lemon and ginger, it is called
     "spicy wine" in one of the manuscripts but is commonly
     known as ginger beer, appropriate in its mildness to the
     innocent character of Christabel.

42. Visiak, E.H.   "Some Coleridge Parallels," *N&Q*, 178
       (1940), 422.

     Here are some obvious parallels between Coleridge's
     poems and those of other poets: "The Ancient Mariner,"
     lines 35-36 and 97-98, and the "Squire's Tale," line
     268, and *Paradise Lost*, XI, 879-880; "Christabel,"
     lines 127-128 and 296, and *Paradise Lost*, II, 884-887,
     and XI, 629; "Dejection," line 39, and *Samson Agonistes*,
     I, 594 (see item 25); "Fears in Solitude," lines 104-107
     and 117, and Plutarch's moral of the frogs.

43. ————. "'Two Voices in the Air' (A Note on 'The Rime
    of the Ancient Mariner')," *N&Q*, 179 (1940), 99.

    The abnormal speed of the ship enables the Mariner to
    hear the spirits and attracts them down below their pro-
    per region so that they perceive him. The explanation
    of the ship's movement resembles the description of air-
    ships by Macmillan and Rudolf Steiner.

44. Wasserman, Earl R. "Coleridge's 'Metrical Experiments,'"
    MLN, 55 (1940), 432-433.

    At least two of the eleven "Metrical Experiments"
    published by E.H. Coleridge are not original. "Songs of
    Shepherds, and Rustical Roundelays" is a popular seven-
    teenth-century lyric, and "When thy Beauty appears" is
    the first stanza of a poem by Thomas Parnell.

<h2 style="text-align:center">1941</h2>

45. Burke, Kenneth. *The Philosophy of Literary Form: Studies
    in Symbolic Action.* Baton Rouge: Louisiana State
    University Press, 1941.

    Consideration of a poet's biography and other poems
    contributes to an understanding of the structural rela-
    tionships within a particular poem. In "The Ancient
    Mariner," for example, Coleridge's marital troubles add
    significance to the strand of actions which begin in
    "The Eolian Harp" with the noontime apologies to Sarah
    and continue with the deflection from the wedding feast;
    the murder of the albatross as a representative of
    Sarah; the punishments inflicted upon the Mariner at
    high noon; and his stated preferences for church,
    prayer, and companionship over marriage. Coleridge's
    suffering from opium helps account for the ambiguity in
    the blessing of the water-snakes, symbolic of the drug,
    and for the cluster of images associating the "silly
    buckets" (1. 297) with the crazy pilot's boy, who takes
    upon himself the worst aspect of the Mariner's lunacy,
    and with the "grey-beard loon" (1. 11), whose cure was
    affected under the aegis of the moon.

46. Copeland, Thomas. "A Woman Wailing for her Demon Lover,"
    RES, 17 (1941), 87-90.

    The source for Coleridge's image of the "Woman wailing
    for her demon-lover" (1. 16) is probably the apocryphal
    story of Sara in the Book of Tobit, on which he was

planning to write an essay at about the time "Kubla Khan"
was composed. Furthermore, reference to this story
occurs in *Paradise Lost*, IV, 168-171, just before the
description of Paradise.

47. De Selincourt, Ernest. "'Lewti,'" *TLS*, December 20,
     1941, p. 643.

     "Lewti" is not the only poem of Wordsworthian origin
     attributed to Coleridge. "Alcaeus to Sappho" is
     Coleridge's rehandling of Wordsworth's "How sweet where
     crimson colours," the manuscript of which is not extant
     but is referred to in a letter from Wordsworth to
     Coleridge. (Cf. items 53, 54, 57.)

48. "From Court to Sanctuary. George Herbert's Songs. An
     Emancipated Spirit," *TLS*, July 12, 1941, pp. 334, 337.

     Coleridge's "Work Without Hope" (11. 1-6) echoes
     Herbert's "Employment (I)" (11. 17-20).

49. Harding, D.W. "The Theme of 'The Ancient Mariner,'"
     Scrutiny, 9 (1941), 334-342.

     The theme of "The Ancient Mariner" is the universal
     human experience of depression, isolation, worthlessness,
     guilt, listlessness, and partial recovery. As emphasized
     by the supernatural machinery, both the depression and
     the partial recovery seem to occur without predictability
     or rational explanation. It is only by a private, irra-
     tional standard that the Mariner deserves punishment for
     the wanton destruction of ties of affection, the sin
     which for Coleridge was the worst of all. Having repre-
     sented this horrifying potentiality, he could not return
     the Mariner to the happy self-sufficiency with which he
     began the voyage.

50. Kitzhaber, Annabel Wetzel. "David Hartley in *Christabel*,"
     RSSCW, 9 (1941), 213-222.

     Begun in 1798, "Christabel" shows the influence of
     Hartley's philosophy in its moral optimism and determinis-
     tic conception of character and development of events.
     The inevitable triumph of good is suggested in Part I
     and fulfilled in the Gillman plan for its conclusion.
     But although Christabel and Geraldine are both passive
     characters, compelled by external forces, Geraldine in
     Part II is not still definitely operating for good.
     Thus, in contrast to "The Ancient Mariner," the parts
     of "Christabel" are of questionable consistency, and the

exposition of Hartley's philosophy is sketchy, for
Coleridge was growing away from the tangible and concrete toward the profound and abstract. Because he
could not express his new ideas clearly enough to write
vivid poetry, he did not finish the poem.

51. Knight, G. Wilson. "Coleridge's Divine Comedy," in *The
     Starlit Dome: Studies in the Poetry of Vision* (Oxford:
     Oxford University Press, 1941), pp. 83-178.

     Coleridge explores hell, purgatory, and paradise re-
     spectively in "Christabel," "The Ancient Mariner," and
     "Kubla Khan." "Christabel" expresses fear of some name-
     less evil, seemingly sexual, in nightmarish images of
     darkness, frightening sounds, and snakes as well as
     images of light and religious grace. The Mariner tells
     of his sin, his loneliness, and his purgatorial redemp-
     tion. His selfish rejection of divine guidance corre-
     sponds to the fall in racial history or to the loss of
     innocence in the maturing personality. His redemption
     comes by way of knowledge of evil, conveyed by the rot-
     ting sea and its associated images, and knowledge of
     death with guilt. After recognizing the beauty of the
     water-snakes, he experiences a sense of purity, freedom,
     and energy and returns to the land and solid fact sug-
     gested by the hermit.
     The paradisal theme in "Kubla Khan" depends upon the
     connotations of the Abyssinian maid, the setting, and
     especially the sacred river and the circular dome. A
     symbol of life, the river originates amid chaotic and
     energetic activity and progresses with uncertainty toward
     eternal nothingness. The dome, built by the powerful,
     Godlike Kubla, images a kind of immortality that tran-
     scends the motion of life and that unites the seemingly
     opposite forces of birth and death, of consciousness and
     unconsciousness, of masculinity and feminity. Coleridge
     expands the transcendental imagery of "Kubla Khan" in
     his two dramas and in his minor naturalistic, psycho-
     logical, and religious poems.

52. McElderry, B.R., Jr. "*Christabel*, Coleridge, and the
     Commentators," *RSSCW*, 9 (1941), 206-212.

     The source studies by Donald Tuttle, Arthur Nethercot,
     and Annabel Kitzhaber should be regarded as supplementary
     to and as harmonious with Gillman's report of Coleridge's
     plan to complete "Christabel." (See items 23, 30, 50.)
     The daemonologies and speculations on superstitions
     concerning vampires and lamias would have helped him in

his transformation of the superficial marvels of ballads
and Gothic romances into an imaginative representation
of Hartley's moral optimism and necessitarianism. These
Hartleian elements and the motif of impersonation would
have been further developed in the concluding episodes.

53. Meyerstein, E.H.W.   "'Lewti,'" *TLS*, December 6, 1941,
        p. 611.

     Southey's annotation in a copy of the second volume of
     the *Annual Anthology*, 1800, testifies that "Lewti" is a
     reworking by Coleridge of an early poem by Wordsworth.
     (Cf. item 54.)

54. ———. "Wordsworth and Coleridge," *TLS*, November 29,
        1941, p. 596.

     De Selincourt's printing in 1940 of Wordsworth's juve-
     nile fragment "Beauty and Moonlight" reveals its identity
     with the short early version of Coleridge's "Lewti" and
     suggests that the extended "Lewti" is a reworking of
     Wordsworth's poem.

55. Pettit, Henry. "Coleridge's Mount Abora," *MLR*, 56
        (1941), 376.

     Light may be thrown on Coleridge's Mount Abora by an
     entry in Cruttwell's *New Universal Gazetteer* (1798):
     "*Abur*, a mountain of Arabia."

56. Sitwell, Osbert. "The Sole Arabian Tree," *TLS*, April 26,
        1941, pp. 199, 206.

     The person from Porlock who interrupted the composi-
     tion of "Kubla Khan" symbolizes the everyday disturbances
     which plague writers. Marco Polo, on the other hand,
     rescues them and inspires such magic as "Kubla Khan" and
     the opening lines of Shakespeare's "The Phoenix and the
     Turtle."

57. Sutherland, James R.   "'Lewti,'" *TLS*, December 6, 1941,
        p. 611.

     De Selincourt's printing of Wordsworth's "Beauty and
     Moonlight" corroborates Southey's statement that it was
     the origin of Coleridge's "Lewti." (Cf. items 54, 53.)

58. Wilkinson, C.H. "The Sole Arabian Tree," *TLS*, May 3,
        1941, pp. 215-216.

In describing how he came to write "Kubla Khan," Coleridge says he fell asleep while reading "Purchas's Pilgrimage," the work published in 1613, and not *Purchas His Pilgrimes*, 1625. (Cf. item 56.)

1942

59. Allen, N.B. "A Note on Coleridge's 'Kubla Khan,'" *MLN*, 57 (1942), 108-113.

"Kubla Khan" is not a fragment but a complete lyric composed of (1) a fragmentary vision (ll. 1-30) in which the images show the dreamer's expanded sense of space and time; (2) an effort to continue the vision (ll. 31-36); and (3) a comment on the loss of vision (ll. 37-54) in which the images, including Coleridge's picture of himself, are outlined and finite.

60. Bonjour, Adrien. *Coleridge's "Hymn before Sunrise": A Study of Facts and Problems Connected with the Poem.* Lausanne: Imprimerie la Concorde, 1942.

A relatively simple poem, Coleridge's "Hymn before Sunrise" presents several complex problems, the most difficult being that of plagiarism. The "Hymn" is obviously an improvement of Brun's shorter "Chamounix beym Sonnenaufgange." Its similarity to the German poem includes even small details like the footnote on Gentiana Major. Along with Coleridge's frequent revisions of the "Hymn" and the combination of inspiration and will in his other poems, this extensive analogy makes carelessness or unconscious reminiscence an unlikely explanation. A conscious borrowing, however, agrees with the scientific and psychological facts--namely, Coleridge's inevitably relaxed moral standard under the influence of opium and his precarious hope in the summer of 1802 that he had not lost his poetic power. Because he wished to restore his friends' confidence, on the eve of the poem's first publication in the *Morning Post* he wrote to Sotheby that he had "involuntarily poured forth a hymn" on top of Mount Scafell and never revealed his indebtedness to the German poem.

In addition to these sources the "Hymn" shows the influences of de Saussure's account of Mount Blanc, Thomson's "Hymn on the Seasons," Helen Maria Williams' *Tour in Switzerland*, and especially Burnet's *Sacred Theory of the Earth*. At one time Coleridge planned to translate into

verse the chapter on "Mountains of the Earth"; Brun's
poem must have called forth some of this material, for
all three works have elements in common.

None of Coleridge's sources, however, exhibits the
unity, harmony, compression, and suggestiveness of the
"Hymn." With great care he revised the poem numerous
times. Besides the eight printed versions, there are
four different manuscripts, three of which can be dated
with certainty and one which internal evidence places
between 1803 and 1809. Of all the changes among these
texts, the most significant is the addition of the passage in which the poet's soul becomes identified with
the mountain (11. 19-23). Although Wordsworth attacked
the sincerity of Coleridge's feeling here, the lines
demonstrate Coleridge's theory of the imagination and
heighten the human associations in the poem.

61.   ————. "A Note on 'Lewti,'" *ES*, 24 (1942), 175-178.

In the successive versions of "Lewti" the heroine's
name presents three variations: Mary, Mary Hutchinson in
Wordsworth's "Beauty and Moonlight" and Mary Evans in
Coleridge's first draft; Cora, perhaps a reminiscence of
a poem entitled "Peru" by Helen Maria Williams; and Lewti,
whose origin remains a mystery. A clue to the identity
of Coleridge's Mary lies in his removal in the second
version of the comparison of her teeth to the white waves
of Tamaha's stream. This is probably a compliment paid
specifically to Mary Evans, since a letter from Coleridge
to her mother indicates that she must have had fine teeth.

62.   Gordon, I.A. "The Case-History of Coleridge's 'Monody
          on the Death of Chatterton,'" *RES*, 18 (1942), 49-71.

Reflecting his moods and stages of literary development,
Coleridge's "Monody" evolved over a period of forty-four
years from the juvenile Pindaric ode of 1790, to the
romantic ode that first appeared in 1794, to the final
couplet-elegy of 1829. The original unpublished "Monody"
shows the influences of Gray, Bowles, and particularly
Thomas Warton, whose uncharitable presentation of Chatterton is countered in phrases echoing "The Suicide." But
the drastic revision of 1794, reprinted here, is indebted
mainly to the language and rhythm of Gray's "Elegy," "The
Bard," and "The Progress of Poesy"--poems which reaffirmed
the conception of Chatterton's poverty, remoteness, and
inspired genius. The version of 1796 adds a new final
section of thirty-six lines in which Chatterton becomes
identified with Coleridge the gloomy Pantisocratic

emigrant. Eliminating some of the personifications and
double epithets, the relatively few changes in 1797 and
1803 indicate the mature Coleridge's lack of interest in
the poem. The 1829 version, however, introduces fifteen
new opening lines, completely alters the first half of
the poem, and allows the "swell and glitter" which the
1797 preface had rejected. It is the 1829 "Monody,"
rather than the one of 1834, which Coleridge considered
final and which should follow "The Garden of Boccaccio"
in any chronological arrangement of his poems.

63. Green, Andrew J. "Essays in Miniature: The Resistless
    Eye," *CE*, 3 (1942), 722-723.

    In "The Ancient Mariner," "Christabel," and "Kubla
    Khan," Coleridge uses the image of the mesmeric power of
    the eye as a poetic medium for his doctrine of philo-
    sophical passivity and for the idea of the divine inspi-
    ration of poetry.

64. Horrell, Joseph. "The Demonic Finale of 'Christabel,'"
    MLR, 37 (1942), 363-364.

    Gillman's account of Coleridge's plan for the comple-
    tion of "Christabel" would harmonize with the poem's
    daemonic background if Geraldine disappeared *with* instead
    of *before* the tolling of the bell. As indicated by
    lines 342-359 and his notes on bells, Coleridge knew
    that church bells especially were inimical to daemons.
    (Cf. items 11, 30.)

1943

65. Basler, Roy P. "Christabel," *SR*, 51 (1943), 73-95.

    In "Christabel," as in some other poems, Coleridge
    used preternatural machinery to suggest the psychological
    theme of the mystery of sexual necessity, or the idea of
    sex as a powerful force which drives people to irrational
    feelings and actions. Like Crashaw's Saint Theresa,
    Christabel goes into the forest to test her love for
    the absent knight. In this domain of preternatural
    creatures she encounters the evil Geraldine, who, in
    hope of transforming herself, enchants Christabel and
    her father. The sexual nature of her enchantment is
    indicated by the preliminary emphasis on physical contact
    (1. 102) and the culminating embrace; the psychologically
    realistic descriptions of Geraldine's desire mixed with

loathing (ll. 255-264), Christabel's trance (ll. 292-
297), and "after-rest" (ll. 312-318); and the erotic implications of the broken reference to the nature of her
dream (l. 252), the emphasis on the "sorrow and shame"
of the circumstance (l. 296), and the use of the phrase
"Thou'st had thy will" (l. 306). As a result of her
enchantment Christabel begins to manifest certain ophidian characteristics, while Geraldine becomes more beautiful and feminine and casts a similar spell on Leoline.
Both Leoline's return to emotional stability and Christabel's rescue could have been accomplished by the lover's
return, the event which Gillman reported to be Coleridge's
plan. Coleridge did not finish the poem, however, because the working out of such a denouement would have
endangered his moral respectability.

66. Beck, Warren. "Personne," *VQR*, 19 (1943), 562-574.

The person from Porlock who interrupted the composition
of "Kubla Khan" was probably a printer or businessman to
whom Coleridge owed money and who was detained for more
than an hour by Coleridge's hypnotic conversation.

67. Brogan, Howard O. "Coleridge's Theory and Use of the
Praeter-Supernatural," *Citadel Bulletin*, 7 (1943), 3-17.

According to Coleridge's theory, the praeter-supernatural, or non-natural realm, should be used to suggest
universal forces which lie beyond human sense; the reactions of the characters should be psychologically true
to life; and the details should never fail to give pleasure. "The Ancient Mariner" exemplifies this theory
most obviously in that the marginal gloss explains and
reinforces the supernatural details and the revisions
tone down details of horror. But "Christabel" lacks
substance and psychological credibility; the praeter-
supernatural becomes an end in itself. "Kubla Khan" is
also just a beautiful fragment.

68. Gay, R.M. "Coleridge's 'Dejection: An Ode,'" *Expl*, 2
(1943), item 14.

Would a psychologist agree with Coleridge's idea in
lines 39-93 that with the afflictions of old age we lose
imagination and joy and must substitute philosophic
resignation to make life bearable?

69. Heidbrink, F.H. "Coleridge's 'Ode on the Departing
Year,'" *Expl*, 2 (1943), item 21.

Coleridge's note, published in the quarto edition of
the poem, makes it clear that "insatiate Hag" (1. 45)
refers to Catherine of Russia and suggests that death
was "twice mortal" (1. 43) because she had committed
mortal sins in public and in private life. Perhaps
Coleridge used the quotation marks to acknowledge the
religious implications of the phrase. (Cf. item 71.)

70. Joughin, G. Louis. "Coleridge's 'Lewti': the Biography
of a Poem," *University of Texas Studies in English*, 23
(1943), 66-93.

A study of the five successive versions of "Lewti"
indicates that the relevant events in Coleridge's life
had less impact on its final form than his own imaginative power. The first manuscript version (1792-94) contains a conventional tribute to Mary Evans, who in the
second draft (ca. July, 1797) becomes Cora, the heroine
of Thelwall's unpublished play "The Incas." Then in the
same manuscript, for an unknown reason and from an unknown source, Cora is replaced by Lewti. (Cf. item 61.)
More extensive changes occur in the poem's structure,
meter and rhyme, grammar, imagery, diction, and dominant
tone. By 1817, "Lewti" has developed an informal structural pattern with a varied refrain, a sense of paragraph
unity, and a basic metrical scheme with free and skillful substitution; it has moved toward stronger sentence
structures, toward a more clearly established point of
view, and toward greater consistency, specificity, and
accuracy.

71. Nethercot, Arthur Hobart. "Coleridge's 'Ode on the
Departing Year,' 43," *Expl*, 1 (1943), item 64.

The phrase "insatiate Hag" (1. 45) does not refer to
Catherine of Russia but to "Conquest" (1. 50). The meaning of "twice mortal mace," however, can only be guessed
at, especially since "twice mortal" is put inside quotation marks in all the early editions of the poem.

72. Sparrow, John. "Jortin and Coleridge," *TLS*, April 3,
1943, p. 163.

The poem "A Wish Written in Jesus Wood, Feb. 10, 1792"
is not an original composition but a translation by
Coleridge of Jortin's "Votum."

1944

73. Beach, Joseph Warren. "Poetry as Realization," in *A
     Romantic View of Poetry: Being Lectures Given at the
     Johns Hopkins University on the Percy Turnbull Memorial
     Foundation in November 1941* (Minneapolis: University
     of Minnesota Press, 1944), pp. 1-22.

     The power of "The Ancient Mariner" is largely due to
     the vivid rendering of the Mariner's bodily sensations
     and his physical distress and relief. His reaction to
     the slimy water-snakes and the phantom ship, his suffer-
     ing from thirst, his eventual release from pain, and his
     experience of sudden changes such as that from movement
     to stillness all give substance to his spiritual adventure.

74. Boas, Louis S. "Coleridge's 'The Ancient Mariner,'
     Part IV," *Expl*, 2 (1944), item 52.

     Interpreted in the light of Wordsworth's 1800 "Preface,"
     "Tintern Abbey," the gloss, and the Mariner's compulsion
     to tell his tale to selected audiences, Part IV is the
     climax of the Mariner's isolation and the beginning of
     his feeling of kinship.

75. Bush, Douglas. "'Pure Serene,'" *TLS*, November 18, 1944,
     p. 559.

     Coleridge's use of the phrase "pure serene" (1. 72) in
     "Hymn before Sunrise" has already been discussed by
     Douglas Bush and J.L. Lowes. (Cf. item 76.)

76. Dudley, O.H.T. "'Pure Serene,'" *TLS*, September 23, 1944,
     p. 463.

     The striking phrase "pure serene" was used independently
     by Cary, Keats, and Coleridge in "Hymn before Sunrise"
     (1. 72). Coleridge's source might have been Suetonius'
     "Life of Augustus."

77. Heidbrink, F.H. "Coleridge's 'Time, Real and Imaginary,'"
     Expl, 3 (1944), item 4.

     "Time, Real and Imaginary" is an allegorical treatment
     of Coleridge's more explicit observations in *Animae
     Poetae* on the relationship of the past, the present, and
     the future. The girl represents the past and the future,
     or imaginary time, while the boy stands for the present,
     or real time.

78. Howarth, R.G. "Coleridge: A Misattribution," *N&Q*, 186
     (1944), 290-291.

     Number 12 of Coleridge's "Metrical Experiments," "Songs
     of Shepherds and Rustical Roundelays," consists of some
     lines from a seventeenth-century lyric, "The Hunting of
     the Gods." (See item 44.)

79. Logan, Sister Eugenia. "An Indebtedness of Coleridge to
     Crashaw," *MLN*, 59 (1944), 551-553.

     Coleridge's threatening "large Black Letter" (1. 7) in
     the sky of "Coeli Enarrant" echoes Crashaw's "large black
     letter" (1. 186) of "In the Glorious Epiphanie of our
     Lord God."

80. Mays, Morley J. "Coleridge's 'Dejection: An Ode,'"
     Expl, 2 (1944), item 27.

     Lines 39-93 belong to a context larger than psychologi-
     cal maturation because Coleridge did not consider old
     age the essential cause of the loss of imagination and
     because he uses "joy" to refer not only to general happi-
     ness but also to poetic creation. (Cf. item 65.)

81. Canceled.

82. Seely, Frederick F. "A Footnote to *The Road to Xanadu*,"
     MLN, 59 (1944), 333-334.

     Parallels between "Chevy Chase" in Percy's *Reliques*
     (11. 165-167 and 129-132) and "The Ancient Mariner"
     (11. 119-121 and 514-515) suggest the influence on
     Coleridge of the rhythms and word patterns of the old
     ballad.

                              1945

83. Bouslog, Charles S. "The Symbol of the Sod-Seat in
     Coleridge," *PMLA*, 60 (1945), 802-810.

     Among Coleridge's personal symbols is the sod-seat of
     camomile ᴗhat he and the Wordsworths built for Sara
     Hutchinson. It is a symbol of his love for her in
     several poems--"Ode to Tranquillity," the original draft
     of "Dejection," "Inscription for a Fountain on a Heath,"
     and "Love's Apparition and Evanishment."

84. Brinkley, R. Florence. "English Book, 1808-1812: *Poems
     By S.T. Coleridge, Esq.*," *Papers of the Bibliographical
     Society of America*, 39 (1945), 163-167.

     Variously described by Coleridge's editors and bibliog-
     raphers, his undated sixteen-page pamphlet, *Poems By S.T.
     Coleridge, Esq.*, contains "Fears in Solitude," "France:
     An Ode," and a considerably revised version of "Frost at
     Midnight." Although the texts of these poems are identi-
     cal with those in the *Poetical Register*, the pamphlet
     was not made up of pages from the *Register* but was
     printed privately for Coleridge by Law and Gilbert some
     time between 1808, when volume 7 of the *Register* was
     expected, and 1812, when it actually appeared.

85. Brown, Huntington. "The Gloss to *The Rime of the Ancient
     Mariner*," *MLQ*, 6 (1945), 319-324.

     The imaginary editor of the gloss serves to distance
     the improbable events of the voyage and to humanize the
     Mariner. As a chorus character, he not only conveys in-
     formation but also wins the reader's sympathy. He is a
     pious seventeenth-century antiquarian who writes in a
     style alternately poetic and pedantic and is thus an
     effective contrast with the minstrel in personality,
     social position, and historical period.

86. Griggs, Earl Leslie. "'The Willing Suspension of Dis-
     belief,'" in *Elizabethan Studies and Other Essays in
     Honor of George F. Reynolds, University of Colorado
     Studies*, Series B, *Studies in the Humanities*, II
     (Boulder: University of Colorado Press, 1945), pp. 272-
     285.

     In "The Ancient Mariner" and "Christabel" Coleridge
     creates the state of willing illusion, or suspension of
     judgment of possibility and reality, by blending familiar,
     realistic details with suggestions of the alien or mys-
     terious. He introduces the Mariner, for example, in a
     present-tense description which combines a realistic
     question with connotations of hypnotism and of olden
     patriarchal times. He holds the reader's attention by
     emphasizing the drama between the Mariner and the Wedding-
     Guest, by gaining sympathy for the Mariner, by subtly
     handling the characterization of Geraldine, and by using
     the principle of contrast throughout both poems.

87. McKeehan, Krene P. "Some Observations on the Vocabulary
     of Landscape Description among the Early Romanticists,"

in *Elizabethan Studies and Other Essays in Honor of
George F. Reynolds, University of Colorado Studies*
Series B, *Studies in the Humanities*, II (Boulder:
University of Colorado Press, 1945), pp. 254-271.

Unlike Wordsworth, Coleridge and his contemporaries
used the adjectives "majestic" and "sublime" rather
loosely, with no particular accuracy. Usually, "majestic"
suggests fearful power, as in "Religious Musings." "Sublime" often refers to mountains, as in "Reflections,"
and is associated with gloom, bleakness, and solemnity,
as in "To the Author of Poems" and in "Lines Written in
the Album."

88. Raven, A.A. "Coleridge's 'Time, Real and Imaginary,'"
     Expl, 3 (1945), item 33.

The poem deals with only two aspects of time. The
girl represents real time because she outstrips the boy
who, as imaginary time, is blind to reality and is com-
paratively stationary, encountering no difficulties which
disturb an even progress. (Cf. item 77.)

88a. Schneider, Elisabeth. "The 'Dream' of 'Kubla Khan,'"
     PMLA, 60 (1945), 784-801.

Modern medical literature casts doubt on a literal interpretation of Coleridge's statement in the 1816 head-
note that "Kubla Khan" is the product of an opium dream.
It has been found, for instance, that opium, of itself,
does not cause dreaming or psychological instability.
Other obstacles to believing in the dream composition of
the poem are the absence of such an unusual experience
from Coleridge's letters and the logical, obvious meaning
of the poem. Drawing his materials from Purchas and
Bartram, the speaker begins describing the strange,
beautiful pleasure grounds but then leaves off, presumably
dissatisfied with his presentation of this paradise.
Only an inner joy or delight could inspire him to re-
create it in truly immortal poetry.

89. Stallknecht, Newton P. "The Moral of 'The Ancient
     Mariner,'" in *Strange Seas of Thought: Studies in
     William Wordsworth's Philosophy of Man and Nature*
     (Durham, North Carolina: Duke University Press, 1945),
     pp. 141-171.

The lines of explicit moral at the end of "The Ancient
Mariner" refer to the idea of imaginative love suggested
earlier by the hidden allegory and stated clearly in the

philosophical passages of the last books of *The Prelude*.
In Wordsworth's terms, the Mariner's suffering of loneliness and despair has resulted from reason's conquest of
feeling. His blessing of the water-snakes indicates the
reawakening of aesthetic love, or primal sympathy for
all life. And his return home corresponds to a renewed
feeling of human fellowship and love; a strengthened religion, symbolized by the Hermit; and a revived mystic
sense of communion.

The Mariner's experience differs from Wordsworth's,
however, in that he continues to live at times under a
spell of horror. This slight difference becomes more
pronounced in "Dejection," where Coleridge denies the
possibility of the renewal of imaginative love and of
the validity of communion.

1946

90.   Dudley, O.H.T.   "The Hornéd Moon," *TLS*, December 7, 1946,
      p. 603.

      Coleridge's sources for the image of the horned moon
      with a star within its nether tip were *The Philosophical
      Transactions of the Royal Society* for 1787 and 1794 and
      Rozier's *Observations sur la Physique*. Besides,
      Coleridge's horned moon was a waning moon that appeared
      in the early morning. (Cf. item 92.)

91.   Maxwell, J.C.   "S.T.C. and Priestly," *TLS*, January 5,
      1946, p. 7.

      In "Ode to the Departing Year" (11. 17-18) Coleridge
      combines the stock image of the nuptial torch with the
      description in Priestley's "Optics" of the joining of
      flames of two candles.

92.   "Off the Track," *TLS*, November 2, 1946, p. 535.

      Though Coleridge's bright star within the nether tip
      of the horned moon is scientifically impossible, it is
      believable within the regions of the troubled soul at
      sea in "The Ancient Mariner."

93.   Starr, Nathan Comfort.   "Coleridge's 'Sir Leoline,'"
      PMLA, 61 (1946), 157-162.

      In addition to Hutchinson's *History of the County of
      Cumberland*, pointed out by A.H. Nethercot (see item 30),
      Coleridge is indebted to Hutchinson's source, Camden's

Britannia, and to Burton's *Anatomy of Melancholy* for the
name and character of Sir Leoline. In these two works
appears the story of the quarrel between King Edward the
Elder and Leolin, Prince of Wales, and of their reconciliation at Aust Cliff on the Severn in Gloucestershire,
a place Coleridge associated with his quarrel and reconciliation with Southey.

94. Warren, Robert Penn. "A Poem of Pure Imagination," *KR*,
     8 (1946), 391-427.

     This essay consists of most of Sections 3, 4, and 5 of
the expanded study of "The Ancient Mariner," entitled "A
Poem of Pure Imagination: An Experiment in Reading,"
which was later published in book form with the text of
the poem. (See item 94a.)

94a. Warren, Robert Penn, ed. *The Rime of the Ancient Mariner*
     by S.T. Coleridge, with an Essay by Robert Penn Warren.
     New York: Reynal and Hitchcock, 1946. Reprinted in
     Selected Essays. New York: Random House, 1958.

     "The Ancient Mariner" conveys Coleridge's general be-
lief in the truth of poetry and in the unity of mind and
of moral and aesthetic values by the fusion of the themes
of the sacramental vision and the imagination. The obvious primary theme of the "one Life" is presented
through the story of crime, punishment, and reconciliation. The severity of the Mariner's punishment, as well
as the death of the crew, is justified when their crimes
are understood as representative of corrupt wills. Symbolically a murder which violates hospitality, gratitude,
and sanctity, the Mariner's unmotivated shooting of the
albatross reenacts the mystery of the fall. The secondary
theme of the imagination is suggested mainly by the image
of moonlight, which dominates the redemption and the
harbor scenes, and by the associated images of the bird,
the wind, and the polar spirit. In contrast, the image
of sunlight symbolizes the understanding and is connected
mainly with the Mariner's crime and suffering and the
phantom ship. The ambiguity of the imagination accounts
for the death of the crew in moonlight, the vengeance of
the polar spirit, the terrifying aspect of the winds and
the land of ice, and the Mariner's continued penance.
The two themes operate together in his crime against the
imagination and God, in the stages of his redemption, in
the polar spirit's obedience to the angelic troop, in
the lighting of the harbor by the moon and the seraphs,
in the sinking of the ship as a repetition of the storm

image and as an act of the angelic troop, and in the
figure of the Hermit as priest of Nature and God.
    This interpretation of the poem has the support of
Coleridge's reply to Mrs. Barbauld, of his remark quoted
by De Quincey connecting the poem with dreams, and of
his theory of the imagination--all of which indicate that
he did intend a moral meaning with relevance to life.
His emphasis on diversity within unity and his distinc-
tion between allegory and symbol provide external reasons for reading the poem on more than one thematic level.

95.   Williams, Ralph. "Coleridge's Parody of Dyer's 'Grongar
        Hill,'" *MLR*, 41 (1946), 61-62.

      "Inside the Coach" (1791) was not published until 1834
      because Coleridge intended it only as an amusing burlesque
      of part of Dyer's poem, not as a higher kind of parody
      conveying some wisdom or criticism.

                              1947

96.   Arnston, Herbert E. "A Probable Borrowing by Coleridge
        from *The Seasons*," *RSSCW* (1947), 201-212.

      That Coleridge was influenced by *The Seasons* is indi-
      cated by his reference to Thomson in the first entry of
      the Gutch memorandum book and by the parallel expressions
      and pictures of the rising sun glistening in the dew in
      lines 98-104 of "Religious Musings" and lines 189-197 and
      1165-71 of *The Seasons*.

97.   Booth, Bradford A. "'Renascence' and 'The Ancient
        Mariner,'" *N&Q*, 192 (1947), 431-432.

      In similar style and structure, Coleridge's "The
      Ancient Mariner" and Edna St. Vincent Millay's "Renascence"
      treat the same revitalizing experience of release upon
      the recognition of beauty.

98.   Fairchild, Hoxie N. "Hartley, Pistorius, and Coleridge,"
        PMLA, 62 (1947), 1010-21.

      In his *Poems* of 1797 Coleridge added a note to line 44
      of "Religious Musings" referring to passages in the 1791
      edition of Hartley's *Observations on Man* and to the
      attached "Notes and Additions" by H.A. Pistorius. Al-
      though he later removed the note, at the time he was
      attracted by the dependence, emphasized by Pistorius,
      of Hartley's religion on his psychology.

99. Griggs, Earl Leslie. "Date Shells and the Eye of the
     Critic," *VQR*, 23 (1947), 297-301.

     Though Warren's thorough and brilliant study of "The
     Ancient Mariner" (see item 94a) does deepen our appreci-
     ation of the poem, it does not sufficiently take into
     account Coleridge's reference, in his reply to Mrs.
     Barbauld, to the miraculous story in "The Arabian Nights"
     by which he must have meant that there should have been
     no moral connection between the slaying of the albatross
     and the following events. Furthermore, Warren's essay
     is excessive in its emphasis on symbols and suspicious
     in its use of Coleridge's later philosophical ideas in
     explanation of an early poem.

100. Grigson, Geoffrey. "'Kubla Khan' in Wales: Hafod and
     the Devil's Bridge," *Cornhill Magazine*, 162 (1947),
     275-283.

     Probably visited twice by Coleridge, Colonel Johnes's
     estate of Hafod House--with its surrounding walls, gar-
     dens, caves, chasm, forests, hills, and the Ystwith
     River--is a likely source for the pleasure dome and
     landscape of "Kubla Khan."

101. Lindsay, Jack. "The Sunset Ship: Keats, Coleridge, and
     Turner," *Life and Letters*, 54 (1947), 199-211.

     In making his phantom ship appear at sunset, Coleridge
     shows a kinship with the Tenebrosi artists, Keats, and
     Mrs. Radcliffe; and in using the sunset ship to suggest
     fear and false hope, he shows an attitude similar to
     Turner's.

102. Whalley, George. "The Mariner and the Albatross," *UTQ*,
     16 (1947), 381-398.

     The profound spiritual and emotional effect of "The
     Ancient Mariner," as well as its moral implications,
     stems from Coleridge's then unconscious projection and
     prophecy of his own inner suffering--his feelings of
     perplexity, loneliness, fear, remorse, dread, and help-
     lessness. Like Coleridge, the Mariner lives a life-in-
     death existence of remorse and aloneness. His isolation
     and sense of homelessness are emphasized even in small
     details like the use of the adjectives "lonely" and
     "lonesome" (11. 364, 446) and the impersonal picture of
     lines 601-609. His passivity, hypnotic power of speech,
     and dreamlike voyage further identify him as Coleridge's
     portrait of himself.

Revisions of the poem, especially the addition of the gloss, sharpened the personal allegory. After the Malta voyage Coleridge recognized that his creativity was beginning to wane and conveyed this realization through the albatross, a symbol of the creative imagination which he had unknowingly destroyed.

103. ————. "Romantic Chasms," *TLS*, June 21, 1947, p. 309.

Dorothy Wordsworth's remarks about the Gothic garden at Crookham recalled to Coleridge's mind both Hafod, which he probably visited in 1794 (see item 100), and Bruce's *Travels*, for the wording in her Alfoxden journal is similar to Coleridge's description of the "deep romantic chasm" (1. 12) in "Kubla Khan."

1948

104. Beatty, Frederika. "A By-Path Along the Road to Xanadu," *CJ*, 44 (1948), 211-212.

Lines 272-281 describing the water-snakes in "The Ancient Mariner" echo the Pyrrhus passage in the *Aeneid*, II, 469-475.

105. Dickson, Arthur. "Coleridge's 'The Ancient Mariner,'" *Expl*, 6 (1948), item 52.

Lines 75-76 do not mean that the albatross participated in the crew's evening prayers (see items 94a, 106) but that for nine consecutive evenings the bird alighted on the ship and remained for the duration of the moonlit night. This sharing of the crew's home makes more heinous the murder of the bird during the ninth night.

106. Harris, Lynn H. "Coleridge's 'The Ancient Mariner,'" *Expl*, 6 (1948), item 32.

Coleridge's reply to Mrs. Barbauld, as well as the concluding moral stanzas, supports a reading of the whole poem, not just Part IV, as illustrating Wordsworth's philosophy of nature expressed in "Lines Written in Early Spring." The action moves from a union of man and nature represented by the albatross, through the Mariner's violation of that union, to the restoration of union. (Cf. item 74.)

107. Kirschbaum, Leo. "Coleridge's 'The Ancient Mariner,'" *Expl*, 7 (1948), item 5.

In the view of Warren (see item 94a) and the crew,
"like God's own head" (1. 97) modifies "The glorious
Sun uprist" (1. 98), but in Coleridge's view it modifies
"Nor dim nor red" (1. 97) and thus points to the irony
of "glorious."

108. Stoll, Elmer Edgar. "Symbolism in Coleridge," *PMLA*,
      63 (1948), 214-233.

"The Ancient Mariner" is a traditional ballad of the
supernatural, significant only for its poetry, structure,
and truth to the legendary experience of cause and con-
sequence. It is thus inappropriate for symbolist critics
such as Knight, Burke, and Warren to read into the poem
present-day ambiguity, Freudian psychology, and Coleridge's philosophy and theology. (See items 51, 45,
94a.) Instead, they should respect Lowes's findings
and consider Coleridge's critical principle that a work
of art is self-contained, his statement of purpose in
Biographia Literaria, and the absence of allegory or
symbolism in the gloss and in the interpretations of
his contemporaries.

109. Tillyard, E.M.W. "Coleridge: *The Rime of the Ancient
      Mariner* 1798," in *Poetry and its Background Illustrated
      by Five Poems 1470-1870* (New York: Macmillan, 1948),
      pp. 66-86.

"The Ancient Mariner" reflects the complexity of the
age in its multiple layers of meaning. On one level,
it is a fascinating story motivated by pride, avenge-
ment, and repentance. On other levels, it presents the
archetypal theme of rebirth, with a modifying emphasis
on the destructive experience, and an allegory of the
mental adventurer whose effort to get behind appearances
implies a criticism of the existing order. In addition
to its diversity, the poem represents the age in its
various strains of religious feeling--pantheism, superstition, and antiquarianism--in its description of
nature as numinous, terrifyingly fantastic, picturesque,
or a correlative of human emotion; in its lack of
politics; and in its focus on an individual's inner
motivation, on intuition and the unconscious, and on a
type of social misfit.

110. Wasserman, Earl R. "Coleridge's 'Metrical Experiments,'"
      MLN, 63 (1948), 491-492.

Number 10 of the "Metrical Experiments," "Experiments
in Metre," was probably borrowed from William Cart-
wright's "Sadness." The discovery of this and other
sources (see items 44, 78) casts doubt on Coleridge's
authorship of nearly all the experiments.

1949

111. Bliss, Hilde Scheuer, and Donald Thayer Bliss.
      "Coleridge's 'Kubla Khan,'" *AI*, 6 (1949), 261-273.

      The meaning of "Kubla Khan" is clarified by the fact
of its dream composition and by Freud's theory that dream
images represent unconscious sexual needs. Accordingly,
many of the images such as the pleasure-dome, in the
inviting description of Kubla's gardens, suggest the
female sexual parts, while words such as "savage"
(1. 14), "waning," and "haunted" (1. 15) imply a quali-
fying uneasiness. Coleridge's orgasm anxiety is indicated by the "lifeless ocean" (1. 28), the ancestral
voices, and the caves of ice inevitably attached to the
pleasure-dome. He could not finish the poem because
its forbidden subject threatened to rise to consciousness.

112. Fairchild, Hoxie N. "Coleridge," in *Religious Trends
      in English Poetry*. Vol. III: *1780-1830, Romantic
      Faith* (New York: Columbia University Press, 1949),
      pp. 263-327.

      Coleridge used opium, religion, metaphysics, and often
poetry as a means of escaping the pains and fears of
the actual world. Certain poems influenced by Words-
worth--such as "This Lime-Tree Bower," "Frost at Midnight," and "France: An Ode"--stand out as exceptions
to this tendency. But the three great poems, especially
"Christabel" and "Kubla Khan," avoid the here-and-now.
Imposing the vividness of the real world on the strange,
old, and faraway, "Christabel" and "Kubla Khan" contain
no ideas, while "The Ancient Mariner" is mainly an allegorical tract on universal benevolence and the religion
of nature.

112a. Martin, Bernard. *The Ancient Mariner and the Authentic
       Narrative*. London: Folcroft, 1949.

       It is generally accepted that in composing "The
Ancient Mariner" Coleridge drew incidents and nautical
images from Cruickshank's dream of a ghostly ship and

from travel literature such as Shelvocke's account of
his captain's shooting an albatross. But for the moral
of the poem Coleridge used John Newton's *Authentic
Narrative* (1764). Unlike the Wandering Jew, Cain, and
Falkenberg, who resemble the Mariner only superficially,
Newton offers a psychological parallel. Both he and
the Mariner commit the crime of blasphemy, or impiety.
Their fellow seamen approve and condemn their crimes,
depending on the weather. They repent spontaneously,
with the results of successful prayer, freedom from the
sign of their crime, church attendance, and a lifelong
penance of public confession. Coleridge must have
known of Newton because of their common interests in
Hannah More, Archbishop Leighton, the abolition movement, and Cowper. And he must have read Newton's popular story, for while he was composing "The Ancient
Mariner," reciting parts of it to Dorothy, and reading
Wordsworth's latest poetry, Dorothy was copying into
her notebook a passage from Newton's fifth letter, and
Wordsworth was using it to describe the Wanderer in
lines that later became part of *The Excursion.*

112b. Nethercot, Arthur H. "Coleridge's 'Christabel' and
      LeFanu's 'Carmilla,'" *MP*, 47 (1949), 32-38.

The theory that Geraldine is a vampire (see item 30)
is supported by the many parallels between "Christabel"
and LeFanu's "Carmilla," a vampire story published in
1872. Both narratives concern the victimization of a
young girl by a female vampire who could be mistaken
for a disguised male or a Lesbian. Most strikingly,
Carmilla and Geraldine resemble each other in their
paradoxical exercise of both attraction and repulsion.
Other similarities between the two stories include the
Gothic castle and the nearby ruins which the vampire
claims as her home, the older man's fascination by the
vampire's charms, the supernatural atmosphere of the
scene in which she first appears, and the use of super-
stitions and minor characters to warn against something
unnatural and menacing.

113. Stevenson, Lionel. "'The Ancient Mariner' as a Dramatic
      Monologue," *Person,* 30 (1949), 34-44.

Coleridge's choice of the ballad form and his stress
on psychological realism in his reviews of Gothic novels
and in his stated plan for "The Ancient Mariner" harmonize with a reading of the poem as a dramatic monologue. Using the method which Browning later developed

more fully, Coleridge creates a character with a mind
totally different from his own who tries superstitiously
to account for the physical and mental tortures which
he endured when his ship was blown off its course, his
fellow mariners all died of exposure and starvation,
and he became increasingly delirious. In this state of
mind, he accepted the killing of the albatross as the
cause of the subsequent disasters, and he attached por-
tentous symbolism to the falling of the dead bird from
his neck into the sea. On the basis of his terrifying
experiences he, not Coleridge, has evolved a creed of
religious dedication to universal love and brotherhood.
The Wedding-Guest is made wiser not so much by this
simply stated moral as by his glimpse into human endur-
ance of extremest hardships.

114.   Tinker, Chauncey B.   "Coleridge's 'Ballad of the Dark
        Ladié,'" *Yale University Library Gazette*, 24 (1949),
        17-20.

        Begun in the productive year 1797-98, Coleridge's
        "Ballad of the Dark Ladié, a Fragment" belongs to a
        group of poems, including "The Ancient Mariner,"
        "Christabel," "Love," and "Kubla Khan" (ll. 14-16),
        which deals with a human victim possessed by an evil
        power that pursues him to his ruin.

115.   Wilcox, Stewart C.   "Coleridge's 'The Ancient Mariner,'"
        Expl, 7 (1949), item 28.

        Lines 97-98 are obscure, but the contrasting "bloody
        sun" (l. 112) and the literary detective work of Lowes
        and Bald (see item 33) support the view of Warren (see
        item 94a) and the crew that "like God's own head" (l. 97)
        goes with "The glorious Sun uprist" (l. 98). (Cf. item
        107.)

116.   Willis, Richard Emerson.   "Another Source of Christabel?"
        N&Q, 194 (1949), 126.

        The opening lines of Joseph Warton's "Ode to Solitude"
        (1746) were probably in the back of Coleridge's mind as
        he began "Christabel."

117.   Wormhoudt, Arthur.   "Coleridge," in *The Demon Lover: A
        Psychoanalytical Approach to Literature* (New York:
        Exposition Press, 1949), pp. 17-50.

        "Christabel" and "The Ancient Mariner" treat one of
        Coleridge's own unconscious tendencies—orally determined

psychic masochism which stems from the infant's reacting
with masochistic passivity and defensive aggression when
frustrated by the mother's withdrawal of the breast.
In "Christabel" this theme is indicated in the following
ways: the opening allusions to the bad mother in the
references to the owl, dog, moonlight, oak tree, woods,
and mistletoe; the associations of Geraldine with the
denying mother in the detail of her horrifying bosom
and in the episodes of her fainting, the dog's growl,
the flaring flame, and her struggle with Christabel's
dead mother; and the defenses against masochistic attachment to the mother in Christabel's silence and giving
Geraldine shelter and in the oedipal pattern manifested
by Leoline's anger, his interpretation of Bracy's dream,
and his daughter's assumption of snakelike characteristics before him.

In "The Ancient Mariner" the masochistic conflict with
the mother is suggested by such actions as the Mariner's
leaving his native country and shooting the albatross,
the sun's rising from the sea and hovering above the
mast, the coming of the hostile storm and ice, the crew's
only reason for speaking, and their punishment of
thirst. In an effort to deny the conflict, the Mariner
finds various defenses: the image of the child as pris-
oner in the phantom bark scene; the heterosexual coitus
fantasy symbolized by the dream of buckets filled with
dew, the storm, and the rocking ship; and, mainly, the
homosexual fantasy personified by the polar spirit and
expressed in the Mariner's blessing the water-snakes,
his pulling at the rope with his nephew, and his relationship with the rest of the crew and the Wedding-Guest.
The seraph-men, the hermit, and the Mariner's preference
for the church indicate the sublimation of the homosexual defense in the asceticism of religion.

1950

118.   Auden, W.H.   *The Enchafed Flood*.   New York: Random
       House, 1950.

The two chapters "The Sea and the Desert" (pp. 3-39)
and "The Stone and the Shell" (pp. 41-90) examine the
Romantic treatment of two pairs of symbols, the desert
and the sea and the stone of abstract geometry and the
shell of imagination.   In the first chapter "The Ancient
Mariner" is mentioned as an example of the Romantic
representation of the sea as a counterfeit desert

and the crew as an irresponsible crowd. In the second
chapter Coleridge's poem is cited for its contrasts of
the albatross and angelic spirits, symbolic of spiritual
visitation, with the water-snakes and polar spirit,
symbolic of unknown powers of human or environmental
nature, and of the comforting moon, associated with salvation, with the hostile sun, associated with fear, and
for its description of the wind, connected variously
with creative powers, delusion, intuitive hope, and
powers of grace and blessing.

119. Boas, Louise Schutz. "Coleridge's 'Ode on the Departing
     Year,' 149-161," *Expl*, 9 (1950), item 15.

     By "the evil thing" (1. 154) Coleridge means the
     slave trade, of the evils of which his "immortal mind"
     (1. 158) is "cleansed" (1. 160).   (Cf. item 122.)

120. Dickson, Arthur. "Coleridge's 'Ode on the Departing
     Year,' 149-161," *Expl*, 9 (1950), item 15.

     In the phrase "the evil thing" (1. 154) Coleridge
     alludes to the story of Achan and "the accursed thing"
     in Joshua 6 and 7, and refers specifically to the busi-
     ness profits for which the war against revolutionary
     France is being waged.   (Cf. items 119, 122.)

121. Fogle, Richard Harter. "The Dejection of Coleridge's
     Ode," *ELH*, 17 (1950), 71-77.

     The poetic structure of Coleridge's ode suggests that
     his dejection is not so deep and unrelieved as the bio-
     graphical and philosophical elements have led critics
     to assume.   During the course of his melancholy intro-
     spection his dulled feelings are awakened and his mind
     regains wholeness.   This rebirth of his imagination is
     objectified by the natural cycle of calm-storm-calm;
     the hopeful image of the moon; the interaction of the
     wind and the lute; the reconciling of grief, fear, and
     delight in the tale of the lost child; and, finally,
     his ability to forget himself in his wish for another's
     peace and joy.

122. Gierasch, Walter. "Coleridge's 'Ode on the Departing
     Year,' 149-161," *Expl*, 8 (1950), item 34.

     In the last stanza of the poem the poet finds himself
     in the position of a prophet whose warnings about En-
     gland's political and military evils are unheeded and
     who must now seek meekness and spiritual contentment.

123.   Meyer, George Wilbur.   "'Resolution and Independence':
       Wordsworth's Answer to Coleridge's 'Dejection: An
       Ode,'" *TSE*, 2 (1950), 49-74.

       Although in its original state of uncontrolled emo-
       tion Coleridge's "Dejection" challenges Wordsworth's
       philosophy of joy, the very existence of its revised
       form testifies to the enduring life of Coleridge's
       "shaping spirit of imagination" and hence of his joy.
       In the published ode (October 4, 1802) Coleridge gener-
       ously admits Wordsworth's triumph in the concluding
       hope that he will continue to "sing his lofty song and
       teach me to rejoice."

124.   Parsons, Coleman O.   "The Mariner and the Albatross,"
       VQR, 26 (1950), 102-123.

       "The Ancient Mariner" does have a moral significance.
       Several strands of evidence outside the poem itself
       point to this conclusion: Coleridge's treatment of re-
       morse as a moral purgative in "Osorio," his verse tra-
       gedy containing phrasing, ideas, and incidents which
       anticipate "The Ancient Mariner"; his belief in the
       value of prayer as a means of retaining one's state of
       grace; and the moral content, similar to that in "The
       Ancient Mariner," of Gothic ballads such as Scott's "The
       Chase, and William and Helen" and of imaginary voyages
       such as Longueville's "The Hermit." Within the poem
       moral significance is conveyed by the albatross, sym-
       bolic of love, and by the Mariner, who manifests his
       dominant trait of self-will most obviously when he shoots
       the bird. As he shifts from the experiential to the
       reflective plane in the moral stanzas, the Mariner
       rightly emphasizes the victorious expression of self-
       lessness in the act of prayer.

125.   Parsons, Howard.   "Coleridge as 'the Wedding Guest' in
       the 'Rime of the Ancient Mariner,'" *N&Q*, 195 (1950),
       251-252.

       The parallels in characterization, ideas, and imagery
       between "The Ancient Mariner" and the "Allegoric Vision,"
       along with Coleridge's statement that he is the listener
       in the "Vision," indicate that he is the Wedding-Guest
       in "The Ancient Mariner."

125a. Smyser, Jane Worthington.   "Coleridge's Use of Words-
       worth's Juvenilia," *PMLA*, 65 (1950), 419-426.

In addition to "Lewti," "Inscription for a Seat by
the Road Side," and "Alcaeus to Sappho," discovered by
de Selincourt, there are several other poems which have
been attributed to Coleridge but which originally belonged to Wordsworth: "To Lesbia"; "Morienti Superstes,"
almost identical with the first eight lines of Wordsworth's poem; and probably "Moriens Superstiti." Except
for "Lewti," which he reworked extensively, Coleridge
never claimed any of these poems. In order to meet his
obligations to the *Morning Post*, he published all of
them, except "The Death of the Starling," which was not
printed in his lifetime, anonymously or pseudonymously.

126. Vivante, Leon. "Samuel Taylor Coleridge: 1772-1834,"
      in *English Poetry and its Contribution to the Knowl-
      edge of a Creative Principle* (London: Faber and
      Faber, 1950), pp. 122-126.

Coleridge displays creative indeterminacy and vitality
except in "Kubla Khan" and even in "The Ancient Mariner,"
in which he is controlled too much by external form.

1951

127. Beres, David. "A Dream, a Vision, and a Poem: A Psycho-
      Analytic Study of the Origins of 'The Rime of the
      Ancient Mariner,'" *IJP-A*, 32 (1951), 97-116.

Coleridge's repressed hostility toward his mother resulted in feelings of guilt and expressed itself in the
oral fixations of concern with food, excessive need for
love and admiration, and infantile relationships with
others. In his poetry it appears mainly in the mother
symbols--the albatross, the spectral woman, and Geral-
dine--who represent love and hate, life and death,
masculine and feminine qualities. The albatross-mother
is associated with food and protection, and the punish-
ments of hunger and loneliness are logical consequences
of the Mariner's killing it. When he restores the
phallic nature of the mother by blessing the water-
snakes, his submission is rewarded with sleep, food,
and satiation. The spectral woman and Geraldine symbolize the mother who was killed and who has returned
to seek vengeance. In the threshold scene Geraldine
acts as the mother in the pain of childbirth and as the
delivered child.

128. Breyer, Bernard R. "Towards an Interpretation of 'Kubla Khan,'" in *English Studies in Honor of James Southall Wilson*, ed. Fredson Bowers, *University of Virginia Studies*, 4 (1951), 277-290.

   "Kubla Khan" is an allegory on the product of the creative imagination, with an introductory note on the creative process and its difficulties. Both Xanadu and poetry, according to Coleridge's theory, are concerned primarily with aesthetic pleasure; both are restricted to natural and supernatural elements and are nourished by the life-stream and the common fountain. According to this interpretation, then, the poem is not incomplete. Coleridge depreciated it possibly because he felt uncomfortable with the daemonic implications of the Mohammedan paradise and the Abyssinian maid.

129. Brooks, E.L. "Coleridge's Second Packet for *Blackwood's Magazine*," *PQ*, 30 (1951), 426-430.

   A series of three articles on witchcraft published in the *London Magazine* during the spring of 1822 could have been among the second group of essays which Coleridge promised to John Wilson but which never appeared in *Blackwood's*. If so, the series would be relevant to a study of "Christabel."

130. Coffin, Tristram P. "Coleridge's Use of the Ballad Stanza in *The Rime of the Ancient Mariner*," *MLQ*, 12 (1951), 437-445.

   Coleridge uses the basic consistency of the ballad stanza, like the wedding feast, to anchor the supernatural story to reality. As the narrative moves into the supernatural realm, he lengthens the regular ballad stanza by repetition of phrases or ideas in order to intensify emotion and to emphasize the strangeness of action. The first expanded stanza occurs, for example, when the storm drives the ship off its course into the mysterious polar regions.

131. Davis, Bertram R. "A Manuscript of 'Kubla Khan,'" *TLS*, January 26, 1951, p. 53.

   Meyerstein's discussion of the Crewe manuscript (see item 137) strengthens the case, argued by Wylie Sypher (see item 31), of its authority about the date and place of composition of the poem.

132. Evans, B. Ifor. "Coleorton Manuscripts of 'Resolution
         and Independence' and 'Ode to Dejection,'" *MLR*, 46
         (1951), 355-360.

         Among Coleridge's letters to the Beaumonts acquired
         from the Coleorton Trustees, there is one with the
         probable date of August 13, 1803, containing "Resolution
         and Independence" followed by an incomplete version of
         "Dejection." As copied respectively by Dorothy Words-
         worth and Coleridge, these manuscript texts differ from
         the final forms of the poems, but the joint presentation
         confirms their close relationship.

133. Fogle, Richard Harter. "The Romantic Unity of 'Kubla
         Khan,'" *CE*, 13 (1951), 13-18. Reprinted in *CE*, 22
         (1960), 112-116.

         "Kubla Khan" concerns the human situation of the im-
         possibility of complete control of the life of nature or
         man. The development of this theme provides an in-
         separable pleasure, symbolizes the Romantic dilemma of
         consciously seeking an unattainable ideal, and embodies
         Coleridge's doctrine of the reconciliation of opposites.
         Within the gardens the main opposites are the dome,
         associated with man and his finite values, and the river,
         suggestive of nonhuman and irrational forces and of
         human life. Because of its shape and religious conno-
         tations the dome does blend with its natural surround-
         ings and with the sacred river, but the impermanence of
         this reconciliation is hinted at by the forests, the
         chasm, the wailing woman, the ancestral voices, and the
         dread in the last lines--all of which are incompatible
         with Kubla's order.

134. Fogle, Stephen F. "The Design of Coleridge's 'Dejec-
         tion,'" *SP*, 48 (1951), 49-55.

         The differences in the two versions of "Dejection"
         illustrate Coleridge's practice of his own artistic
         principles as well as the more obvious need to conceal
         his love for Sara Hutchinson. The removal of all refer-
         ences to her and to his marital unhappiness resulted in
         the simplification and clarification of the cause of
         his dejection, in a more consistent tone, and in the
         increased importance of the storm as a way of unifying
         the structure of the ode and of symbolizing the develop-
         ment of his own emotions.

135. Jones, Edgar. "A New Reading of 'Christabel,'"
         Cambridge Journal, 5 (1951), 97-110.

The pattern of "Christabel" is inevitable and logical when Geraldine is seen as a simple, rather than a composite, character. Viewing her as possessed by a demon-lover accounts for her evil and supernatural qualities as well as certain difficulties presented by the text: her feigning of weakness so that Christabel must carry her over the threshold, her fear at the appearance of Christabel's mother on the daughter's wedding day, her promise to requite Christabel, the physical deformity which she bears with shame, the shrinking away from her own impending desecration of Christabel, the embrace of the snake and the dove in Bracy's dream, Christabel's hissing while under the spell of Geraldine's influence, and her earlier fears for her real lover. The demon-lover must have been on Coleridge's mind because the figure appears again in "Kubla Khan," where it is unrelated to its surroundings. In Part II the pattern is weakened slightly by the intrusion of the actual world, definite localization, extraneous supernatural machinery, and the author's own feelings.

136. Kahn, Sholom J. "Psychology in Coleridge's Poetry," *JAAC*, 9 (1951), 208-226.

The distinctive characteristic of much of Coleridge's poetry is its perceptive, scientific treatment of psychological themes, especially those of dreams and madness. In poems like "The Ancient Mariner" and "Dejection" the use of psychology is particularly successful, although the less familiar dream poems should also be studied for a full understanding of Coleridge's poetic and personal development.

137. Meyerstein, E.H.W. "A Manuscript of 'Kubla Khan,'" *TLS*, January 12, 1951, p. 21.

Its neat appearance and at least two variants from the 1834 text (l. 7 "compass'd" and l. 41 "Amara" changed to "Amora") suggest that the Crewe manuscript is a fair copy of the poem made before Coleridge sent it to the printer in 1816.

138. ———. "A Manuscript of 'Kubla Khan,'" *TLS*, February 9, 1951, p. 85.

Omitted from the earlier collation of the Crewe manuscript of "Kubla Khan" is the variant in line 13, "a green hill." (See items 131, 31.)

139. Milner, R.H. "Coleridge's 'Sacred River,'" *TLS*, May 18, 1951, p. 309.

   The sacred river Styx, described by Hesiod in the *Theogony*, is the most probable source of Coleridge's subterranean river in "Kubla Khan."

140. Parsons, Howard. "The Sources of Coleridge's 'Kubla Khan,'" *N&Q*, 196 (1951), 233-235.

   The source of most lines of "Kubla Khan" is *Paradise Lost*. The lines of descriptive scenery, for example, come from *Paradise Lost*, IV, 132-231; other parallels include the following: line 2 and I, 710-719; lines 12-16 and IX, 444, 499-504, 549, 733-734; lines 29-30 and I, 661-662; lines 37-48 and I, 711-712, 710-719, II, 552-555; lines 48-54 and I, 56, 192-195, IV, 977-979, V, 346-347, 526-529.

140a. Peckham, Morse. "Toward a Theory of Romanticism," *PMLA*, 66 (1951), 5-23. Reprinted in *The Triumph of Romanticism: Collected Essays*. Columbia, South Carolina: University of South Carolina Press, 1970.

   The meaning of "The Ancient Mariner," as well as its relation to *The Prelude* and *Sartor Resartus*, can be illuminated by an understanding of Positive Romanticism as dynamic organicism and of Negative Romanticism as the absence of any cosmic order at all. Like Wordsworth's and Carlyle's work, Coleridge's concerns the experience of spiritual death and rebirth. The Mariner moves from despair, guilt, and alienation to love, forgiveness, and partial reacceptance. In spontaneously blessing the water-snakes, receiving the refreshment and help of nature, and retelling his story, he affirms the values of dynamic organicism--the unconscious mind, the living universe, diversitarianism, and the creative imagination.

141. Rossiter, A.P. "Coleridge's 'Hymn before Sunrise,'" *TLS*, September 28, 1951, p. 613.

   In addition to the well-known sources, Brun's "Chamounix beym Sonnenaufgange" and his own experience on Scafell, Coleridge's "Hymn before Sunrise" draws upon his visit to the Newlands Fall and Brun's notes to her poem.

142. ————. "Coleridge's 'Hymn before Sunrise,'" *TLS*, October 26, 1951, p. 677.

The darkness at the opening of Coleridge's "Hymn before Sunrise" can be traced to a stanza in Brun's "Der
Alpenmorgen," while the rosy light comes from another
description of Mont Blanc in the second of her Genfersee
poems. (Cf. item 141.)

143. RØstvig, Maren-Sofie. "Another Source for Some Stanzas
      of *The Rime of the Ancient Mariner*," *MLN*, 66 (1951),
      543-546.

      Since Coleridge, Wordsworth, and Lamb all knew and
      appreciated Charles Cotton, a seventeenth-century nature
      poet, it is likely that certain phrases and rhythms in
      Cotton's description in "Winter" of a storm and of the
      sudden appearance of a ship influenced lines 145-148,
      151-153, and 314-322 in the 1798 version of "The Ancient
      Mariner."

144. Smith, J. Percy. "Criticism and *Christabel*," *UTQ*, 21
      (1951), 14-26.

      The first reviews of "Christabel" attacked Coleridge
      personally and faulted the poem for obscenity, incom-
      prehensibility, and unorthodox versification. There
      were sympathetic voices--the *European Magazine*, Thomas
      Love Peacock's unpublished "Essay on Fashionable
      Literature," Leigh Hunt's metrical analysis in "An
      answer to the Question, What is Poetry?" and John Wil-
      son's review of a new edition of Coleridge's poems.
      But not until John Sterling's article in 1828 did
      "Christabel" receive its due recognition. Echoing
      Coleridge's own critical principles, Sterling's treat-
      ment is concerned with the aesthetic experience of the
      poem rather than a rationalistic or moralistic explana-
      tion of it. In this respect his essay, supplemented
      by Ada L.F. Snell's 1929 study of the meter, offers the
      best criticism of "Christabel," superior to the early
      reviews as well as the interpretations by critics like
      James Gillman, H.D. Traill, J.M. Robertson, John Living-
      ston Lowes, and Arthur Nethercot. (See item 30.)

                              1952

145. Bramwell, James. "'Kubla Khan'--Coleridge's Fall?"
      Neuphilologische Mitteilungen, 53 (1952), 449-466.

      Moving from impersonal vision to self-awareness,
      "Kubla Khan" is a dream-fable symbolizing Coleridge's

fall from an opium paradise and his inability to regain
its spiritual harmony and creative vision. The dream
begins in a mood of oriental serenity but then descends
(1. 12) to a more complex, personal level, suggesting
the unpleasant sensation of struggling for breath
(1. 18), the downhill course of Coleridge's life and
creative energy (1. 28), his realization of the possibility of an invasion of the dream, and his feeling of
guilt for deliberately seeking escape by means of opium
(1. 30). In lines 31-36 he attempts to save the dream;
and in lines 37-47 he associates his lack of success
with the failure to sustain his vision in "Christabel"
and the resulting feelings of guilt, disharmony, and
loneliness. He then refers to his estranged friends as
"all who heard" (1. 48) and, in the imagery describing
the poet with flashing eyes and floating hair, pictures
himself as intoxicated, mistrusted, dreaded, and therefore isolated.

146.   Emmet, Dorothy E. "Coleridge on the Growth of the
       Mind," *Bulletin of the John Rylands Library*, 34
       (1952), 276-295.

       The heart of Coleridge's metaphysical interest was
his attempt to understand the creative growth of the
mind--the fundamental condition for which is the combination of activity and receptivity he calls joy. It is
this state of consciousness, rather than a projectionist
or realist philosophy, which is described in "Dejection"
and which begins to be renewed in that poem (1. 118) and
in "The Ancient Mariner" (1. 282).

147.   Hopwood, V.G. "The Interpretation of Dream and Poetry,"
       UTQ, 21 (1952), 128-139.

       "The Ancient Mariner" illustrates the loosening of
ordinary moral and physical laws common to both poetry
and dream but also the purpose and unity, the contribution of each part to the whole, which distinguishes
poetry from dream.

147a. Patterson, Charles I. "An Unidentified Criticism by
       Coleridge Related to 'Christabel,'" *PMLA*, 67 (1952),
       973-988.

       Coleridge's review of Bishop Samuel Horsley's *On the
Prosodies of the Greek and Latin Languages* sheds light
on his metrical theory and on his practice in "Christabel" of adapting classical quantitative verse to English

accentual prosody. Written just before Part I of the
poem, Coleridge's essay makes clear that by "accent" in
his Preface he meant a beat which would coincide sometimes with lexical accent and at other times with
metrical stress, coming to rest on a monosyllable even
when it functions as a preposition. Since the time
values of English syllables vary widely, he regarded
the line rather than the metrical foot as the sole unit
of measure. Thus, in "Christabel" he attempted to make
the total time of each line the same by regularly using
four strong beats and by varying the number of unaccented
syllables in accordance with meaning and character. He
associated anapests-running-into-amphibrachs, for example, with Sir Leoline and Lord Roland (ll. 162-163); but
when Sir Leoline forgets his age and develops a romantic
passion for Geraldine, Coleridge appropriately retained
the swift anapests (ll. 445-446).

148. Raysor, Thomas M. "Coleridge's Comment on the Moral of
     The Ancient Mariner," *PQ*, 31 (1952), 88-91.

     Coleridge's comment on the moral of "The Ancient
     Mariner" shows sounder critical judgment in the version
     published in August, 1834, in the *Quarterly Review* than
     in the altered account published in *Table Talk* (1835),
     under the date May 31, 1830. In the more credible re-
     port of the conversation with Mrs. Barbauld, Coleridge
     criticizes only the stanzas of explicit moral, but in
     the *Table Talk* version he regrets the moral cause of
     action which gives the poem its narrative structure and
     its appeal to human feeling.

                            1953

149. Bouslog, Charles S. "Coleridge and Mithraic Symbolism,"
     N&Q, 198 (1953), 66-67.

     Coleridge's private symbols for Sara Hutchinson in-
     clude the cherub and the two torch-bearers, one with
     his torch inverted and the other with an upright torch.
     These figures come from Mithraic slabs which he probably
     saw in the Mediterranean.

150. Daniel, Robert. "Odes to Dejection," *KR*, 15 (1953),
     129-140.

     Coleridge's "Dejection" is the earliest of the roman-
     tic odes to dejection--meditative lyrics in which a

strongly individualized speaker in a vivid setting
laments his sense of loss when confronted with such
unpleasant facts as old age and death without the comfort of religious faith. Influenced by Coleridge's
poem, Keats's "Ode to a Nightingale" echoes some of its
phrases and adopts its associational structure and os-
cillating movement between pain and anodyne.

151. House, Humphry. *Coleridge: The Clark Lectures 1951-52*.
      London: Rupert Hart-Davis, 1953.

The very early poems, influenced by Milton, show
Coleridge's anguish over the patriotic dilemma and his
attempt to combine political and philosophically religious themes. In the Conversation Poems he turns from
verse propaganda to autobiographical subjects treated in
the informal style of Cowper. "Frost at Midnight" is
the finest poem in this group. "The Eolian Harp" is
thrown off balance by the rejection, in the last section, of the experience of harmony (11. 26-33, added in
1817) and of the Neoplatonist speculation (11. 44-48).
But the major revisions of "Frost at Midnight" contribute to its achievement of seriousness and unity. In
contrast to a similar situation in *The Task*, the move-
ments of the mind in time and space provide organization
and leave the significant impression of the mind's very
being.

"The Ancient Mariner" is contemporary with "Frost at
Midnight" but very different from the style of the Conversation Poems. It assimilates features of Gothic
horror and the traditional ballads, modifying them to
suit the overall purpose of showing the interpenetration
of two aspects of reality, the visible bodily world of
the wedding feast and the invisible spirit world of the
tale. Besides conveying the Mariner's spiritual states,
the elements of nature provide the means through which
he is acted upon by the invisible world, changed from a
normally happy man who is at one with society and its
values to a wanderer who is half outcast and half
participator. A large part of his experience involves
error, incomprehensibility, and frustration. Out of
ignorance, he thoughtlessly shoots the albatross--an act
which gradually acquires meaning at the animal, human,
and spiritual levels. His sinful ignorance is made more
apparent by the behavior of the crew who do not know,
for one thing, the dual nature of the tropical sun. He
does not understand why he blesses the water-snakes,
and his one deliberate, tremendous effort leads ironically to the climax of the disaster. The horror of the

deaths and curses is later brought home by the activity
of the reanimated bodies. This event, as well as other
miscellaneous detail in sections V and VI, and "the
theme of the imagination" are not given a coherent convincing explanation by Robert Penn Warren's too rigid
scheme of symbolic reference. The imagery of the mist,
the moon, and the albatross points to values which are
of great concern but which are mysterious and indefinite.
"Kubla Khan" does concern imaginative creativity of
the more specifically poetic kind. It is a statement of
the fulfillment, the ecstasy of poetic creation. The
words "Could" (1. 42) and "once" (1. 38) must receive
slight emphasis and thus refer to the possibility and
the delight of creative achievement. Evidence for this
interpretation lies in the biographically relevant
facts and in certain verbal details such as the light
and fast meter and the connection between "that dome"
(1. 47) and the beautifully described dome of Part I.
The dome is consistently treated as an emblem of fulfillment and satisfaction; the river is invariably
called "sacred," suggesting the energy and life upon
which Kubla's ideal activity depends. Aware of its
possible destruction, he himself has created the miraculous union of pleasure and sacredness, warmth and coldness, softness and hardness. And in Part II it is the
poet who has achieved this fusion and is thus regarded
as a seer deserving the ritual dread.
Because of the relation between the two parts and the
precision and clarity of the description, "Kubla Khan"
cannot be considered a fragment. But the two parts of
"Christabel" are very different, one of the most obvious
inconsistencies being the shift in Part II to the detailed geography of the Lake District. Part I is devoted
mainly to the creation of a vague, mysterious atmosphere
through the suggestion in the description of slight distortion, contrast, or surprise and through the strange
dominating character of Geraldine. A number of passages,
including lines 256-262 added in 1828, indicate that
she is at the mercy of some evil influence. Apparently,
though, it was Christabel and her vicarious suffering
which Coleridge intended to be the central interest.
He could not complete the poem because he was trying to
explore the complex overlapping of sex and religion in
the phenomenon of martyrdom, a serious psychological
problem only hinted at in the stories of Gothic horror.
Unlike "Christabel," "Dejection" is not a fragment.
But by comparison with "Frost at Midnight," "The Ancient
Mariner," and "Kubla Khan," it is not an artistic whole.

In omitting the personal detail of the verse letter, Coleridge altered its sequence, direction, and tone. One of the most important differences is that in the original version the weather parallels the argument so that the description of the wind's activity precedes the deepest self-analysis and the long undivided realization of the power of joy which ends the poem. This feeling of love and joy, even in the published poem, is strong enough to minimize the tone of self-pity which obtrudes in "Pains of Sleep" and "Work without Hope."

152.   Mercer, Dorothy F. "The Symbolism of 'Kubla Khan,'"
       JAAC, 12 (1953), 44-66.

       Two of the most significant influences on "Kubla Khan" were the developing concept of the imagination and the sequence of imagery in Jacob Boehme's formulation of the continuous circular movement of the seven fountain spirits which govern life. These qualities have parallels in "Kubla Khan." The fountain, for example, is Boehme's fourth form, the abyss of God, which contains the potentiality of both wrath and love and out of which arise self-knowledge, free will, and imagination. The dome and the "mingled measure" (1. 33) correspond to the seventh form, or paradise, in which all qualities are in equilibrium. Standing apart from the seven forms, the Abyssinian maid functions as Boehme's heavenly Virgin, as wisdom drawing the poet to herself. She also represents the imagination, a concept important to Boehme as well as to Coleridge and his age. It is through the creative imagination that the seven nature forms or the opposites within the poem can be seen as one continuous redemptive process. It is through the secondary imagination that Kubla recreates his experience and achieves the paradisal consciousness conveyed by the images of the poem. Its incantatory quality suggests the passive aspect of the imagination.

153.   Raysor, Thomas M. "Notes on Coleridge's 'Lewti,'" *PQ*,
       32 (1953), 207-210.

       Similarities of the cloud images in a notebook fragment (No. 16), "Lewti," "Christabel" suggest a similar date, placing the earlier limit of the period in which "Lewti" could have been written at the end of 1797 or possibly in the early months of 1798.

154.   Rossiter, A.P. "Coleridge's *Soother in Absence*," *TLS*,
       May 8, 1953, p. 301.

A survey of Coleridge's references to the projected "Soother in Absence" suggests that it was to be a collection of love poems, mainly connected with Sara Hutchinson, rather than a work subtitled "My Life and Thoughts."

155. Schneider, Elisabeth. *Coleridge, Opium, and "Kubla Khan."* Chicago: University of Chicago Press, 1953.

The fragment of "Kubla Khan" is not an opium dream but a conscious, logical composition within the tradition of pseudo-oriental writing. In addition to the medical improbabilities (see item 88a), several textual and biographical circumstances discourage belief in the dream composition. In providing an earlier version of the poem, the Crewe manuscript indicates that Coleridge did revise both the text and the story of its composition. The phrasing in the 1816 account reflects Darwin's definitions in the *Zoonomia* of true sleep and sleeping dreams. The use of fictional dreams was in vogue at the time, and Coleridge could easily have gotten the idea from his dreams of *Paradise Lost* and of his epitaph and from the report of Mrs. Robinson's dictation of "The Maniac" while half-awake. Besides, if he really had such an extraordinary dream experience, it is unlikely that he would have kept quiet about it for sixteen years, not mentioning it in letters or notebooks, in the conversation with Clement Carlyon on dreams and poetry, or on the occasion recorded by John Payne Collier when he recited the poem.

Instead of an actual dream, "Kubla Khan" grew out of a contemporary literary tradition within which the most influential works were Landor's *Gebir*, Wieland's *Oberon*, and Southey's *Thalaba*. This group of interrelated poems, presided over by Milton, had already synthesized the miscellaneous travellers and geographers discussed by Lowes and contained almost every image and many specific phrases used by Coleridge. In *Thalaba*, for example, occurs a "stately" bridge-arch-pleasure building, reflected in midstream, with cool, dim lower chambers and iced foods which contrast with the tropical climate outside.

Chronologically, however, *Thalaba* and *Gebir* are possible sources only if "Kubla Khan" was written in 1799-1800, not in 1797-98 as has been commonly thought. Although the evidence is inconclusive, the new dating is more plausible for several reasons. (1) Of Coleridge's own statements, the most accurate is the retrospective

note of 1810 summarizing his quarrel with Lloyd and
connecting it with his retirement near Porlock and the
beginning of his addiction to opium. These circumstances, as well as his inability to finish "Christabel,"
are more easily placeable after his return from Germany,
in the months between late September, 1799, and June 2,
1800, than in 1797 or 1798. (2) Of the references to
the poem by others, the earliest occurs in a poem by
"Perdita" Robinson, written in October, 1800. Though
Dorothy Wordsworth's use of the word "Kubla" may imply
the existence of the poem in 1798, this is unlikely
since it is not mentioned by Greenough and Carlyon in
their accounts of Coleridge in Germany or by Southey
during the autumn of 1799 when Coleridge was writing
for the *Annual Anthology* and the *Morning Post*. (3) The
circumstances of Coleridge's life and reading point to
the later date. During the year 1799 he encountered
scenery resembling the dominant features of Kubla's
landscape. The evidence here includes his tours of the
German Harz region, south Devon, and the Lake District;
his reunion with Southey, during which time he must
have read part of *Thalaba* and some verses by William
Taylor containing an incident about a girl and an Abyssinian bishop; Wordsworth's letter describing the waterfall Hardraw Force; and two articles in the *Monthly
Magazine* on Bristol. He was also reading Purchas'
Pilgrimage and *Pilgrimes*, *Gebir*, the *Aeneid*, Collins'
odes, and Milton's prose and poetry. (4) Finally, the
imagery, language, and versification of "Kubla Khan"
resemble the poetry of 1799-1800. During this period
Coleridge's alterations and expansions of German poems,
as well as original poems like "Ode to the Duchess of
Devonshire," show an interest in the words and images
prominent in "Kubla Khan." Especially significant are
the words and phrases which occur for the first time--
"ancestral," "midway," "momently," "intermit," "loud"
music, and "such a deep delight"--and the irregular
metrical pattern, unlike anything in the poetry of
1797-98.

The logic and clarity of the poem itself (see item
88a), with its complex musical pattern and its departure
from Coleridge's usual style of description, suggest a
conscious, deliberate composition. Its poetic significance does not lie in its wholeness or in its symbolism.
The images of the ancestral voices and the wailing woman,
as well as the division into two parts, make the poem
read like a fragment with a postscript added at some
later time. Coleridge called it a "fragment," and no

evidence indicates that he regarded it as having any
hidden meaning. He did write symbolic poems, but he
always made the significance of images explicit and in
theory insisted on "translucence," or intelligiblity.
It is not symbolism that accounts for the poem's affec-
tive quality but partly the complexities and unifica-
tions of its verse pattern. The predominance of *ae* and
other modified *a* sounds, inclosed assonance (ll. 1, 3,
4), and the foreshadowing of the terminal rhyme by a
preceding echo of assonance or alliteration--these devices give to the stale material an air of mysterious
meaning.

Another part of the poem's special character is its
oscillation. Interpreted as a magic or "dream" quality,
this ambivalence originated in a deliberate attempt to
effect Lessing's notions of "beauty in motion" and the
"charm of words" rather than a clearly painted scene.
It is developed by the sound pattern, the imagery, the
movement, and the meaning. In fact, the poem's deepest
meaning, to some extent inherent in the subject of paradise, is the oscillation between giving and taking away,
between bright affirmation and sunless negation.

156. ————. "Notes on *Christabel*," *PQ*, 32 (1953), 197-206.

Circumstances surrounding the sources and date of
"Christabel" strengthen the beliefs that it is rooted
in contemporary as well as older literature and that
both Part I and Part II were written as they now stand
in late 1799-1800. Geraldine seems related to the vampire in Southey's notes for *Thalaba* and to the seps, a
mythical serpent, in his "Ode" of December 19, 1799;
like Geraldine, these creatures had the power to compel
imitation of themselves in their victims. Other serpents with blinking eyes, swelling necks, and the power
of fascination appear respectively in Landor's *Gebir*,
Thalaba, and the account in the *Monthly Magazine* in
1798 of a "Journey from New York to Philadelphia and
the Brandywine." The name Leoline is also a link with
Thalaba, since according to his notes Southey at one
time considered using the story of some "Leoline and
Lady." Besides the sharing of these names, there are
other indications that Part I was not completed in its
final form until after Coleridge's return from Germany
in the summer of 1799--namely, the lateness of the
spring of 1799 and the probable reflection of it in "The
Three Graves" (ll. 470-473) as well as in "Christabel"
(1. 22), the visual discrepancies in the opening scene,
and the use in Part I of unrhymed lines in rhymed verse
(ll. 94, 173).

1954

157. Ford, Newell F. "Kenneth Burke and Robert Penn Warren:
      Criticism by Obsessive Metaphor," *JEGP*, 53 (1954),
      172-177.

      Instead of using logic and textual evidence, Burke and
      Warren employ the trite "aegis" metaphor in their argu-
      ments that the sun and moon in "The Ancient Mariner"
      symbolize malign and benign agents. (See items 45, 94a.)
      Their symbolic method of analysis is inappropriate for
      a ballad of the supernatural, and their interpretations
      do not harmonize with the meaning and purpose of the
      poem as defined by Coleridge's and Wordsworth's accounts
      of its genesis, Coleridge's gloss, and his statement to
      Mrs. Barbauld on the moral.

158. Griggs, Earl Leslie. "Notes Concerning Certain Poems by
      Samuel Taylor Coleridge," *MLN*, 69 (1954), 27-31.

      Several assumptions about the Coleridge canon are in-
      correct. For example, his first published poem is not
      "To Fortune," but rather is "Genevieve," which, originally
      entitled "Irregular Sonnet" and signed "C-AEtatis 14,"
      appeared in the *Morning Chronicle* on July 15, 1793.
      (Cf. item 221.) "The Faded Flower" was probably written
      by Southey. Similarly, "To Lord Stanhope" must not be-
      long to Coleridge, since five weeks after its publica-
      tion he promised to send George Dyer a sonnet on Stanhope.
      In another letter to Dyer he mentioned enclosing three
      epigrams, probably those which appeared anonymously in
      the *Monthly Magazine* for April and June, 1804.

159. Nelson, William. "A Coleridge 'Borrowing,'" *TLS*,
      June 11, 1954, p. 377.

      Lines 414-417 of "The Ancient Mariner" about the
      ocean's obedience to the moon derive from the 49th
      stanza of Sir John Davies' *Orchestra, or a Poeme of
      Dauncing.*

160. Whalley, George. "Coleridge, Southey and 'Joan of Arc,'"
      N&QNS, 1 (1954), 67-69.

      Collaborating with Southey in the writing of "Joan of
      Arc," Coleridge composed a long note on II, 34, refuting
      the mechanistic philosophy of Hartley; another note in
      IV, 489; passages in Book II; and five lines in Book IV.

161. White, Alison. "Coleridge's *The Rime of the Ancient Mariner*, 198," *Expl*, 13 (1954), item 11.

Life-in-Death's whistling three times suggests a witch's intention of confounding the Trinity.

162. Wilcox, Stewart C. "The Water Imagery of the *Ancient Mariner*," *Person*, 35 (1954), 285-292.

The images of water and dryness are among the contrasting image patterns which develop the theological theme of the Mariner's redemption. In the passages preceding his baptismal regeneration, his aloneness and helplessness are indicated by the images of thirst and spiritual dryness (11. 119-122, 162-166, 245-247); in the redemption scene his perception of beauty is associated with the water, burning under the moonlight (11. 270-271); and afterward his joy and spiritual and physical refreshment are conveyed by the images of dew and rain (11. 297-300).

1955

163. Cannon, Garland H. "A New, Probable Source for 'Kubla Khan,'" *CE*, 17 (1955), 136-142.

William Jones's "A Hymn to Ganga," which appeared in *The Asiatick Miscellany* of 1785, is a likely source for "Kubla Khan" since Coleridge had probably read the hymn, along with an Indian map from which he remembered the Abor Hills and drew the name "Abora" (1. 41), and since the two poems have the following resemblances: the subject of a sacred river; an omniscient point of view which late in the poem changes to the first-person observer; a concluding note of frustration; the inclusion of a sun-ice contrast, war prophecies, a heavenly song, and a love-sick woman; and similar imagery, particularly that describing the river's origin, its surrounding land, and its eventual merging with the ocean.

164. Coburn, Kathleen. "Coleridge and Wordsworth and 'the Supernatural,'" *UTQ*, 25 (1955), 121-130.

Wordsworth's literal and factual treatment in *Peter Bell* and *The White Doe* of material similar to that in "The Ancient Mariner" and "Christabel" emphasizes Coleridge's use of the supernatural to symbolize such inner experiences as fear, guilt, and loneliness. He

could not finish "Christabel" because it was too close
to his own experience of desolation and dejection.

165.   Fogle, Richard Harter. "Coleridge's Conversation
        Poems," *TSE*, 5 (1955), 103-110.

        Most of the Conversation Poems are fine poems of their
        kind. Their occasional instances of false grandeur stem
        from Coleridge's effort to give dignity and significance
        to the meditations of a private person in unremarkable
        circumstances. Although they imitate the random associa-
        tive processes of a relaxed mind, they are not natural
        and spontaneous but are organized by a central philo-
        sophical idea into a circular structure with a return,
        such as the revised ending of "Frost at Midnight,"
        which is also a synthesis.

166.   French, Warren G. "Coleridge's 'Christabel,'" *Expl*, 8
        (1955), item 48.

        Though a devout Christian, Christabel could have been
        influenced by local Druidical traditions in choosing to
        pray under an oak tree in Northern England during the
        season of Be'il-tin, the principal Druidical festival.

167.   Gersh, Gabriel. "Palaces of Pleasure," *Commonweal*, 63
        (1955), 33-35.

        Unlike the modern pleasure resort, Kubla Khan's plea-
        sure dome depends on a sense of man's littleness and
        weakness against the power and mystery of the universe.

168.   Kreuzer, James R. "Diction," in *Elements of Poetry*
        (New York: Macmillan, 1955), pp. 8-12.

        In lines 1-15 of "The Ancient Mariner" Coleridge uses
        both connotative and denotative diction to make credible
        the strangeness of the Mariner and to establish the van-
        tage point in reality.

169.   Marsh, Florence G. "Coleridge: 'A Mountain-Birth,'"
        N&QNS, 2 (1955), 261-262.

        Two parallel passages from other poems by Coleridge
        support Humphry House's reading of line 129 of "Dejec-
        tion" but make improbable his suggestion of the reminis-
        cence of Horace. (See item 151.)

170.   Mary Eleanor, S.H.C.J., Mother. "Strange Voyages:
        Coleridge and Rimbaud," *Renascence*, 8 (1955), 64-70, 87.

The differences between Coleridge's treatment of the
voyage symbol in "The Ancient Mariner" and Rimbaud's in
"Bateau ivre" stem partly from Coleridge's romantic
transcendentalism. This viewpoint accounts, for example,
for the emphasis on intuition in the scene of the Mariner lying in a trance while supernatural forces propel
his ship and in his act of blessing the water-snakes
"unawares." It explains the significance of the fact
that the same water-snakes constitute both torment and
release, depending on the Mariner's attitude toward them.

171. Piper, H.W. *Nature and the Supernatural in "The Ancient
     Mariner."* Folcroft, Pennsylvania: Folcroft Press,
     1955.

     Drawing details such as the fatal tropic heat and the
     phosphorescence in which the water-snakes move from
     Darwin's *The Botanic Garden* and the moral from Words-
     worth's "Lines Left upon a Seat in a Yew-Tree," in "The
     Ancient Mariner" Coleridge abandons the argumentative
     tone of the early poems and presents imaginatively the
     Unitarian view of nature as composed of living intelli-
     gent forces. Under God's direction of these forces,
     the Mariner comes to understand the physical world as
     possessing a life like his own and learns to talk about
     it in supernatural terms. The polar spirit, for example,
     produces the wind which returns him, and the spirits who
     descend to work the ship display all the characteristics
     of electricity.

172. Schanzer, Ernest. "Shakespeare, Lowes, and 'The Ancient
     Mariner,'" *N&QNS*, 2 (1955), 260-261.

     In his search for sources for "The Ancient Mariner"
     Lowes overlooked two obvious ones: Casca's description
     of supernatural incidents in *Julius Caesar* (I.iii.15
     ff.) for the detail in the 1798 text of the flaming arms
     and *The Tempest* for the aerial spirits and the themes of
     supernatural manipulation of the weather, life-in-death,
     and release by repentance.

173. Schneider, Elisabeth. "The Unknown Reviewer of
     'Christabel': Jeffrey, Hazlitt, Tom Moore," *PMLA*, 70
     (1955), 417-432.

     The notorious review of "Christabel" in the *Edinburgh
     Review* for September, 1816, has been ascribed to Francis
     Jeffrey and more commonly to William Hazlitt. Jeffrey,
     however, specifically denied being the author; and

though Coleridge at first suspected Hazlitt, in the
closing chapter of *Biographia Literaria* he was not sure.
A more likely candidate is Tom Moore, the Irish poet to
whom the review is assigned by T.F. Dibdin in his
Reminiscences and by Jeffrey's biographer Lord Cockburn.
In addition to the general similarities of opinions,
tone, and style, the review resembles Moore's other
writing in its technical interest in versification and
its highly individual use of the term "couplet."

174.   Whalley, George. *Coleridge and Sara Hutchinson and the
       Asra Poems.* London: Routledge & Kegan Paul, 1955.

       Chapter 1, "'Sara's Poets'" (pp. 1-32), provides a
transcript of Coleridge's poems in Sara's manuscript
book and attempts to establish their dates and biographical significance. Chapter 3, "The Asra Poems"
(pp. 97-141), relates the poems in Sara's book to the
Asra poems. Although the book preserves new variants
as well as hitherto unpublished verse, it is important
mainly as a record of Coleridge's association with
Sara. It contains the following seemingly miscellaneous
group of Coleridge's poems which Sara copied into her
book from 1801 to 1810: "A Soliloquy of the Full Moon,"
"The Language of Birds," "Tranquillity--an Ode," "Ode
after Bathing," "Inscription for a Fountain," "The
Picture," "Song from Lessing," "Psyche," "Hope and
Time," "The Keepsake," and "The Devil's Thoughts."
       These poems are not so obviously for or about Sara
as the more personal "Letter" addressed to her; nevertheless, they should be considered as Asra poems not
only on the basis of their inclusion in Sara's book but
also on the authority of Coleridge's own arrangement of
his poems in *Sibylline Leaves* and subsequent editions and
and on the internal evidence of theme and imagery.
Deeply submerged in such personal images as the moon,
the sod-seat, the sound of bees, and the cone of sand,
the theme of the poems is Coleridge's love for Asra.
Two of the poems, "Tranquillity" and "Ode after Bathing,"
celebrate his happy visit with the Hutchinsons in July
and August, 1801. The most personal of all, "The Keepsake," recalls another visit through the reference to
Sara as "Emmeline" and the phrase, reworked from a prose
account, "The Entrancement of that Maiden kiss."

1956

175. Beaty, Frederick L. "Two Manuscript Poems of Coleridge," *RES*, NS 7 (1956), 185–187.

An unpublished manuscript in the Cornell Library contains Coleridge's "The Knight's Tomb," his scansion of it, and his account of his grievance against Scott for incorrectly quoting the last three lines in *Ivanhoe* and *Castle Dangerous*. On the back of the half-sheet is a portion of "Youth and Age," transcribed by Joseph Henry Green.

176. Beyer, Werner W. "The Background of Coleridge's 'Cain,' Precursor of 'The Ancient Mariner,'" *N&QNS*, 3 (1956), 32–34, 82–84.

Though "The Wanderings of Cain" has been traditionally associated with Gessner's *Death of Abel* and with the Valley of Stones, it more closely resembles certain features of Wieland's *Oberon*, all of which had earlier been presented (see item 35) except for the wandering hero's eventual regeneration through the influences of innocence and natural beauty and the traits, actions, and functions of the three characters.

177. Bishop, Morchard. "The Farmhouse of Kubla Khan," *TLS*, May 10, 1957, p. 293.

The farmhouse at which Coleridge wrote "Kubla Khan" is less likely to be Ash or Twitchin than Broomstreet because of its verbal resemblance to the word "Brimstone," the name quoted in an unused entry of *Table Talk*; its accessibility to the traveller taking Coleridge's frequented cliff-path from Porlock Weir to the Devonshire border or to the businessman from Porlock, possibly on horseback; its "lonely" appearance in an open area; and its proximity to deep romantic chasms and "a sunless sea" (1. 5).

178. Bonnerot, Lewis. "The Two Worlds of Coleridge: Some Aspects of His Attitude to Nature," in *Essays by Divers Hands, Being the Transactions of the Royal Society of Literature of the United Kingdom*, NS 28 (1956), 93–105.

In theme and structure the Quantock Poems express Coleridge's conflicting aspirations toward the vast sublime world of the imagination and the little secure world of domesticity. In "Kubla Khan," however, the

world of dreams and imagination remains unchecked and
makes possible the successful building of the perfect
work of art, or the "stately pleasure dome."

179.   Bowen, Hoyt E.   "Coleridge's 'The Rime of the Ancient
       Mariner,' 198," *Expl*, 15 (1956), item 9.

       In its context, Life-in-Death's whistling three times
is probably connected with the superstition of sailors
that whistling aboard ship calls up the wind. (Cf.
item 161.)

180.   Jordan, Hoover H.   "Thomas Moore and the Review of
       'Christabel,'" *MP*, 54 (1956), 95-105.

       A thorough analysis of internal evidence shows that
the ideas and style of the unknown reviewer of "Christabel" are not those of Thomas Moore but of Hazlitt and
Jeffrey. Traces of Hazlitt, for instance, appear in
the use of brilliance as a standard of excellence, in
objections to such things as suddenness of transition,
in the reference to Byron and to Coleridge's other
"fine" verses, and in the preference for alliteration
and balanced sentence structure. Key words in the
review--like "extravagance," "raving," "drivelling,"
"shuffling," and "incongruity"--abound in the writings
of Hazlitt and Jeffrey but not in those of Moore.
Other characteristics typical of Jeffrey include the
condescension toward Byron and the "new school" of Lake
poets, the charge of intelligibility, the selection of
musical poets, and the flippancy of tone. Moore, on
the other hand, genuinely admired Byron and the Lake
poets, approved of irregular verse patterns, and in his
reviews usually found something pleasant to say. In
style his writing is marked by allusions, quotations,
plays on words, and much imagery--features which are
absent from the review of "Christabel." (Cf. item 173.)

181.   Mayo, Robert.   "Two Early Coleridge Poems," *Bodleian
       Library Record*, 5 (1956), 311-318.

       Heretofore unnoticed, two of Coleridge's early poems
appeared in successive numbers of the *Weekly Entertainer*
for October, 1793. Later printed in the *Cambridge
Intelligencer* and included in the first volume of *Poems*,
"Absence, an Ode" is Coleridge's second published poem.
"Absence, a Poem," given here, is a combination of the
manuscript poem "Effusion at Evening" and "Lines on an
Autumnal Evening." It--and probably the first poem too--
is a love poem addressed to Fanny Nesbitt.

182.   Schulze, Fritz W.   "Wordsworthian and Coleridgian Texts
       (1784-1822) Mostly Unidentified or Displaced," in
       Strena Anglica, Festschrift für Otto Ritter, ed.
       Gerhard Dietrich and Fritz W. Schulze (Halle: Niemeyer,
       1956), pp. 225-258.

       Formerly unidentified literary sources for some of
       Coleridge's poems include the following: Wordsworth's
       translation of Virgil's *Georgics*, IV, 511-515, for "The
       Hour We Shall Meet Again"; Wordsworth's *Septimi Gades*
       for "Lines Written at Shurton Bars"; Navagero's imita-
       tion of Anacreon's 46th Ode for "The Rose"; Moore's
       rendering of Anacreon's 49th Ode for "An Ode in the
       Manner of Anacreon"; Wordsworth's "Lines Written as a
       School Exercise," an Anacreontic "Imitation," "Beauty
       and Moonlight," and *Septimi Gades* for "Lewti"; Cole-
       ridge's own "A Thought Suggested by a View on Saddle
       Back" for lines 40 ff. about the "storm-Blast" in "The
       Ancient Mariner"; Thomas Warton's "Pastoral in the
       Manner of Spenser" for the hoar frost image in line 260
       of "The Ancient Mariner"; Wordsworth's reporting of
       Shelvocke's *Voyage* for the simile of the painted ship
       in "The Ancient Mariner."

183.   Seronsy, Cecil C.   "Dual Patterning in 'The Rime of the
       Ancient Mariner,'" *N&QNS*, 3 (1956), 497-499.

       The structural principle of dual patterning appears
       in the two rhyming lines which divide the ballad stanza
       into two statements; in the two-part structure of each
       line reinforced by two main stresses, the caesura, a
       repeated word or its variant, alliteration, assonance,
       internal rhyme, and chiasmus; and in paired images and
       details.   This pattern harmonizes with the dual aspects
       of the story and creates an angular, disjointed move-
       ment suitable to the supernatural atmosphere.

184.   Smith, Bernard.   "Coleridge's *Ancient Mariner* and Cook's
       Second Voyage," *Journal of the Warburg and Courtauld
       Institute*, 19 (1956), 117-154.

       A major source of the pattern, events, and imagery in
       "The Ancient Mariner" is the accounts of Cook's second
       voyage, especially the *Journal* kept by William Wales,
       astronomer and meterologist who taught mathematics at
       Christ's Hospital when Coleridge was there.   According
       to the *Journal*, the *Resolution* followed the course of
       the Mariner's ship in Parts I and II and encountered
       the same events in the same sequence--the fair weather

which became stormy and fitful, the mast-high ice which
surrounded the ship and made a lasting impression on
the crew with the sound of its splitting and the reflection of light, the shooting of an albatross by a crew-
man who later experienced guilt and remorse, the calm
and heat, the water-snakes, and the formation of dew on
the sails. Both the *Journal* and the poem record the
phenomenon of the rotting phosphorent sea illuminated
by agitation, the *aurora australis*, and the moon partly
covered by mist or fog. The image of an obscured
heavenly body, as well as the whirlwind-waterspout
image, occurs first in the Christ's Hospital poems at
a time when association with Wales was promoting Coleridge's interest in science and travel. This interest
is the real genesis of "The Ancient Mariner" but is
ignored in Lowes's explanation.

185.   Tomlinson, Charles. "S.T. Coleridge: 'Christabel,'" in
    Interpretations: Essays on Twelve English Poems, ed.
    John Wain (London: Routledge & Kegan Paul, 1956),
    pp. 86-112.

    The basic pattern of the tale of terror is the strug-
gle between evil and innocence. In Coleridge's poem
this conflict is successfully expressed in the theme of
division within the self and within intimate relationships. With respect to Christabel especially, the total
disintegration of personality and will is subtly and
completely developed by the cumulative series of instances of Geraldine's character as a fatal woman and
by the following images of incipient disease and unfulfilled potential: the gray cloud which nearly hides the
sky, the full moon that is dulled, the spring that has
not yet arrived, the groaning toothless mastiff, the
one red leaf, and the snake coiled around the bird,
which recalls the picture of Geraldine sleeping with
Christabel. Lines 227-228 and 329-331 are ironic, suggesting that the blue sky of helpful saints and spirits
no longer operates upon the world below.

186.   Whalley, George. "Coleridge's Sheet of Sonnets, 1796,"
    TLS, November 23, 1956, p. 697.

    Coleridge's untitled pamphlet contained an essay on
the sonnet followed by twenty-eight sonnets, one of
which is Anna Seward's and four of which are Lloyd's.
The fact that Coleridge purposefully bound two of the
three known copies of this little anthology with Bowles's
Sonnets has been virtually unnoticed.

187. Whitesell, J. Edwin. "'The Rime of the Ancient Mariner,'
      Line 142, *N&QNS*, 3 (1956), 34-35.

      When he wrote line 142, Coleridge remembered the an-
      cient punishment of fastening a dead person to the body
      of a criminal until infection and eventual death
      resulted.

188. Wright, John K. "From 'Kubla Khan' to Florida,"
      American Quarterly, 8 (1956), 76-80.

      With the publication in 1943 of Francis Harper's
      annotated edition of Bartram's *Travels in Georgia and
      Florida, 1773-74: A Report to Dr. John Fothergill*, it is
      possible to identify the exact localities, visited and
      described by Bartram, which influenced some of the
      images of "Kubla Khan." The Manatee Spring, for exam-
      ple, helped create the image of the fountain and the
      shadow of Kubla's pleasure dome, and Salt Springs Run
      helped suggest the river Alph.

189. Canceled.

                              1957

190. Abrams, M.H. "The Correspondent Breeze: A Romantic
      Metaphor," *KR*, 19 (1957), 113-130.

      As the speaker in Coleridge's "Dejection" moves from
      apathy through mounting passion and imaginative power
      to peace, he demonstrates the romantic use of the rising
      wind as a metaphor for the renewal of a sense of com-
      munity, of life and emotional vigor, and of creative
      inspiration.

191. Canceled.

192. Bostetter, Edward E. "*Christabel*: The Vision of Fear,"
      PQ, 36 (1957), 183-194.

      Coleridge's other poems like "The Pains of Sleep,"
      his letters, and his notebooks indicate that he associ-
      ated "Christabel" with his own life. Aware of his
      morally ambiguous nature, in the phrase "O sorrow and
      shame" (1. 674) he links himself with both Geraldine
      and Christabel. Geraldine resembles the loathly ladies
      of his dreams. She becomes increasingly malevolent as
      she is seen from Christabel's fearful perspective, the
      "vision of fear" (1. 453) which paralyzes her will and

which Coleridge called "sleep of the spirit," or madness. Her dreams are like the fiendish dreams recorded
in his notebooks, and her desolation in the final scene
was his own. He left the poem unfinished because he
could not confront the hopelessness of extricating her
from further enslavement. He could not answer the disturbing question in "The Conclusion to Part II" about
the relationship of love and hate in human nature.

193. Coburn, Kathleen. "Coleridge Redivivus," in *The Major
      English Romantic Poets: A Symposium in Reappraisal*,
      ed. Clarence D. Thorpe, Carlos Baker, and Bennett
      Weaver (Carbondale: Southern Illinois University
      Press, 1957), pp. 113-125.

Although Coleridge cannot be credited with any one
particular system, he did work out a way of looking at
various kinds of thought and experience which illumi-
nates and integrates them. In the *Treatise on Method*
he explained this process as dependent on a unifying
act of mind, or initiative, the importance of which he
had recognized earlier in poetry. "The Ancient Mariner,"
"Kubla Khan," "Christabel," and "Dejection" are all
based on the paralyzing disintegration resulting from
the loss of the initiative.

194. Erdman, David V. "The Case for Internal Evidence (3):
      Newspaper Sonnets Put to the Concordance Test: Can
      They Be Attributed to Coleridge?" *BNYPL*, 61 (1957),
      508-516, 611-620; 62 (1958), 6-49.

The concordance test of seven newspaper sonnets, all
potentially Coleridge's, indicates that three of them
are probably his, while another one cannot be claimed
or rejected with certainty. The "Sonnet. To Mrs.
Siddons," signed "Fontrose," was published in the
Morning Chronicle for January 29, 1795, directly under
the last of a series of eleven "Sonnets on Eminent
Characters," signed "S.T.C." In contrast to Wordsworth's
poems and to the earlier Siddons sonnet, signed by
Coleridge but actually contributed by Lamb, this poem
shares associated word clusters with a number of Coleridge's other poems and shows his characteristic use of
italics in the closing couplet. Two sonnets to Lord
Stanhope, published in January and February of 1795,
form a linked progression with a third Stanhope poem
known to be Coleridge's; and all of the Stanhope poems
use the Coleridgean metaphor comparing the patriot and
the blazing sun. The case for Coleridge's authorship

of the second one, however, is slightly weakened by two
of his letters which could be interpreted as external
evidence that he wrote only the third Stanhope sonnet.
Finally, an unsigned "Sonnet," beginning "Blaze on,
blaze on, thou fiercely flaming fire," appeared in the
Morning Post for April 12, 1798; its images and phrases
occur in earlier or contemporaneous poems by Coleridge,
but these resonances lack sufficient complexity and
variation to be admitted as evidence of his authorship.

195. Fogle, Richard Harter. "The Genre of *The Ancient
Mariner*," *TSE*, 7 (1957), 111-124.

"The Ancient Mariner" is a poem in the romantic genre,
which for Coleridge meant a poem of purest imagination
that depends for its effectiveness on a sense of inevi-
tability and on the principles of dramatic illusion,
proportion, and sameness in difference. The recognizable truth of the human experience is presented in an
impossible setting, and the ballad meter is varied in
pace and intensity. The Mariner is the ideal romantic
poet, since he holds the attention of an unwilling
listener and awakens the imagination with the tale of
his insensitive negation of the living spirit. The life
of his romantic universe is conveyed partly by the existence of invisible beings, the most powerful of whom
are associated with the land to which he returns.

196. Johnson, S.F. "The Case for Internal Evidence (2): An
Uncollected Early Poem by Coleridge," *BNYPL*, 61 (1957),
505-507.

The verbal parallels from Coleridge's known early
verse support the external evidence for his authorship
of "Lines on the Portrait of a Lady," a poem with the
signature of "S." which appeared in the *Watchman* for
March 17, 1796, along with two other poems, signed respectively "T." and "C.," attributed to Coleridge. (Cf.
item 21.)

197. Kroeber, Karl. "'The Rime of the Ancient Mariner' as
Stylized Epic," *Transactions, Wisconsin Academy of
Sciences, Arts, and Letters*, 46 (1957), 179-187.

Reading "The Ancient Mariner" as a stylized epic of
quest clarifies its archetypal significance and its unified total design and condensed symbolism which distinguish it from other ballads of the supernatural. The
poem is epical in theme; and like *The Odyssey* and the

Babylonian *Gilgamesh*, it treats the motifs of the night
journey, the important return home, the crime which
brings about death of the hero's companions, supernatural assistance, prophetic visions, and the concluding rejection of the sensuous life. The Mariner,
Odysseus, and Gilgamesh are all willful men who have seen
and experienced strange things.

198. Langbaum, Robert. "The Dramatic Lyric and the Lyrical
      Drama," in *The Poetry of Experience: The Dramatic
      Monologue in Modern Literary Tradition* (New York:
      Random House, 1957), pp. 38-74.

      Imitating the structure of experience, "Frost at Mid-
      night" concerns the poet's gain in perception as his
      understanding of the mystery of process expands from an
      awareness of the silent workings of frost to his child's
      breathing, his own thinking, and finally to the deeper,
      wider mystery of permanence.

199. Ober, Warren U. "Original Versions of Two Coleridge
      Couplets," *N&QNS*, 4 (1957), 454-455.

      "The Homeric Hexameter" and "The Ovidian Elegiac Metre"
      exist in their original versions in an unpublished manu-
      script in the Mitchell Library.

200. ————. "'The Rime of the Ancient Mariner' and Pinck-
      ard's 'Notes on the West Indies,'" *N&QNS*, 4 (1957),
      380-382.

      Two of Dr. George Pinckard's 1796 letters to an un-
      known London friend resemble "The Ancient Mariner" in
      certain details--a ship approaching the observer with
      full sails in the apparent calm, a ship moving without
      resistance, colorful dolphins, lights on the sea at
      night, and the presence of the sun and moon. It is
      therefore possible that Coleridge read these letters
      before they were included in the published collection,
      Notes on the West Indies (1806).

201. Patrick, John M. "Ammianus and Alpheus: The Sacred
      River," *MLN*, 72 (1957), 335-337.

      The ancient writer Ammianus Marcellinus, whose works
      Coleridge probably knew, not only associates the
      Alpheus with the Nile in passages which resemble the
      description of the sacred river in "Kubla Khan" but
      also mentions a river called Abora.

202. Purser, J.W.R. "Interpretation of *The Ancient Mariner*,"
      RES, 8 (1957), 249-256.

      The main theme of the poem is the Mariner's reluctant
      endurance of the life-in-death existence to which his
      destiny has called him. In killing the albatross he
      rebels against the intrusion of spiritual values and
      consequently suffers from fear, loneliness, and a loath-
      ing of the world and himself. Recovery from such des-
      pair comes gradually as he learns to live the spiritual
      life by surrendering himself to love.

203. Smith, Charles J. "Wordsworth and Coleridge: The Growth
      of a Theme," *SP*, 54 (1957), 53-64.

      "The Ancient Mariner" is a symbolic treatment of the
      theme which runs through most of Wordsworth's and Cole-
      ridge's major poems during the 1790's--the theme of
      crime, punishment, curse, remorse, and regeneration.
      In contrast to Peter Bell, whose remorse is awakened by
      nature, the Mariner is brought to remorse by super-
      natural manifestations.

204. Suther, Marshall. "On the Interpretation of 'Kubla
      Khan,'" *BuR*, 7 (1957), 1-19.

      In *Coleridge, Opium, and Kubla Khan*, Elisabeth
      Schneider argues that the poem is a fragment and that
      it is not susceptible to a symbolic interpretation.
      (See item 155.) But her treatment of these critical
      problems is unconvincing. In the first place, Coleridge
      called the poem a "fragment," meaning that he planned to
      add something to it, not that it was aesthetically in-
      complete. Second, he did write symbolic poetry, poetry
      which characteristically delivers its meaning by impli-
      cation, for poetry which operates otherwise is another
      form of discourse. Finally, in theory he disapproved of
      explicit, obvious meanings, although the major images
      of "Kubla Khan" appear in other poems in which the sym-
      bolism is relatively open and consistent.

205. Woodring, Carl R. "Coleridge and Mary Hutchinson,"
      N&QNS, 4 (1957), 213-214.

      George Whalley's emphasis on Coleridge's early affec-
      tion for Mary Hutchinson as well as Sara (see item 174)
      is based partly on an error in the transcription of the
      verse letter to Asra. He and others (see items 15, 151)
      print "the eye-lash" (1. 107) for "thy eye-lash."

206. Wordsworth, Jonathan. "Some Unpublished Coleridge
      Marginalia," *TLS*, June 14, 1957, p. 369.

      Printed here for the first time, Coleridge's annota-
      tions for Hugh James Rose, in an 1812 edition of the
      Friend, are mainly philosophical except for a comment
      on the psychological rather than poetic merits of "The
      Three Graves" and several corrections to the text of
      "Hymn before Sunrise."

                              1958

207. Chayes, Irene H. "Coleridge, Metempsychosis, and
      'Almost all the followers of Fenelon,'" *ELH*, 25 (1958),
      290-315.

      Coleridge's revision of Ramsay's doctrine of metem-
      psychosis appears specifically in two minor poems, the
      second sonnet on the birth of his son Hartley (1796)
      and "The Snow-Drop" (1800), and indirectly in "The
      Ancient Mariner" and "Christabel." In a letter comment
      attached to the Hartley sonnet, Coleridge attributed its
      philosophical idea to Fenelon, an oblique reference to
      Andrew Michael Ramsay, friend and biographer of Fenelon,
      whose major work Coleridge had just been reading and
      whose explanation of infant death as caused by purity
      illuminates the conclusion of the poem and gives it a
      unity that is not readily apparent in the text.
          Like Hartley, the polar spirit is a Ramsayan degraded
      intelligence. In carrying out divine justice he perse-
      cutes the Mariner for violating the law of order, or
      love, for breaking the chain of metempsychosis which
      binds together all beings. With the corpse of the alba-
      tross hung around his neck, the Mariner himself suggests
      a degraded intelligence in bondage to an animal body
      until he becomes worthy of a higher state and is set
      free.
          Geraldine is a spirit from another world who becomes
      a martyr in descending to her reptilian state and then,
      in order to achieve some undisclosed task, victimizes
      Christabel in exchanging personalities with her. This
      rivalry dramatizes the conflict between Coleridge's
      emotional attraction to heterodoxy and his critical
      belief in orthodoxy.

208. Coburn, Kathleen. "Original Versions of Two Coleridge
      Couplets," *N&QNS*, 5 (1958), 225-226.

Since "The Ovidian Elegiac Metre" and another variant
version of "The Homeric Hexameter" also exist in a manuscript in the Huntington Library, it cannot be determined
whether the Mitchell Library versions are the originals.
(Cf. item 199.)

209. Erdman, David V. "Coleridge as Nehemiah Higginbottom,"
     MLN, 73 (1958), 569–580.

An examination of the Higginbottom sonnets and of the
context of their publication shows that Coleridge's
mockery was directed not at Southey but mainly at himself. The first sonnet is a parody of the language and
the melancholy brooding in several of his early poems,
especially "Monody"; the third sonnet, "On a Ruined
House in a Romantic Country," ridicules the swelling
diction and imagery of "Lines Written at Shurton Bars,"
"To the Nightingale," "An Effusion at Evening," and,
most obviously, the first draft of "Lewti," an almost
unchanged transcription of Wordsworth's notebook fragment "Beauty and Moonlight." The second sonnet, "To
Simplicity," is a satiric attack upon the style of
Charles Lloyd, though Southey could easily have supposed
that he was Coleridge's target since this and the other
sonnets appeared in the *Monthly Magazine* for November
1797, just after the *Anti-Jacobin Review* had begun its
parodies of Southey.

210. ————. "Unrecorded Coleridge Variants," *SB*, 11 (1958),
     143–162.

Since no systematic examination of the periodical
files has ever been made, this report supplies a needed
chronological list of all variants in text, title, and
signature of all Coleridge poems first published in
British newspapers from 1793 to 1820.

211. Erdman, David V., ed. "A New Discovery: The First Re-
     view of *Christabel*," *Texas Studies in English*, 37
     (1958), 53–60.

The first review of the *Christabel* volume has been
recently discovered in the London *Times* of May 20, 1816,
and in a partial reprint in the *Courier* of June 4. Its
extensive circulation and perceptive enthusiasm accounts
for the rapid sale of the book in spite of the hostile
reviews and for the reference in the manuscript defense
of "Christabel" (see item 27) to contradictory opinions,
equally confident and authoritative, neutralizing each

other. Its author, probably Henry Crabb Robinson, re-
spectfully doubts that Coleridge will ever finish the
poem or that the principle of scanning by accents instead
of syllables is really new. But he praises the richness
and variety of the meter, the human interest, the subtle
suggestion of Christabel's moral sensitivity, the skillful use of superstition, and the memorable exactness of
visual and auditory imagery.

212. Gardner, W.H. "The Poet and the Albatross (A Study in
      Symbolic Suggestion)," *English Studies in Africa*, 1
      (1958), 102-125.

      The facts of Coleridge's biography, as well as his
Platonic view of literature, point to the likelihood
that the Mariner's voyage has metaphysical and theological parallels with the life of man. The equator, for
example, suggests the median of maturity, after which
the worldly and unworldly pressures drive man into the
region of ice and fog, into the realization of his
physical and spiritual vulnerability and of the necessity of partial renunciation of the sensual life before
faith can begin to redeem him. In killing the albatross
the Mariner rejects the relief of Christ's love and joy
and consequently suffers the divine retribution of the
bloody sun. He begins to allow grace to redeem him when
he bites his arm in a Christlike act of self-sacrifice,
and with the rushing out of the stars he enters the
penitential, purgatorial phase of his redemption. The
familiar landmarks of his home country suggest his re-
habilitation, while the seraphs indicate the promise of
final redemption and resurrection. The sinking of his
ship parallels the conversions of Saul and Augustine of
Hippo; his wandering and strange power of speech symbolize the missionary wanderings and gift of tongues of
Christ's early disciples.

213. Marsh, Florence G. "Christabel and Coleridge's 'Recipe'
      for Romance Poems," *N&QNS*, 5 (1958), 475-476.

      Coleridge probably left "Christabel" unfinished be-
cause he knew its faults. He linked it with romances
like Scott's "The Lady of the Lake," which he ridiculed
for, among other things, its formulaic use of place
names, nomenclature of heraldry and arms, mixture of
styles, and employment of a bard, rhyme, moralizing,
and Gothic incidents and characters.

214. Canceled.

215. Canceled.

1959

216. Abrew, Kamal De. "Coleridge's 'Ancient Mariner'--Rime
or Ballad?" *University of Ceylon Review*, 17 (1959),
90-98.

A contradiction seems to exist between the Christian
view of the Mariner as moving from sin to penance and
restoration and a realistic description of his psychological experience of suffering, numbness, and impossible
complete recovery. But the contradiction can be resolved by interpreting the moral stanzas as a statement
of the wisdom which he has gained but ironically cannot
use. The ballad form is appropriate, since folk literature is characterized by its embodiment of such simple
truths.

216a. Beer, J.B. *Coleridge the Visionary*. London: Chatto &
Windus, 1959.

After the failure of the Pantisocracy, Coleridge became particularly interested in the writings of Boehme
and Berkeley, in the myths of Cupid-Psyche and Osiris-
Isis, and in the traditions surrounding sun-worship and
the mysterious race of Abyssinians. Drawing support
from these studies, he responded to the romantic predicament with his own myth of evil and redemption which
provided the intellectual structure for his greatest
poems. In his visionary moods he speculated that,
having deprived himself of the true vision of God and
the universe, man either fears or misuses his daemonic
powers. But still remembering his lost glory, he feels
both fear and attraction for objects associated with it.
The Mariner shoots the albatross, for example, because,
as the mist emphasizes, he is unaware of the inner harmony of the universe. Cut off from the light of God,
he experiences only the heat of his presence, his guilty
conscience perceiving the sun as a Typhonian image of
anger and retribution and the water-snakes as loathsome
and corrupt. When he blesses them, they, along with the
spring and the Isis-like moon, become images of redemption which foreshadow his vision of the sun as the
source of light and harmony and of the harmony of all
human beings among themselves and with God. But the
vision is not permanent. In fact, it is part of the
Mariner's curse that he must live with the memory of
blessedness.

In "Christabel" evil is again represented as a lapse
of daemonic energies. The idea that evil is a distortion of good is suggested by images such as the veiled
moon, clouds, mist, and owls as well as by the ambivalent behavior of Geraldine. The focus of attention,
however, is more on the redemption of such evil.
Christabel--whose character parallels in some respects
Crashaw's St. Theresa, Isis, and Psyche--is intended to
accept the evil, to subsume it, and eventually to
transform it. But the task of making this process take
place in her unconscious proved too demanding for
Coleridge to finish the poem.

"Kubla Khan" is a finished poem, regardless of
Coleridge's method of composition or his probable plans
for expansion. As it is, several patterns of meaning
bind the images together in a compact, logical structure. Associations with the tradition of sun-worship,
for example, allow the images of the first two stanzas
to indicate that Xanadu is a lost paradise. Kubla resembles the violent sons of Cain and Ham who feared and
propitiated the sun as a substitute for the lost
Shechinah: a man of commanding genius who remembers
the lost glory, he strives to re-create the paradisal
garden. But he can impose his will on nature only
temporarily, for the threat of destruction is implicit
in his own precarious position as well as in the river,
which denies immortality as it flows down to a sunless
sea, and in the dome, which suggests false values in
its separation from the world. These ominous hints become explicit in the ambivalent images of the second
stanza, particularly in the destructive Typhonian fountain and the ancestral voices. In contrast to this lost
paradise stands the vision of static harmony in the
third stanza (ll. 31-36) and of paradise regained in
the fourth stanza. Flux and permanence and reason and
nature are now reconciled; a measured harmony replaces
the tumult. Associated with the troglodyte guardians
of ancient truth, the Abyssinian maid also functions as
an Isis-figure who thus complements the wailing woman
and who could redeem the poet to the unfallen condition
of the inspired bard of absolute genius.

217.   Bishop, Morchard. "Captain James and Ivor James," *TLS*,
       January 16, 1959, p. 35.

       In *The Source of "The Ancient Mariner"* (1890), Ivor
James attempts to prove Coleridge's debt to *The Strange
and Dangerous Voyage of Captaine Thomas James* (1633).

Lowes and others have regarded this evidence seriously,
but a presentation copy of Ivor James's pamphlet reveals that it was a literary hoax, motivated by ancestor-
worship and the desire to amuse the Fortnightly Literary
Club of Cardiff.

218.   ————.   "Notes of Two Coleridges," *BNYPL*, 63 (1959),
       531-533.

Coleridge's two natures are seen in the tension between fun and propriety that exists in a witty distich,
printed here for the first time, which he wrote on
September 20, 1830, on the flyleaf of his copy of
Kenilworth.

219.   Durr, R.A.   "'This Lime-Tree Bower My Prison' and a
       Recurrent Action in Coleridge," *ELH*, 26 (1959), 514-
       530.

Coleridge's main concern, in poetry and in prose, is
the action, illustrated fully in "This Lime-Tree Bower,"
of multeity coming into unity, of the soul losing its
individuality and finding its true being in the one Life
of God. Like the Mariner and the poet of "Frost at Midnight" and "Dejection," the speaker in "This Lime-Tree
Bower" moves out of his despondency and loneliness into
unitive joy by means of an imaginative act of mind. As
in "Fears in Solitude" and "Reflections" his transformation is imaged by an emergence out of a dell onto a sudden expanse of prospect. There, in the soft, diffusive
light appropriate to the imagination, his liberated mind
perceives the presence of the one Life. Typically, his
thoughts then return to the bower at noon, but in his
mood of delight he can now appreciate its loveliness as
the patterns of light and shade change with the passage
of time. At sunset he can identify with the rook, a
symbol of his own loving, soaring spirit.

220.   Icban-Castro, Rosalina.   "The Crucifixion Story in
       Coleridge's 'The Rime of the Ancient Mariner,'"
       Diliman Review, 7 (1959), 326-333.

A restatement of Coleridge's religious philosophy in
the archaic language of long ago, "The Ancient Mariner"
is based on the Gospel account of Christ's crucifixion
and man's salvation, for in both stories occur the words
"cross" and "blood"; the numbers three, seven, and nine;
the themes of thirst, loneliness, and forgiveness; the
scene of casting dice, or lots; the parallel actions of
the Mariner and mankind and of the albatross and Christ.

221. MacGillivray, J.R. "A New and Early Poem by Coleridge,"
      BNYPL, 63 (1959), 153-154.

      The four-stanza love poem printed here may be Cole-
      ridge's first published poem. Signed "S.T.C.," "The
      Abode of Love" appeared in the *Cambridge Chronicle* for
      July 31, 1790, at a time when he was in love with Mary
      Evans. It uses rhyme words that are particularly char-
      acteristic of his early verse. (Cf. item 158.)

222. Marsh, Florence G. "The Ocean-Desert: *The Ancient
      Mariner* and *The Waste Land*," *EIC*, 9 (1959), 126-133.

      Comparison of "The Waste Land" and "The Ancient
      Mariner" clarifies the meaning of some of the latter's
      images and symbols. Both poems are concerned with the
      theme of spiritual dryness, which in "The Ancient Mari-
      ner" is suggested by the images of the unmoving ship,
      beating sun, and rotting water. The protagonists in
      both poems are incapable of love--hence the significance
      of the ice surrounding the Mariner's ship, his crime,
      and the resulting absence of wind and rain. Though the
      Mariner does eventually feel the wind and rain, as with
      the protagonist in "The Waste Land," his recovery of
      life and spontaneous feeling is only partial.

223. Marshall, William H. "The Structure of Coleridge's
      'Reflections on Having Left a Place of Retirement,'"
      N&QNS, 6 (1959), 319-321.

      "Reflections" is not merely a personal description of
      the poet's reluctance to leave his Clevedon cottage, for
      the implicit comparison of the speaker to Adam and to
      Christ makes it an account of the paradise that all men
      have lost and must regain. The antithesis between man
      fallen and man redeemed prepares for the millennial
      image at the end, providing the structural unity and the
      fusion of seventeenth- and eighteenth-century sensibili-
      ties that Max F. Schulz found missing. (See item 228.)

224. Moorman, Charles. "The Imagery of 'Kubla Khan,'" *N&QNS*,
      6 (1959), 321-324.

      Although the images of "Kubla Khan" do not reflect a
      completed idea, they do convey meaning in suggesting
      the process of imagination in which opposites are recon-
      ciled. In the first section (11. 1-30) the major oppo-
      sites of pleasure and pain are developed by a number of
      lesser pairs of opposites which establish the kind of
      ground necessary for the pleasure dome. The complete

reconciliation of these opposites in the second section
(11. 31-36) defines the ideal poem, impossible for
Coleridge himself (11. 37-54).

225. Ober, Warren U. "Southey, Coleridge, and 'Kubla Khan,'"
     JEGP, 58 (1959), 414-422.

Apparently recorded for possible use in the writing of
Thalaba, ten Common-Place Book entries, which Southey
quoted from travel literature of Asia and Africa, support
some of Elisabeth Schneider's conclusions about "Kubla
Khan" and provide previously unrecognized sources for
the following details: the pleasure-dome, the wailing
woman, the river, the chasm, the description of the
grounds in lines 6-9, and possibly the dulcimer, the
"honey-dew" (1. 53), and the Khan himself. Other images
such as the "caves of ice" (1. 36) and the poet's
"floating hair" (1. 50) resemble features of Sir William
Jones's *The Palace of Fortune: An Indian Tale*, also one
of Southey's sources for *Thalaba*.

226. Piper, Herbert W. "The Pantheistic Sources of Cole-
     ridge's Early Poetry," *JHI*, 20 (1959), 47-59.

In his early poetry Coleridge develops the idea,
drawn mainly from Priestley and Darwin, that the natural
world consisted of active, intelligent, purposive
monads which, when organized, formed part of the Divine
Mind. Identifying the monads with Darwin's spirits of
the elements, he shows them at work in the process of
eternal good. In "The Destiny of Nations" the spirits
of the stars and northern lights lead the Lapps to superstition, the first step to religion; and in the second
part of "Religious Musings" the French Revolution is
interpreted as the beginning of the Millennium and of
the events prophesied in Revelation.

227. Robinson, A.M. Lewin. "A Coleridge Poem," *TLS*, July 31,
     1959, p. 447.

Information is requested on the history of a Coleridge
poem, written in 1814, which appeared in the 1852 edition
of his poems as "A Hymn" and in the *Cape of Good Hope
Literary Gazette* for October 1, 1852, as "God Omni-
present." (Cf. item 4.)

228. Schulz, Max F. "Coleridge, Milton, and Lost Paradise,"
     N&QNS, 6 (1959), 143-144.

Although his abandonment of his rustic retreat at
Clevedon parallels Adam's eviction from Eden, Coleridge's
treatment of this theme in "Reflections" is secular, his

style is an incongruous mixture of Miltonic sublimity
and conversational informality, and his attitude alternates between anticipation and nostalgia. These differences result from his incomplete assimilation of
the seventeenth-century spirit.

229.   ———. "Oneness and Multeity in Coleridge's Poems,"
        TSE, 9 (1959), 53-60.

        Like his philosophy and literary criticism, Coleridge's
        poetry is governed by his idealistic sense of the simul-
        taneous oneness and multeity of life. In "A Day-Dream,"
        for example, the waking-dreaming mind of the poet fuses
        past and present into one continuous moment and then
        realizes that his musings are a part of the still sounds
        of nature. [In "This Lime-Tree Bower" the closing image
        of the rook unites the actual surroundings of the speaker
        and the mentally reconstructed prospects of the sight-
        seers as the silent contemplation of Lamb and Coleridge
        merges with the noisy flight of the bird.] Similarly,
        the Ancient Mariner finds relief when he reaches out to
        participate in the calm, happy disposition of the moon,
        the stars, and the sea-snakes.

229a.   Werkmeister, Lucyle. "Coleridge's 'Anthem': Another
        Debt to Bowles," *JEGP*, 58 (1959), 270-275.

        Although it cannot be definitively dated, Coleridge's
        "Anthem for the Children of Christ's Hospital" is ob-
        viously an adaptation of Bowles's 1790 pamphlet entitled
        Verses on the Philanthropic Society. Coleridge's poem
        substitutes a stanzaic form for Bowles's heroic couplets
        and praises God instead of a benevolent society; but
        like the *Verses*, it concerns early vice caused by human
        suffering and corrected by moral and religious instruc-
        tion. It echoes Bowles's phrases in such expressions
        as "Want's dark vale" (1. 22) and uses his metaphors
        comparing suffering and vice with winter tempests,
        clouds, and darkness; virtue and happiness with sun-
        light and moonlight; and the effect of benevolence upon
        the poor with a cave suddenly penetrated by beams of
        light.

230.   Woodring, Carl R. "Coleridge and the Khan," *EIC*, 9
        (1959), 361-368.

        In the fragment of "Kubla Khan," the profane, pride-
        ful, and impercipient Khan is not emblematic of the
        sacred poet but a contrast to him. While the poet takes
        "deep delight" (1. 44) in creating a lasting union of
        opposites, Kubla builds a temporary pleasure dome which
        Coleridge associated with the ice palace of the despised
        Russian Empress Catherine and with unwholesome pleasures.

1960

231. Ahmad, Munir. "Coleridge and the Brahman Creed (Re-
      flections of Indian Thought in Coleridge's Poetry),"
      IJES, 1 (1960), 18-37.

      Coleridge responded to the contemporary interest in
      the East by planning his own poem on India and by seek-
      ing pleasure through opium and "bhang," a drug prepared
      from Indian hemp. More particularly, his knowledge of
      Hindu thought and mythology is reflected in his poetry--
      in the pantheism of "The Eolian Harp" and "The Destiny
      of Nations"; in the daemonic agencies of "The Ancient
      Mariner"; in the principles of transmigration which
      help explain the personalities of Geraldine, Christabel's
      mother, and Geraldine's captors; in the advocacy of
      action-in-inaction, deep self-possession, and intense
      repose in "Kubla Khan."

232. Angus, Douglas. "The Theme of Love and Guilt in
      Coleridge's Three Major Poems," *JEGP*, 59 (1960),
      655-668.

      Coleridge's three major poems reflect his narcissistic
      need for sympathy and mother love and his strongly de-
      veloped oedipal guilt. Though he had tried to present
      a world dominated by love, in these poems he allows the
      emergence of his real belief in a world of loneliness,
      fear, guilt, and evil. Symbolizing an ambiguous reac-
      tion to the mother caused by guilt, good and bad in-
      fluences compete for the soul of the central character;
      and in each case the evil involves isolation brought
      about by a feminine figure. In "The Ancient Mariner"
      the gentle spirit wins and saves the Mariner from his
      life among the dead. But in "Christabel" the good
      mother is dead and loses the battle to the eternal
      witch figure Geraldine, who represents a repressed,
      guilt-laden incestuous attachment to the mother. And
      in "Kubla Khan" evil has already taken over the soul
      of the narrator, for whom the pleasure dome and the
      damsel are lost.

233. Brett, R.L. "Coleridge's *The Rime of the Ancient
      Mariner*," in *Reason and Imagination* (London: Oxford
      University Press, 1960), pp. 78-107.

      A study of "The Ancient Mariner" in light of Cole-
      ridge's poetic theory leads to the conclusion that the
      meaning of the poem is expressed in its symbols. The
      geographical voyage is also a spiritual adventure,
      having the life-death structure of the Lazarus story,
      in which the nature of sin is suggested by the Mariner's
      motiveless crime and the resulting spiritual death.

Breaking his isolation, the grace of God appears in the
Mariner's spontaneous act of blessing the water-snakes
and in the following image of rain. These symbolic
events occur in a dramatic context created by several
conscious artistic devices--namely, the old seaman himself whose appearance and manner help the listener
accept his tale, the speed of the narrative and its
use of the historic present tense, the intrusive questions of the Wedding-Guest and noises from the celebration of life.

234. Cameron, Kenneth Walter. "Schiller's 'Die Ideale' and
      the Odes of Coleridge and Wordsworth," *Emerson Society
      Quarterly*, No. 19 (1960), 36-37.

Although Schiller's short poem "Die Ideale" cannot be
considered a certain source for Coleridge's "Dejection,"
it is possible that Coleridge knew it well.

235. Coburn, Kathleen. "Poet into Public Servant," *PTRSC*,
      54 (1960), 1-11.

During the little-known period in which Coleridge was
a civil servant in Malta, he came to identify himself
more and more with the wandering Mariner, and his notebooks reflect the same back and forth movement between
outer and inner worlds that we see in the poem.

236. Creed, Howard. "'The Rime of the Ancient Mariner': A
      Rereading," *EJ*, 49 (1960), 215-222, 228.

After adequate preparation, a classroom discussion of
"The Ancient Mariner" should include these topics: circumstances and purpose of its composition, Coleridge's
romantic theory of the imagination and the oneness of
the world, the significance of the framework in pointing
to a unity which is more inclusive than that of marriage,
the propriety of willful selfishness punished by complete isolation, the special insight belonging to the
Mariner-poet as both a blessing and a curse, the merging
of natural and supernatural imagery, the function of
the archaic diction, variations in the ballad stanza,
and flaws such as the confusion in the gloss about just
when the ship reaches the line.

237. Emerson, Francis Willard. "Joseph Sterling's 'Cambuscan'
      in Coleridge's 'Kubla Khan,'" *N&QNS*, 7 (1960), 102-103.

Joseph Sterling's "Cambuscan, or the Squire's Tale of
Chaucer," published in 1785, influenced Coleridge's version of Purchas as well as certain expressions in his

description of Kubla's palace ground (11. 1, 2, 8-11, 13-16, and 31-32).

238. Fleissner, Robert F. "'Kubla Khan' and 'Tom Jones': An Unnoticed Parallel," *N&QNS*, 7 (1960), 103-105.

It is likely that Fielding's picturesque account of Squire Allworthy's estate influenced Coleridge's description of the landscape of "Kubla Khan." Evidence for this possibility lies in Coleridge's familiarity with *Tom Jones*; the resemblance of both scenes to the fashionable eighteenth-century garden; the inclusion in both works of a stately structure, an enchanted spot, a reference to a hill and then to mountain scenery; and especially the correspondence of words and phrases such as "miles," "meander," and "mazy."

239. Gérard, Albert. "Clevedon Revisited: Further Reflections on Coleridge's 'Reflections on Having Left a Place of Retirement,'" *N&QNS*, 7 (1960), 101-102.

The reason for the failure of "Reflections" is not that it lacks a recognizable structure. Its complex design results from the intertwining of three distinguishable patterns: (1) the theme of retirement (11. 1-14), the theme of the active life (11. 43-62), and the combination of these in the last paragraph; (2) a series of contractions and expansions; and (3) an ascending spiral-like movement from natural piety through cosmic vision to humanitarian action. The poem fails because the emotional emphasis does not coincide with the structural emphasis.

240. ———. "The Systolic Rhythm: The Structure of Coleridge's Conversation Poems," *EIC*, 10 (1960), 307-317.

The inner structural rhythm of the Conversation Poems shows one of the deepest urges in the Romantic mind, the desire to extend the self beyond immediate experience. Within an overall pattern of ascension, the mind of the speaker moves in a heartbeat rhythm of systole and diastole, contraction and expansion. In "The Eolian Harp," for example, his attention alternates between his particular situation and the various worlds of perceptual nature, fanciful reverie, intellectual speculation, and religious faith. His effort to find some spiritual value in his experience is suggested partly by the images of widening perspective, the allegorizing of natural objects, and the similes which dematerialize the harp's melody. Clearly, Coleridge intended the last section to be climactic; but like the last section of "Reflections," it is anticlimactic because it

expresses an attitude which clashes with his deeply
felt experience. In "This Lime-Tree Bower," however,
he achieved a perfect blending of thought and feeling,
imagery and structure.

241.   Gose, Elliott B., Jr. "Coleridge and the Luminous Gloom:
        An Analysis of the 'Symbolical Language' in 'The Rime
        of the Ancient Mariner,'" *PMLA*, 75 (1960), 238-244.

        A phrase from Coleridge's Notebook Number Five, the
        "luminous gloom," suggests the penetration of dark
        shadows by the light of the sun. In "The Ancient Mari-
        ner" this image of the sun, with its qualities of heat
        and redness, symbolizes God and is important in the
        Mariner's conversion and in the harbor scene, while the
        moon, with its contrasting qualities of coldness and
        whiteness, symbolizes mutable nature and is connected
        with the storm in Parts I and V, with the Nightmare
        woman, and with the Mariner's compulsion to tell his
        tale.

242.   Gunstan, David. "A Second Look at the Albatross," *DR*,
        40 (1960), 206-211.

        Coleridge's poem created the superstition about the
        evil consequences of killing an albatross. Before 1798,
        sailors killed the bird for sport and for various uses
        of its oily vomit, feathers, and feet. Even in Shel-
        vocke's *A Voyage Round the World by Way of the Great
        South Sea* (1757), the albatross was suspected as a bird
        of ill omen, and nothing came of killing it.

243.   Harrison, Thomas P. "Bird of Paradise: Phoenix Redivi-
        vus," *Isis*, 51 (1960), 173-180.

        Unlike Wordsworth, Coleridge prefers to use the fic-
        tions associated with the bird of paradise. The notions
        that they have no feet, spend their lives in perpetual
        flight, and feed on dew appear in lines 23-25 of "The
        Eolian Harp."

244.   Heninger, S.K., Jr. "A Jungian Reading of 'Kubla Khan,'"
        JAAC, 18 (1960), 358-367.

        "Kubla Khan" concerns the failure of Kubla's attempt
        at a process which both Coleridge and Jung called "indi-
        viduation," the integration of opposing forces within
        the psyche. In constructing his "mandala" (a geometric
        figure based on the number four, considered by Jung as
        an archetypal symbol of the self), Kubla hopes to

reconcile the conscious and the unconscious, the sun
and the moon, the pleasure-dome and the River Alph. He
brings these disparate elements together (11. 25-26),
but the result is only an intermingling followed by the
tumultuous disappearance of the river and the destruction of the pleasure-dome. In the despondent epilogue
the figures of the Abyssinian maid and the poet are
associated with the unconscious.

245. Kroeber, Karl. *Romantic Narrative Art*. Madison:
     University of Wisconsin Press, 1960.

     Coleridge's poems illustrate several major trends in
     Romantic narrative art. With its complicated structure,
     intricate symbolic pattern, and subtle metrical varia-
     tion, "The Ancient Mariner" contributed to the estab-
     lishment of the literary ballad, its success owing
     partly to an imaginative rather than antiquarian in-
     terest in a primitive mentality. "Kubla Khan" shows
     the sense of incompleteness in the early visionary lyric
     which resulted from a conflict between the inner order
     and the objective narrative order. "Christabel" exem-
     plifies the tendencies of the poetic tale to make the
     narrative an end in itself, to shift the perspective,
     and to emphasize pictorial beauty, timelessness, and
     stylized characters involved in a representative moral
     problem.

246. Landon, Carol. "Wordsworth, Coleridge, and the *Morning
     Post*: An Early Version of 'The Seven Sisters,'" *RES*,
     NS 11 (1960), 392-402.

     Among the contributions to the *Morning Post* provided
     by Wordsworth but evidently submitted by Coleridge is
     "The Solitude of Binnorie, or the Seven Daughters of
     Lord Archibald Campbell," a poem which Wordsworth in-
     cluded in his *Poems in Two Volumes* (1807) under the
     title "The Seven Sisters." The *Morning Post* version
     has a prefatory note probably written by Coleridge.
     Signed "M.H." for "Mountain Hermit" or "Mary Hutchinson,"
     the note praises Mary Robinson's "The Haunted Beach"
     and suggests that "The Solitude of Binnorie," as well
     as "Alcaeus to Sappho" and "The Mad Monk," was part of
     an exchange of compliments with Mary Robinson.

247. Marshall, William H. "A Coleridgean Borrowing from
     Plato," *CJ*, 55 (1960), 371-372.

     Plato's myth of the den gives unity to the first
     part of "The Destiny of Nations."

248. Parrish, Stephen Maxfield, and David V. Erdman. "Who
      Wrote 'The Mad Monk'? A Debate," *BNYPL*, 64 (1960),
      209-237.

      The authorship of "The Mad Monk" is here debated, and
      two more explanations are offered for the similarity of
      its second stanza to the first stanza of Wordsworth's
      "Intimations" ode. Instead of accepting the common
      assumption that Wordsworth borrowed from Coleridge,
      Parrish argues that "The Mad Monk" is by Wordsworth and
      that in the ode he was using his own earlier poem. The
      biographical circumstances surrounding the publication
      of "The Mad Monk" in the *Morning Post* suggest that it
      was among the poems by Wordsworth which Coleridge
      touched up, signed pseudonymously, and mailed to Stuart
      in the letter of October 7, 1800. Coleridge must have
      sent it to Mrs. Robinson, too, since her daughter re-
      printed it in *The Wild Wreath* (1804) under his name,
      without his permission to include any of his poems.
      Furthermore, there is internal evidence of Wordsworth's
      authorship. Its Gothic qualities and Sicilian setting
      are characteristic of Wordsworth's early verse and
      interests; its form, theme, and tone resemble his later
      poem "'Tis said, that some have died for love"; and its
      language--particularly in lines 21-24, which recapitu-
      late "Strange Fits of Passion Have I Known"--passes the
      concordance test as Wordsworth's.
      Erdman, on the other hand, believes that these
      Wordsworthian elements constitute a parody by Coleridge
      of Wordsworth's then-current poetry. Removed from a
      serious context in poems like "'Tis said," the hermit's
      disturbing view of nature and his jealous cry of agony
      (11. 36-37) have the effect of burlesque. His Words-
      worthian-Radcliffean vocabulary implies mockery. With
      deliberate impropriety, he uses some phrases which never
      occur in Wordsworth's poetry before 1805. Instead of a
      true Wordsworthian rustic, he is the guilty monk of
      Mrs. Radcliffe's *The Italian* or, as the signature sug-
      gests, the fellow poet of Cassiani junior, who later
      removed the outward trappings of parody, identified
      himself as Coleridge, and, in spite of his initial re-
      fusal, sent "The Mad Monk" to Miss Robinson.

249. Canceled.

250. Schulz, Max F. "S.T. Coleridge and the Poem as Improvi-
      sation," *TSE*, 10 (1960), 83-99.

Coleridge reached the furthest point in his effort to
combine spontaneity and form in the improvisation poems
--"A Tombless Epitaph," "The Reproof and Reply," "Sancti
Dominici Pallium," "A Character," "Duty Surviving Self-
Love," "Lines Suggested by the Last Words of Berengarius
ob. Anno. Dom. 1088," and "The Improvisatore." Although
these poems suffer from a lack of universal interest
and vitality as well as from the improvisator's social
unimportance and egocentricity, they are significant in
their use of the improvisator to provide both subject
and structure. They retain the solo performance of the
improvisator while suggesting an unrehearsed exchange
of talk by means of the imagined speech of a second
person, a scene description, or a prose preamble.

251. Suther, Marshall. *The Dark Night of Samuel Taylor
      Coleridge*. New York: Columbia University Press, 1960.

Coleridge failed to write any more great poetry·after
1802 not because of his preoccupation with philosophy
and theology or the interference of personal misfortunes
but because of his confusion of the poetic experience
of nature with the mystical experience of God. In most
of the poems preceding "Dejection" he expected nature
to be immediately and personally active in the trans-
mission of the divine presence. And he often used the
images of light and wind to suggest the atmosphere
appropriate to its action upon him. Actual experience,
however, did not fulfill his expectation, so that by
the time of "Dejection" he can no longer respond to
nature. He is no longer capable of the experience which
results in the creation of a poem.
    This reversal of his earlier position is evidenced in
the ode particularly by the tone and the change in his
use of the light and wind images. He conveys a tone of
protestation in his effort at the beginning of stanza 1
to be casual and detached, in the insistence of emphatic
expressions such as "our life alone" (1. 48) and "soul
itself" (1. 56), and in the piling up of images to
represent the soul's contribution to the poetic experience. (The multiplication of images may also indicate
his feeling that the light symbol is no longer adequate
or fully appropriate.) The "fair luminous cloud" (1. 54)
has now become associated with the mind's activity, and
the accustomed wind of inspiration has become a "deadly
storm." Coleridge's exploration of the possibilities
of the poetic experience as distinguished from the
artistic elaboration of it places him among the Romantic

poets, its destructive effects making his development
more similar to Rimbaud's than to that of his English
contemporaries.

252.   Ware, Malcolm.   "'The Rime of the Ancient Mariner': A
       Discourse on Prayer?" *RES*, 11 (1960), 303-304.

       The Mariner's spiritual progress closely parallels
       Coleridge's five stages of prayer.   Thus the emphasis
       of the concluding moral lies appropriately on prayer.

253.   Werkmeister, Lucyle.   "Coleridge, Bowles, and 'Feelings
       of the Heart,'" *Anglia*, 77 (1960), 55-73.

       Coleridge's early poetry substantiates his claim in
       Biographia that Bowles's poetry freed him from his en-
       slavement to metaphysics and encouraged his development
       of "feelings of the heart."   In poems such as "On Seeing
       a Youth Affectionately Welcomed by a Sister," written
       before his discovery of Bowles, Coleridge insists on
       the necessity of family attachments; yet his stoic em-
       phasis on reason made it intellectually impossible for
       him to acknowledge his "original tendencies" toward
       poetry and nature or to regard feelings as anything
       other than symptoms of moral weakness.   After 1789, how-
       ever, he accepted Bowles's view that pity is the real
       force in feeling and a strong incentive to virtue.   Al-
       though his expression of this idea differs from Bowles's,
       he uses the word "pity" frequently; and in the 1790 ver-
       sion of "Monody" he pictures Chatterton as being moved
       by pity and as representing the true poet whose powers
       of pity emanate directly from God.

                              1961

254.   Ahmad, Munir.   "A Probable Indian Source of a Coleridge
       Verse Fragment," *N&QNS*, 8 (1961), 217-218.

       Coleridge's knowledge of Eastern philosophical litera-
       ture and his plan to write an Indian poem increase the
       probability that he used the description of the Banian
       tree and the meditative Fakir, published in *The Oriental
       Collections*, in the fragmentary verses which begin, "As
       some vast Tropic tree, itself a wood."

255.   Bloom, Harold.   "Samuel Taylor Coleridge," in *The
       Visionary Company: A Reading of Romantic Poetry*
       (Garden City, New York: Doubleday, 1961), pp. 199-237.

In "The Eolian Harp" Coleridge fears the moral consequences of indulging his imagination. But on rare occasions he does liberate himself into his potential of
pure imagination: in "Frost at Midnight" with its analogy
of frost and memory; in "The Nightingale" with its contrast of the moon's effect on the passive nightingales
and on the imaginative child; in the visionary world of
"The Ancient Mariner" with its sacramental moment in
which the Mariner imaginatively perceives the connection
of all phenomena, acts, and things; in "Christabel" with
its near alliance of innocence and evil and its consequent distrust of the imagination; in "Kubla Khan" with
its triumphal chant asserting the possibility of an
imaginative paradise which would be more lasting than
Kubla's reconciliation of opposites; in the moment of
self-transcendance in "France: An Ode"; in "Dejection"
with its image of the eddy which summarizes the suggestion throughout the poem of the flux of nature; in the
"fair constellated foam" (1. 97) of "To William Wordsworth"; and in the moonlight vision of human time in
"Limbo." The interchange of light in these poems suggests the potency of the imagination and the one Life
of the phenomenal universe.

256. Bowra, C.M. "The Ancient Mariner," in *The Romantic
      Imagination* (New York: Oxford University Press, 1961),
      pp. 51-75.

Coleridge makes the supernatural events of "The
Ancient Mariner" seem convincing by exploiting the
familiar experience of dreaming, by describing nature
realistically, and by giving his characters universally
human emotions and sensations. To this, he adds a
mythological dimension with the theme of crime and
punishment, suggesting the irrationality and frivolity
of crime, the corruption, helplessness, and isolation
of guilt, and the criminal's need for confession.

257. Buckley, Vincent. "Coleridge: Vision and Actuality,"
      Melbourne Critical Review, 4 (1961), 3-17.

The most important quality of Coleridge's poetry is
its sensuousness, or vision of the actual world. In
the Conversation Poems this actualizing energy shows up
in the control and economy with which Coleridge explores
the process of reverie, in the tone of direct address,
in the movement of the verse, and in the references to
real scenes and persons. The vigor of "Kubla Khan" lies
in its dramatic organization of images and rhythmic

variation. Especially in the first four parts, "The
Ancient Mariner" develops the visionary significance of
events through the controlled use of actual details and
rhythmic flexibility and the juxtaposition of opposites.
The lack of actuality and concentration in the last
three parts helps to explain the weakness of the theme
of restored harmony.

258. Byers, John R., Jr. "Coleridge's 'Time, Real and
      Imaginary,'" *Expl*, 19 (1961), item 46.

      Recognizing the importance of both of Coleridge's
      notes on the poem, of all three divisions of time, and
      of the setting, one may interpret the race as represen-
      tative of the passing of time, the girl as symbolic of
      real time and of the present and the past, and the boy
      as standing for the future and for imaginary time.
      (Cf. items 77, 88.)

259. Erdman, David V. "Lost Poem Found: The Cooperative
      Pursuit & Recapture of an Escaped Coleridge 'Sonnet'
      of 72 lines," *BNYPL*, 65 (1961), 249-268.

      Through the cooperative efforts of several scholars
      the newspaper text of Coleridge's "The Snow-Drop" has
      been found in the *Express and Evening Chronicle* for
      January 6-9, 1798. Though not a "sonnet," it is ap-
      parently the poem referred to in the Coleridge-Robinson
      anecdote reported by Carlyon and Greenough. It is
      signed by "Francini"; and, as shown by the collation of
      the two texts printed here in parallel columns, it is
      the same as the "Zagri" poem in the Berg Collection
      manuscript, the most extensive revisions being the
      addition of a ninth stanza and the replacement of the
      howling storm with the thawing by day and freezing by
      night.

260. ————, Lucyle Werkmeister, and R.S. Woof. "Unrecorded
      Coleridge Variants: Additions and Corrections," *SB*,
      14 (1961), 236-245.

      This report corrects errors and ambiguities in the
      original list (see item 211) and adds other variants as
      a result of a more extensive survey of the newspapers.

261. Farrison, W. Edward. "Coleridge's *Christabel*, 'The
      Conclusion to Part II,'" *CLAJ*, 5 (1961), 83-94.

      Inspired by the child Hartley, the twenty-two lines
      which form the "Conclusion to Part II' were probably

composed as a part of "Christabel," even though their
only manuscript source is Coleridge's letter to Southey
of May 6, 1801. During the eight months before the
date of this letter, Coleridge was busy planning to
finish and publish the poem and constantly had it on his
mind. After publication he made a number of changes
but none in these lines. Apparently he felt that they
belonged to the poem as they were because they continue
the theme of Christabel's infancy and childhood and
because, like the first conclusion, they function as a
summary of much of the action of the preceding part.
Walking with Geraldine outside the castle, Leoline reflects in these concluding lines on the events of the
morning, on Christabel's jealous behavior in contrast
to his memory of her childhood, and on his inner conflict between paternal and romantic love.

262. Garvin, Katharine. "Snakes in the Grass (with Particular
      Attention to Satan, *Lamia*, *Christabel*)," *REL*, 2 (1961),
      11-27.

      The character of Geraldine is best explained by the
      mythological conception of the lamia, a combination of
      daemon and vampire. Although it does not harmonize
      with Gillman's summary of the conclusion, it does
      account for other details such as Geraldine's dependence
      on the imprudence of Christabel, her fear of the good
      mother's spirit, her withered bosom, her ability to
      assume either sex, and her devouring of Christabel's
      soul.

263. Gérard, Albert. "Counterfeiting Infinity: 'The Eolian
      Harp' and the Growth of Coleridge's Mind," *JEGP*, 60
      (1961), 411-422.

      Though it was a strong temptation, the idea of the one
      Life in "The Eolian Harp" (11. 26-29, 44-48) was cer-
      tainly not a definite and firmly held conviction for
      Coleridge in 1795. The statement in lines 44-48 is
      ambiguous: it is surrounded with connotations of diffi-
      dence, and the phrasing is hypothetical. Because of
      its pantheistic overtones it is dismissed as "unhallow'd"
      and "vain." But by 1797, he was able to reconcile his
      intuition of unity with Christian transcendentalism.
      The conception of nature as symbolic occurs in "This
      Lime-Tree Bower," in the 1817 addition to "The Eolian
      Harp," in "The Destiny of Nations," and in the striking
      phrase "counterfeit infinity" that appears in the letter
      of October 14, 1797, to John Thelwall. Earlier, in a

notebook entry of 1796, Coleridge had used the same
phrase to refer to the falsity of identifying nature
and spirit and to the philosophical uncertainty exem-
plified in "The Eolian Harp."

264.   Gettmann, Royal A., ed.   *"The Rime of the Ancient Mari-
       ner": A Handbook.*   San Francisco: Wadsworth Publishing
       Co., 1961.

This collection includes excerpts from Coleridge's
own statements and those of his contemporaries as well
as items 13, 49, 103, 164, 94a, 51, 108, 118, 130, 151
summarized above and Maud Bodkin's essay in *Archetypal
Patterns in Poetry: Psychological Studies of Imagination*
(London, 1934).

265.   Little, Geoffrey L.   "Christabess: By S.T. Colebritche,
       Esq.," *MLR*, 56 (1961), 215-220.

Among the early attacks on "Christabel," the anonymous
parody "Christabess: By S.T. Colebritche, Esq." deserves
consideration for its accusations of plagiarism and inappropriate versification and for its major intention
of showing that, when stripped of its Gothic trappings,
the poem lacks human interest.   (See also items 144, 30.)

266.   Marshall, William H.   "Coleridge, the Mariner, and
       Dramatic Irony," *Person*, 42 (1961), 524-532.

A simple medieval man, the Mariner interprets his experiences as a believer in anthropomorphism, which
Coleridge then regarded as superstition.   It is the
Mariner, not Coleridge, who considers the shooting of
the albatross a trivial act, who finds evidence for
universal retribution and supernatural intercession,
and who ironically bases his moral conclusions on inadequate support.

267.   ———.   "The Structure of Coleridge's 'The Eolian
       Harp,'" *MLN*, 76 (1961), 229-232.

"The Eolian Harp" is constructed upon the interaction
of two motifs--the moved and the mover, implicit in the
title as the harp and the breeze and developed in the
poem as the passive and the active, the actual and the
potential, the extensional and the imaginable, and the
female and the male.   Each of these motifs becomes dominant during two phases of the poem, creating an alter-
nating pattern of four phases (11. 1-25, 26-33, 34-43,
44-48), and then merges with the other in the last phase

as mind, or understanding, becomes the moved and faith, an aspect of reason, becomes the mover.

268. Sastri, P.S. "The Moon in Coleridge's Poetry," *IJES*, 11 (1961), 59-77.

Coleridge's poetry shows an ambivalent attitude toward the moon. It represents the creative imagination as well as wild-working fancy, redemption, joy, music, paradise, divine grace, wisdom, mysticism, and the life of the spirit as well as the dark and sinister, the mysterious, and the preternatural.

269. Schulz, Max F. "Coleridge's 'Apologetic' Prefaces," *TSE*, 11 (1961), 53-64.

Coleridge's prefaces are complex. With variable effectiveness they apologize for the faults of the fragments, juvenilia, and impromptus which they introduce while, at the same time, managing indirect praise of the poet and the poems. The prefaces to poems such as "Kubla Khan," "Fire, Famine, and Slaughter," and "The Blossoming of the Solitary Date-Tree" simultaneously absolve Coleridge of responsibility for their defects and call attention to his poetic achievement by deft use of the motifs of hard luck, youth, spontaneous composition, and favorable reception by illustrious friends.

270. Ware, J. Garth. "Coleridge's Great Poems Reflecting the Mother Imago," *AI*, 18 (1961), 331-352.

Coleridge's usually repressed fantasy of the good-bad-omnipotent mother appears with increasing clarity in his three major poems. In "The Ancient Mariner" it is represented by the figure of Life-in-Death and by the image of the moon. In "Kubla Khan" it accounts for such ambivalent imagery as that in lines 14-16 and for the intermingling of male and female sexual imagery in the third stanza. In "Christabel" it moves toward consciousness in the shocking description of Geraldine undressing, and it explains the presence within Christabel and Geraldine of both male and female traits, of both good and evil motives. Christabel, for example, has a masculine name and is associated with the masculine symbols of the oak and its mistletoe; her behavior arouses suspicion when she goes to the forest to pray instead of to the chapel and then invites Geraldine to sleep with her.

271. Ware, Malcolm. "Coleridge's 'Spectre-Bark': A Slave
      Ship?" *PQ*, 40 (1961), 589-593.

      In one of his essays in *Winter Nights: or, Fire-Side
      Lucubrations* (1820), Nathan Drake refers to "The Ancient
      Mariner" in connection with the superstition that slave
      ships would be stricken with the pestilence and con-
      demned to a period of spectral voyaging. This interpre-
      tation of the spectre-bark has the support of Coleridge's
      concern with the slavery question, his knowledge of
      other works which treat the theme of slavery in a simi-
      lar dramatic context, and his probable intention in the
      stated moral of stressing the natural bonds of man to
      man and of giving universality and scope to his allegory.

272. Watson, George. "The Meaning of 'Kubla Khan,'" *REL*, 2
      (1961), 21-29.

      "Kubla Khan" is a poem about two kinds of poetry--
      fanciful poetry, represented by the precise, matter-of-
      fact tone of lines 1-36, and imaginative poetry, sug-
      gested in the last paragraph by the Platonic allusion
      to poetic inspiration. Associated with the inferior
      poetry, Kubla is an arrogant tyrant who has degraded
      the natural river of imagination for his own artificial
      pleasure.

273. Werkmeister, Lucyle. "The Early Coleridge: His 'Rage
      for Metaphysics,'" *HTR*, 54 (1961), 99-123.

      Corroborating Coleridge's account of his early "rage
      for metaphysics," the poems of 1787 to 1791 express
      Plotinian views on suffering, virtue, and freedom.
      "Easter Holidays," for example, reflects the Plotinian
      solution to the problem of suffering: although everyone
      is subject to misfortunes, only the vicious suffer be-
      cause of them. "To the Evening Star" mentions a virtuous
      maid who will be rewarded by becoming a planetary soul,
      and "Quae Nocent Docent" refers to the concept of vir-
      tue as activity. In "Progress of Vice," "Honour," and
      "On Imitation" the fall is seen as inevitable, and
      habitual vice is explained as motivated by necessity
      rather than the expectation of pleasure. In these and
      other poems written after 1789 Coleridge becomes less
      dependent on Plotinus, introducing the idea of guilt as
      a necessary concomitant of suffering and, in "Happiness"
      and "Anthem for the Children of Christ's Hospital,"
      coloring the Plotinian thought with an attitude of
      Christian resignation.

274. Wilcox, Stewart C. "The Arguments and Motto of *The Ancient Mariner*," *MLQ*, 22 (1961), 264-268.

Coleridge's revisions of "The Ancient Mariner" help establish its thematic significance. The Argument of 1800, for example, calls attention to the Mariner's cruelty and inhospitality; and this, together with the symbolic representation of the albatross in the text, sufficiently accounts for the gravity of the Mariner's crime. The Motto, added in 1817, does not mention the fish or the term "Seraphic Philosophy," included in the full text of the passage from Burnet, which might have suggested Coleridge's water-snakes and his use of seraphic angels instead of some other kind.

275. Woodring, Carl R. *Politics in the Poetry of Coleridge*. Madison: The University of Wisconsin Press, 1961.

Except for the three major poems which only indirectly demonstrate against the times, most of Coleridge's poems are consciously political. Much of the figurative language as well as the subjects of various poetic genres shows political inspiration and purpose. Neutral words like "social," "state," "government," "nation," and "people" have emotional significance, and terms like "despot," "tyrant," "monarch," and "king" are treated more or less synonymously in the early poems. (This consistently negative attitude would suggest condemnation of the potentate Kubla Khan and his dome of wealth and pleasure.) Feelings of humanitarian pity and benevolence, of indignation at ambition and the continued war, and of distrust of commercial wealth are expressed in partisan phrases, in the many metaphors involving freedom and restraint, and in the suggestions of Pantisocracy conveyed in images of quiet vales enclosing toil, health, love, peace, and equality.

Political forces operate even more obviously in the laudatory newspaper sonnets, the partisan *jeux d'esprit*, and the exalted odes. Influenced by Milton, Bowles, and the newspapers, the series of sonnets on eminent contemporaries recognizes the ideal of the Patriot Sage in particular men—Erskine, Burke, Priestley, Kosciusko, La Fayette, Godwin, Bowles, Southey, Sheridan, and Stanhope. Among other looser poems of praise are the verses to the Duchess of Devonshire and Mary ("Perdita") Robinson, whom Coleridge commended in "To the Snow-Drop" as a fellow poet of the Opposition. He reprinted some of the journalistic poems in *Sibylline Leaves*, including odes on the Departing Year and France; "Fears in

Solitude"; "Fire, Famine, and Slaughter," showing how
Colin Clout and his fellow rustics fare under Pitt;
"The Raven," a political fable in which C.J. Fox is represented by the Raven, Burke by the Woodman, and the
Whig party or the British state by the oak; "Parliamen-
tary Oscillators," an effort to influence the vote
against Pitt's proposal to triple the assessed taxes;
"Recantation: Illustrated in the Story of the Mad Ox,"
charging Pitt with needlessly provoking the Revolution-
ists until all of France went mad; and "The Devil's
Thoughts," a sharp satire written in collaboration with
Southey. The best of these is "France: An Ode." Responding to Bonaparte's invasion of Switzerland, Coleridge weaves the themes of liberty, light, sound, and
the elements of Nature into a renunciation of government
as a source of freedom and a reliance instead on the
morality of the individual who creatively perceives the
free natural elements.

1962

276.   Bishop, Morchard.   "MS. of 'Kubla Khan,'" *TLS*, Febru-
       ary 23, 1962, p. 121.

       The importance of the Crewe manuscript has been recog-
       nized since 1938, but there is no reason to believe
       that its account of the composition of "Kubla Khan" is
       more valid than that of the 1816 Preface. (See item
       283.)

277.   Blackstone, Bernard.   "Little Boy Lost," in *The Lost
       Travellers: A Romantic Theme with Variations* (London:
       Longmans, 1962), pp. 140-180.

       Recurring throughout Coleridge's poetry are images of
       trance, or suspended motion, such as the unquivering
       flame and silent icicles in "Frost at Midnight," and
       movements of various mental travellers from psychologi-
       cal restriction to expansion and heightened awareness.
       The first half of "The Ancient Mariner," for example,
       is masculine, silent, and constrictive; the second part
       is feminine, musical, and expansive. The Virgin inter-
       venes in the place of the nightmare figure Life-in-
       Death, and the self-forgetful act of blessing replaces
       the Mariner's selfish shooting of the albatross. This
       crime is a projection of the motiveless evil of the
       whole crew of mutineers.

278. Bostetter, Edward E. "The Nightmare World of *The
      Ancient Mariner*," *SIR*, 1 (1962), 241-254.

      The world of "The Ancient Mariner" is not the orderly,
      benevolent one of Coleridge's formal philosophy but the
      grim, capricious one of his unconscious fears. Chance
      determines the punishment of the Mariner and his ship-
      mates; compulsion motivates his acts of crime and bless-
      ing; arbitrariness characterizes the action of the
      supernatural hierarchy. Such a world makes full redemp-
      tion impossible and the moral stanzas ironic.

279. Carswell, John. "'Kubla Khan,'" *TLS*, March 16, 1962,
      p. 185.

      Coleridge's description of the river in "Kubla Khan"
      must have been influenced by Fielding's rhythm and use
      of "amazing" in his account in *Tom Jones* of Squire All-
      worthy's Somerset estate. (Cf. item 238.)

280. Dowden, Wilfred S. "Thomas Moore and the Review of
      'Christabel,'" *MP*, 60 (1962), 47-50.

      In two unpublished letters--one to Jeffrey of May 23,
      1816, and another to Murray of December 24, 1816--Moore
      states that he had given up his intention of reviewing
      "Christabel." Other circumstances used by Elisabeth
      Schneider to implicate Moore (see item 288) actually
      tend to absolve him: the record in his diary of the
      bantering conversations in which he denied having written
      "A Vision; by the Author of Christabel"; the letter to
      Leigh Hunt of August 19, 1813, in which he wished to
      acknowledge "Little Man and Little Soul"; the letters
      which concern attempts to keep secret the plan and title
      of *Lalla Rookh*; and his open, honest dealings with
      Murray. (See also items 173, 180.)

281. Fogle, Richard Harter. *The Idea of Coleridge's Criti-
      cism.* Berkeley: University of California Press, 1962.

      Chapter 2, "Coleridge on Organic Unity: Life" (pp. 18-
      33), uses the structure and representation of nature in
      "This Lime-Tree Bower" as an example of Coleridge's
      theory of organic unity, a process that evolves in dis-
      tinct steps toward a reconciliation of opposites.
      Within the circular movement of the poem the poet pro-
      gresses from discontent through imaginative joy to an
      appreciation of the limited but genuine value of the
      bower. His feelings are expressed through the natural
      scenes of their setting--the deep, narrow dell, the

animated, colorful landscape, and the lime tree bower
with its distinctive yet harmonious objects and hues
which reconcile the extremes of deprivation and fullness. In their different degrees all three scenes have
life, variety, and unity.

Chapter 7, "'Christabel'" (pp. 130-159), illustrates
the dialectic method of Coleridge's Shakespearean criticism with an interpretation of that poem as the inevitable conflict of innocence and evil, brought about to
some extent by the carelessness of innocence but mainly
by the confusing complexity of evil. In contrast to
Spenser's allegorical representation of single qualities
in Archimago and the false Duessa, Coleridge's portrayal
of evil is ambiguous. Geraldine is both victim and
agent; she seems real without being specifically identified. In her waking dreams Christabel somehow links
Geraldine with her mother--an association with goodness
that is reinforced by the descriptions of Geraldine's
eyes as both small and large, dull and bright and of
her body as both ugly and beautiful, old and young. In
addition to their thematic importance, these few parti-
culars, along with the references to dreams and the
hypnotic effect of the meter, help secure the suspension
of everyday judgment required by a poem of the supernatural.

282.   Maxwell, J.C.   "'Kubla Khan,'" *TLS*, March 23, 1962,
          p. 201.

The parallel between *Tom Jones* and "Kubla Khan" (see
item 279) is also discussed by Robert Fleissner (in
item 238).

283.   "MS. of 'Kubla Khan,'" *TLS*, February 16, 1962, p. 112.

The Crewe manuscript is valuable mainly because of
the signed note relating circumstances of composition
which differ from those given in the 1816 Preface.

284.   Owen, Charles A., Jr.   "Structure in 'The Ancient
          Mariner,'" *CE*, 23 (1962), 261-267.

The meaning of the poem is partly defined by the
interrelationships of three structural elements--the
Mariner's narrative, the dialogue between him and the
Wedding-Guest, and the narrative of encounter. The
dialogue, for instance, dramatizes the conflict between
the common and the extraordinary and the main action
of conversion which are repeated in the Mariner's

narrative. The oversimplified account of vivid past
events reflects his conversion and his continuing effort
to understand it as well as the skilled manipulation of
audience gained from telling it many times.

285.   Piper, Herbert W. *The Active Universe: Pantheism and
       the Concept of Imagination in the English Romantic
       Poets.* New York: Oxford University Press, 1962.

       Chapter 2, "Coleridge: the Unitarian Poet 1794-6"
       (pp. 29-59), considers Unitarianism and Coleridge's
       early use of it, a subject treated in the earlier essay.
       (See item 226.)
       Chapter 4, "Nature and Imagination in *The Ancient
       Mariner*" (pp. 85-105), presents the material of the
       earlier lecture. (See item 171.) To this it adds more
       discussion of the idea of the imagination as a moral
       force for both Wordsworth and Coleridge and a qualifi-
       cation to D.W. Harding's explanation of the theme.
       (See item 49.)

286.   Purves, Alan C.   "Formal Structure in 'Kubla Khan,'"
       SIR, 1 (1962), 187-191.

       The regularity of the structure, particularly the
       versification, indicates the completeness and unity of
       "Kubla Khan" and reinforces its meaning. Section III
       (11. 12-24) of the first part (11. 1-36), for instance,
       is the same length as section VII (11. 42-54) of the
       second part (11. 37-54), since both sections deal with
       forces of creation. But the omission in section VII of
       the rhyme schemes in the first part associated with the
       physical surroundings of the dome, as well as the
       change from pentameters in section III to tetrameters
       in section VII, indicates the difference between the
       mode of creation of the ordinary man and that of the
       poet.

287.   Rowell, Charles H.   "Coleridge's Symbolic Albatross,"
       CLAJ, 6 (1962), 133-135.

       The qualities suggested by the color white, the role
       of savior, and the reminders of the crucifixion make
       the albatross a Christ symbol.

288.   Schneider, Elisabeth.   "Tom Moore and the *Edinburgh*
       Review of *Christabel*," *PMLA*, 77 (1962), 71-76.

       A reexamination of the evidence points even more
       strongly to Moore, rather than Hazlitt or Jeffrey, as

the author of the *Edinburgh* review of "Christabel."
In addition to the facts presented earlier (see item
173) are some unpublished letters of Moore and Hazlitt.
Moore's two letters disclose his intention of writing
a scornful article; their denials of carrying out this
plan are not very convincing in light of Moore's admitted practice of concealing his authorship when success was questionable. Hazlitt's eighteen letters
confirm every contribution to the *Edinburgh* known to be
his, but none mentions "Christabel." Also relevant are
the following unnoticed parallels between the review
and Moore's other writing: the coterie joke referring
to Lady Caroline Lamb as the "mastiff bitch"; the ridi-
cule of Coleridge's introduction to "Kubla Khan" and
his use of the term "psychological curiosity"; the in-
nuendo in the choice of the word "leap"; the use of the
classical tag "the irritable race of poets" and of
"couplet" in unusual ways; the elision in "driv'ling";
and the allusions to the advertisement of "Christabel"
in the *Morning Chronicle*, for which Moore was writing
in 1816, and to "Martinus Scriblerus'" "Bathos: or the
Art of Sinking," a known favorite of Moore. Finally,
the odd selection of "the corner of a newspaper" as a
standard of poetic quality is suitable only for Moore,
the most successful newspaper poet of the day, who constantly thought of success in these terms. (Cf. items
180, 280.)

289. Stevenson, Warren. *"Christabel*: A Re-interpretation,"
        Alphabet, No. 4 (1962), 18-35.

      On the level of subconscious symbolism, "Christabel"
depicts the psychic conflict and poetic rivalry of
Wordsworth and Coleridge. Represented by the image of
the snake coiled around the dove, their relationship
was one in which the more passive Coleridge tried un-
successfully to imitate the style of the older, taller
Wordsworth, who successfully infused his best poetry
with the philosophic awareness derived from Coleridge.
Beginning with Wordsworth's rejection of "Christabel"
from the second edition of the *Lyrical Ballads*, Coleridge felt discouraged and betrayed. His eventual loss
of poetic power and his fearful dreams identify him
with Christabel in her silence, suffering a "vision of
fear" (1. 453) and vicariously atoning for the sin of
Geraldine. Similarly, Wordsworth is linked to Geraldine
by her sinking weariness; her association with the five
senses (the "warriors" 1. 81), the oak tree, and the

Druids; and her deformity, which symbolizes Coleridge's
unconscious apprehension of the "hidden vice" that made
Wordsworth unfit for the title of divinely inspired poet.

290. Woof, R.S. "Wordsworth's Poetry and Stuart's Newspapers:
      1797-1803," *SB*, 15 (1962), 149-189.

      Presented here is an annotated checklist of over forty
      poems, later attributed to Wordsworth, which appeared in
      Daniel Stuart's newspapers, the *Morning Post* and the
      Courier, during the six years from December, 1797, to
      December, 1803. Three of these are now judged to be
      Coleridge's: "The Old Man of the Alps" and "Lewti,"
      both signed "Nicias Erythraeus," and "The Mad Monk," a
      parody of Mrs. Radcliffe signed "CASSIANI jun." (Cf.
      item 248.) On the other hand, the two fragments "The
      hour-bell sounds" and "Yet thou art happier far than
      she," presented as one poem by E.H. Coleridge, are now
      thought to be two separate poems by Wordsworth. Others,
      including "Translation of a Celebrated Greek Song,"
      "Inscription for a Seat by a Road Side," and "Alcaeus
      to Sappho," were revised for publication by Coleridge.

                            1963

291. Beer, J.B. "Coleridge and Boehme's *Aurora*," *N&QNS*, 10
      (1963), 183-187.

      In view of the poetic contexts in which it appears,
      Coleridge's theory of light and sound does find its
      imaginative ground in the passage cited in *Coleridge
      the Visionary* (see item 216a) in which Boehme describes
      angels and the ways in which they communicate with each
      other. Of the passages in *Aurora* that would have sug-
      gested the theory in more detail, there are two which
      are more convincing than those suggested by Duane B.
      Schneider. (See item 304.) And not just three but all
      the lines in a notebook entry bearing on "Kubla Khan"
      and "The Ancient Mariner" were derived from *Aurora*.

292. Beyer, Werner W. *The Enchanted Forest*. New York:
      Barnes & Noble, 1963.

      This study provides a summary of *Oberon*, includes the
      evidence for Wieland's influence on "Cain," presented
      previously in items 35 and 176, and extends the con-
      sideration of Wieland's influence to "Kubla Khan" and
      "Christabel." The following paragraphs summarize the

additions to item 24 and the chapters on "Kubla Khan"
and "Christabel."

With functional daemonic machinery and a sequence of
thematic episodes parallel to that in "The Ancient
Mariner," *Oberon* provided a matrix within which Coleridge
could organize previously unrelated literary and psychological experiences. Like "The Ancient Mariner," the
central part of *Oberon* begins with an interrupted wedding and the departure of a ship, followed by a wilful
crime on shipboard that releases daemonic vengeance,
public condemnation of the sinner, gambling for his
fate, and a frightful illusion at sundown. After a
lengthy penance Huon meets the once-worldly hermit whose
saintly intervention and life story probably helped
Coleridge to conceive the turning point of his poem.
Both hermits live in a forest above the sea and, before
hearing their confessions, mistake the sinners for
ghosts. Furthermore, Wieland's hermit is like the
Mariner--particularly in his lonely survival of the
death by plague of his loved ones, his experience during
sleep of seeing the heavenly faces of the dead and hearing angelic voices, his feeling that he is a blessed
ghost, and his discovery of the sacramental unity of
life in a vision of the beauty of heavenly light. Other
light imagery appears in both poems at the welcoming
and--along with the bird who makes the breeze blow,
the personification of the storm, the two aerial voices,
and the daemonically propelled homeward voyage--consti-
tutes part of the daemonic machinery which is strikingly
similar to Wieland's.

Unlike the other poems of 1797-98, "Kubla Khan" does
not treat the theme of sin and penance. But its four
scenes do roughly parallel the sequence in *Oberon*.
Wieland describes a paradise, for example, which has
been decreed by Titania and contains her moon cavern,
her fountains of delight, and a tumultuous river that
runs near bottomless caverns to the sea. An ancient
fir forest and rocky cliffs surround it, and nearby
lies a fertile plain with numerous rivers and cedar-
covered slopes. Titania herself resembles the "woman
wailing for her demon-lover" (1. 16), as does Rezia in
her frantic search for her lost child. The "Ancestral
voices" (1. 30) heard by Kubla have their parallel in
the voices of the dead heard by the hermit which seem
to prophesy his death and in the voices of her kidnappers heard by Rezia amid the deafening tumult of a
waterfall. The seer at the end is both a poet and the
visionary Huon, daemonically favored and guided. Like

Huon, he is inspired by a damsel and replies to her
song. His rapture corresponds to Huon's and Rezia's delight when they are being borne through the air to
Oberon's palace, and his awed observers may be the enchanted dancers, victims of Oberon's punitive power.

For "Christabel," *Oberon* did not provide a complete
narrative sequence, but it did offer suggestions for
certain incidents and characters, especially the vampiric
serpent-daemon Geraldine. She seems to be a daemon who
has fallen from grace and is therefore, unlike Oberon,
intimidated by the divine. She resembles him in being
both malevolent and benevolent, in having certain daemonic powers, and in acknowledging heavenly beings.
She is caught in a strait between good and evil because
she is a composite of the gentle Titania and the beautiful lamia-like temptress Almansaris, who is herself both
gentle and savage. Huon's mysterious nocturnal encounter
with her suggests Geraldine's meeting with Christabel.
And Geraldine's kidnapping recreates his abandonment
under a tree, his moaning and being carried in a trance
across "the shade of night," as well as Rezia's brutal
abduction by a band of pirates. The circumstantial details of Rezia's life and her premonitory fears of ruina-
tion and snakebite reappear in the characterization of
Christabel. Her attack resembles the kidnapping of the
devout Lady Angela on a moonlit night by a werwolf who
later arises fresh and strong from a miraculous sleep.
The fact that *Oberon* ends with reconciliation and redemption supports other indications that in Part II,
Coleridge must have veered from his original intentions.
More important, however, is the emphasis which such
literary influences place on the role of the conscious
in Coleridge's creative process.

293.   Bostetter, Edward E. "Coleridge," in *The Romantic
       Ventriloquists: Wordsworth, Coleridge, Keats, Shelley,
       Byron* (Seattle: University of Washington Press, 1963),
       pp. 82-135.

This chapter extends the idea, first developed in
item 278, of the conflict between Coleridge's desire to
affirm a benevolent universe and his imaginative perception of evil. "Kubla Khan" ends with frustration and
uncertainty because he believes that the realization of
his poetic power depends upon revival of the confidence
and faith expressed in the frenzied, striving rhetoric
of his early poems. "The Ancient Mariner" presents a
universe of unpredictable, despotic forces, including

the Mariner's own sadistic impulse which Coleridge saw
in himself as well. He manages to reach a more or less
positive resolution, but in "Christabel" he could not
devise an ending in which good prevailed. Evil victimizes
both Christabel and Geraldine and, in the conclusion to
Part II, intermixes with good in Coleridge's personal
experience. On the evidence of "Dejection," he has not
lost his poetic imagination but the power to control its
direction.

294.   Bouslog, Charles S.   "Structure and Theme in Coleridge's
        'Dejection: An Ode,'" *MLQ*, 24 (1963), 42-52.

Originally a verse letter to Sara Hutchinson, Coleridge's "Dejection" suffers from the structural and
thematic changes which are frequently concerned with
concealment rather than aesthetics. Although the revised structure is more obviously logical than the
associational thought sequence of the longer letter,
the last three stanzas of the ode are forced, rhetorical,
and intrusive--particularly the reference to the lost
child and the wishes for the mysterious "Lady." In its
final, generalized form the poem deals only with Coleridge's inability to respond to nature. It omits personal material such as the hints of domestic discord,
the ill effects on him of his children, and the references to Mary and Sara Hutchinson. Instead of being
mentioned directly, these details are reduced to a private symbolism meaningful only to a few intimate friends.

295.   Braekman, W.   "An Unpublished Poem by S.T. Coleridge,"
        N&QNS, 10 (1963), 181-182.

Printed here for the first time is Coleridge's "Lines
sent with a collection of MSS. to John May Esqr.," a
poem dated May 31, 1812, found among the British Museum
manuscripts in a collection known as *"Farewell to Eton,*
and many other poems, by various members of the Coleridge
family."

296.   Doughty, Oswald.   "Coleridge and a Poet's Poet: William
        Lisle Bowles," *EM*, 14 (1963), 94-114.

In *Biographia Literaria* and elsewhere Coleridge publicly
declared his indebtedness to Bowles's critical principles
as well as to his poetry. The young Coleridge was attracted by Bowles's contemporaneity and sensitivity and by
the intimacy and simplicity of his sonnets. As Coleridge
matured, his opinion became more detached and critical;

but he never renounced Bowles's influence, and in later
years while living at Calne he cultivated the vicar's
friendship.

297.   Dunlap, Rhodes.   "Verses by Coleridge," *PQ*, 42 (1963),
       282-284.

       Now in a manuscript in the University of Iowa Library,
       the six unpublished lines which Coleridge dated Septem-
       ber 23, 1833, are typical of his late religious verse,
       though perhaps they echo the earlier "Hymn before Sun-
       rise" and "Dejection."

298.   Gerber, Richard.   "Keys to 'Kubla Khan,'" *ES*, 44 (1963),
       321-341.

       The myth of the earth- and mother-goddess Cybele fig-
       ures significantly in the four parts of the sonata-like
       movement of "Kubla Khan." The fusion in Coleridge's
       dreaming mind of Cybele, or Kubele, and Kubla explains
       the association in lines 1-5 of Kubla, his dome, walls,
       and towers with Alph and the caverns and the shift
       within the second part (ll. 6-30) to the savage yet holy
       and enchanted landscape of ancient forests, a woman
       wailing for her demon lover, the waning moon, and the
       panting earth. In lines 31-36 the oppositions between
       the worlds of Kubla and Cybele become miraculously rec-
       onciled: the caverns and the tumult become the caves
       and the musical measure. In the coda of lines 37-54
       Cybele and her priests explain the references to the
       Abyssinian maid, who is a part of the general transfor-
       mation to harmony and to the ecstatic poet.

299.   Harding, D.W.   "The Theme of 'The Ancient Mariner,'" in
       Experience into Words: Essays on Poetry (London:
       Chatto & Windus, 1963), pp. 53-71.

       This article is a revised version of item 49 with
       further emphasis on the private nature of the Mariner's
       guilt and on the fortuitousness of his act of blessing.
       In addition, it qualifies Lowes's statement of theme and
       evaluates psychoanalytic studies such as those of David
       Beres and Maud Bodkin. Beres's Freudian interpretation
       of the albatross (see item 127) and Bodkin's importation
       of the Jungian idea of rebirth exemplify the inaccurate,
       imprecise handling of text often characteristic of psycho-
       analytic criticism.

300.   Maxwell, J.C.   "Coleridge: A False Attribution," *N&QNS*,
       10 (1963), 182.

Attributed to Coleridge, the poem "The Cherub" is
really a truncated version of James Hogg's parody of
Coleridge.

301. Pafford, Ward. "Coleridge's Wedding-Guest," *SP*, 60
      (1963), 618-626.

The Wedding-Guest functions as an obvious foil for the
Mariner and, at the same time, reinforces the theme of
love since his experience parallels the Mariner's. When
the Mariner stops him, he displays the qualities of
pride, arrogance, and cruel whimsy which motivated the
Mariner's crime. From flippancy, his attitude gradually
progresses to nearly complete passiveness, modified by
occasional fearful protests arising from his childish,
superstitious nature and by the concern and sympathy
shown at the end of Part I. By the end of the Mariner's
story, each has moved toward the other, the Mariner using
simple, direct moralizing to reach his hearer's limited
understanding and the Wedding-Guest becoming wiser and
less worldly.

302. Ridenour, George M. "Source and Allusion in Some Poems
      of Coleridge," *SP*, 60 (1963), 73-95.

Awareness of source and allusion in some of Coleridge's
poems increases our understanding of the poems and our
respect for the poet. A reading of the German originals,
for instance, can make us sensitive to the significant
omissions in "On a Cataract" and "Catullian Hendecasyl-
lables." A comparison of "First Advent of Love" with
Sidney's *Arcadia*, Book I, reveals the originality with
which Coleridge uses the conventional combination of
the delicate and the vigorous. Cowper's "Retirement"
(ll. 347-364) makes explicit the religious context of
stanza 4 of "Dejection," a poem which is itself a commentary on the movement from passivity to activity in "The
Garden of Boccaccio." Another dialogue is that between
"Constancy to an Ideal Object" and *The Prelude*, VIII,
397-405, the result being an emphasis on Coleridge's
suggestion of the illusory quality of the imaginative
experience. Finally, Boehme's *Forty Questions Concerning
the Soul, The Threefold Life of Man*, and *Election of
Grace* not only add enrichment but contribute to the
meaning of Coleridge's "Ode to the Departing Year,"
"Limbo," and "Ne Plus Ultra," each of which shows a
Boehmenist preoccupation with the nature of time and
eternity.

303. Rodway, Allan Edwin. "Radical Romantic Poets: Coleridge,"
      in *The Romantic Conflict* (London: Chatto & Windus,
      1963), pp. 159-175.

      During the period of social conflict from 1797 to 1803,
      Coleridge wrote his best poetry--the three major poems
      and the less imaginative "Dejection" and "Frost at Mid-
      night." "The Ancient Mariner" and "Kubla Khan" are dream
      poems to be experienced rather than interpreted. The
      Mariner's shipmates, for example, are reminiscent but
      not consciously symbolic of the mob or public opinion;
      the sun peering through the grate hints at an outer con-
      flict; the albatross at times has symbolic significance,
      but in other contexts it is just a companionable bird;
      the sense of stillness and potentiality conveyed at one
      point by the silent sea later becomes a sort of death.
      The course of the river in "Kubla Khan" has several
      parallels, the strongest of which is the overthrow of
      tyranny.

304. Schneider, Duane B. "Coleridge's Light-Sound Theory,"
      N&QNS, 10 (1963), 182-183.

      Certain passages from Jacob Boehme's *Aurora* describing
      the sixth property of sound seem more probable as a
      source for Coleridge's theory of the relationship between
      light and sound than the passage cited by J.B. Beer in
      Coleridge the Visionary. (See item 216a.)

305. ————. "The Structure of 'Kubla Khan,'" *American Notes
      and Queries*, 1 (1963), 68-70.

      The dialectical structure of thesis (ll. 1-11), an-
      tithesis (ll. 12-30), and synthesis (ll. 31-36) prepares
      for the ultimate reconciliation of opposites in the image
      of the sunny palace which contains suggestions of dark-
      ness, decay, and death.

306. Schulz, Max F. *The Poetic Voices of Coleridge: A Study
      of His Desire for Spontaneity and Passion for Order.*
      Detroit: Wayne State University Press, 1963.

      Coleridge's poems exhibit at least seven different
      modes, or voices--farrago, prophecy, ventriloquism, con-
      versation, dream, confession, and improvisation. In
      each of them he tries to combine spontaneity and form
      and to reproduce the natural cadences of speech. The
      farrago poems include such youthful efforts as "Sonnets
      Attempted in the Manner of Contemporary Writers," "To a

Young Friend Who Had Declared His Intention of Writing
No More Poetry," "Lines Composed in a Concert-Room," and
"A Christmas Carol." Treating themes of political and
social reform, friendship, and poetry, they distort for
ironic effect the inflated rhetoric and digressive
thought of the poetry of sentiment. They remain ineffective, however, without the unity of tone necessary for
immediately apparent, sharply realized satire.

The prophecy poems rely initially on the tradition of
sublimity but derive their unity increasingly from the
poetic material rather than from the external form of
the ode. The unity of "Dejection," for example, stems
from the image of the storm, supported by the motifs of
fertility-sterility and freedom-restriction. The nature
imagery objectifies Coleridge's ambivalent feelings and
suggests his increased dejection and continued constric-
tion of imagination. In "Hymn before Sunrise" the com-
prehensiveness of the mountain reconciles the opposites
of light and dark, animate and inanimate, silence and
sound, and so provides an emblem of the poet's consciousness.

By imitating the colloquial diction and stark action
of the ballad, the ventriloquism poems affect a simplicity and naturalness unavailable to the farrago and
prophecy poems. But only in "The Ancient Mariner" and
Part I of "Christabel" does this affected simplicity
become transformed into the genuine inflection of Coleridge's own voice. The success of these efforts is due
largely to the fusion of two kinds of poetry, or two
points of view--the balladic and the lyrical. In "The
Ancient Mariner," for example, the incidents of the
albatross and the water-snakes have both narrative and
moral significance. With other details, though--such
as the presence of the Wedding-Guest and the death of
the crew under the star-dogged moon--only the primary
view operates. And the dominance of the lyrical elements in the second half of the poem foreshadows the
sacrifice in "Christabel," Part II, of narrative movement and realism to the use of the preternatural, elab-
orately detailed landscapes, and well-expressed sentiments.

The Conversation Poems probably achieve the most satisfying balance of spontaneity and form. Addressing a
friend or relative, they convey the spontaneity of conversation through brevity, apparent lack of structure,
and the natural rhythms of speech which characterize
their blank verse. At the same time, they impose order
and control through a circular pattern of mood and

thought: the philosophy of the one Life, which gives
unity to such an apparently digressive poem as "The
Nightingale"; a cluster of images--including harp, wind,
sun or moon, and their reflected lights--expressive of
this philosophy; and a central unifying image such as
the silence in "Frost at Midnight." Each of the poems
traces two calm-exaltation-calm parabolas within which
the centrifugal-centripetal action of the poet's mind
advances his understanding beyond what it was at the
starting point. At the beginning of "Frost at Midnight,"
for example, the silence disturbs him, but by the end
he understands that the silent formation of frost, the
quiet breathing of Hartley, and the growth of his own
thought are all related by means of the eternal processes
of life in nature and man.

Like the Conversation Poems, the dream poems are
characterized by two cycles of mental contraction and
expansion, a retrospective mood, and a low-keyed tone.
They reproduce the spontaneity of the reverie without
its lack of unity, since the poet's response to his day-
dream gives it wholeness and his dominant sensations control the flow of images. Feelings of warmth and tranquility appear in each of the three scenes of "A Day-
Dream" and help explain the association of the flickering
lights of the glowworm and the stars with the sparkling
fountain and the dancing flames. Such merging of past
and present, of mental impression and external object,
distinguishes most of the dream poems from the Conversation Poems. In "Kubla Khan," however, the visionary
past stands in static opposition to the present actuality. Unlike the dreamer-poet, whose reverie is forever
vanishing, Kubla has been able to give actuality to his
dreams in the form of a paradise which for a time reconciles the measurable and the immeasurable, the temporal
and the eternal.

In contrast to the serenity and the wholeness of the
dream poems are the melancholy sense of isolation and
the inconclusiveness of the confession poems. As in
"The Pains of Sleep," Coleridge looks to the past in an
unsuccessful effort to discover reasons for his present
hopelessness. When he attempts in "Youth and Age" only
to dramatize his feelings of inadequacy, he manages to
avoid the usual inconclusiveness and uncertainty of tone
and direction. He universalizes his particular experience of growing old in a pleasing harmony of the thesis-
antithesis-synthesis structure and the body-nature
imagery. (For a summary of Schulz's discussion of the
improvisation poems, see item 250. Chapter VIII, "The

Improvisation Voice," is a revision of his earlier
article, with only a few stylistic changes and added
details on the history of the publication of "The Blossoming of the Solitary Date-Tree.")

Even the more formal songs, which critics tend to ignore, show the reconciliation of spontaneity and form
and of sound and sense which characterizes Coleridge's
best poetry. Glycine's song is typical of the others
in this respect as well as in its carefully structured
communication of the transience of life. In conclusion,
each of Coleridge's poems follows a specific form, but
the most successful ones combine the conversational mode
of development, the reminiscent point of view, and the
one Life frame of reference.

307. Skeat, T.C.   "'Kubla Khan,'" *British Museum Quarterly*,
      26 (1963), 77-83.

In the now freely available Crewe manuscript of "Kubla
Khan," Coleridge has written an alternative account of
its composition which tends to support studies of its
unity and sources and to discredit the accuracy of the
details in the defensive Preface of 1816.

308. Smith, Gayle S.   "A Reappraisal of the Moral Stanzas in
      The Rime of the Ancient Mariner," *SIR*, 3 (1963), 42-52.

Incongruous in tone and content with the central moral
vision, the two stanzas of explicit moral are part of
the comic framework. As a reminder of the commonplace
world, they intensify the sublime experience which
neither the Mariner nor his listener understands.

309. Smith, Raymond J., Jr.   "The Imagery of 'Christabel,'"
      McNeese Review, 14 (1963), 32-44.

The imagery of "Christabel" functions to unify its
parts, including the Conclusion to Part II. Throughout
the poem, Coleridge uses color imagery: red and blue,
associated with Christabel, suggest vitality and grace,
while green and white, associated with Geraldine, con-
note false vitality and death. In Part I images such as
the veiled moon, the nearly-still wind, and the silent
birds convey Christabel's temporary spiritual isolation;
the impotent mastiff, the ineffectual gate, and the for-
gotten shield suggest her lack of physical protection.
In Part II the central image of the snake-dove struggle
underlines her inner conflict as well as the outward
conflict between her and Geraldine for the confidence of

the Baron. It also activates earlier snake images and
lends an ironic tone to later snake and dove figures.

310. Werkmeister, Lucyle. "Some Whys and Wherefores of Coleridge's 'Lines Composed in a Concert-Room,'" *MP*, 60
(1963), 201-205.

On the basis of its political and biographical allusions and its emphasis on the importance of feelings,
Coleridge's "Lines Composed in a Concert-Room" should be
dated late April or early May, 1789. The "lady," the
"pert Captain," and the "primmer Priest" of the opening
lines refer to Mary Wells, Edward Topham, and the Rev.
Charles Este--all associated with the *World*--while in
the closing lines "Freedom's latest foe," the *World*,
opposes "Freedom's center," the spurious *Star*. In the
central part of the poem the speaker wants to leave the
people in the concert room, who are incapable of responding to music or nature, for an area recognizable as
Ottery and for the company of those whose feelings are
uncorrupted--the Rev. Fulwood Smerdon, and "Anne," Coleridge's sister who died in 1791. (Cf. item 275.)

1964

311. Berkoben, Lawrence D. "*Christabel*: A Variety of Evil
Experience," *MLQ*, 25 (1964), 400-411.

The naive speaker of "Christabel" contributes to its
blurred distinctions of good and evil by his ambiguous
attitudes toward the protagonists and by his narrative
technique. He frequently asks a rhetorical question and
answers it, a device which helps develop the echo motif
seen in Christabel's response to Geraldine's repeated
request to stretch forth her hand; in her imitation of
Geraldine's ophidian traits; and in the images of the
cock answering the owls, the mastiff groaning at the
sound of the clock, and, most explicitly, the distortion
by the sinful ghosts and the devil of the peal of the
matin bell. Such distortions of goodness presented a
moral problem which Coleridge could never solve.

312. Braekman, W. "A Reconsideration of the Genesis of S.T.
Coleridge's Poem '.On Taking Leave of ----,'" *N&QNS*,
11 (1964), 21-24.

The original version of Coleridge's "On Taking Leave
of ----" is not the longer "To Two Sisters," contributed

to the *Courier* for December 10, 1807, but the short farewell "To M.M. and C.B.," dated November 22, 1807, discovered among a collection of autographs recently acquired
by the British Museum.

313.   Buchan, A.M.   "The Sad Wisdom of the Mariner," *SP*, 61
       (1964), 669-688.

From the Mariner's tale, the Wedding-Guest learns the
sad truth that man's destiny is controlled by mysterious,
omnipotent spirits and that his sensory impressions and
emotions are far more effective than his will and reason.
On the few occasions when the Mariner does exert himself,
his action is meaningless, without reason, justification,
or approval. He lays his hand on the Wedding-Guest to
detain him, but he tells his story because he is driven
by an anguish he can neither understand nor restrain.
He shoots the albatross for no reason at all but then
feels responsible for a willful crime. He inflicts pain
on himself in order to hail a ship, the spectre-bark.
He blesses the water-snakes, but he was "unaware" and
gives the credit to his kind saints. He joins the dead
sailors in working the tackle; but the routine is pointless, and his nephew does not speak to him. Finally,
he picks up the oars to help row the pilot's boat but
terrifies those who have come to save him.
     In his literary criticism, Coleridge continued to
recognize the chaotic world below the will and reason;
and though he had moments of joy and calm like that in
"Frost at Midnight," he could never really share Wordsworth's trust in the sensory world.

314.   Chayes, Irene H.   "Rhetoric as Drama: An Approach to the
       Romantic Ode," *PMLA*, 79 (1964), 67-79.

The merging of rhetorical and dramatic structure which
distinguishes the Romantic ode first appeared in Coleridge's "Dejection," where, by means of the rhetorical
progression in stanza 7, the speaker moves outward in a
reversal of direction that leads to the threshold of
creativity. Expressing the anguish which he has been
unable to feel, the borrowed image of the screaming
lost child at the end of the stanza suggests that his
emotions have been awakened and purged but that an actual
revival of his lost creativity is still in the future.

315.   Empson, William.   "The Ancient Mariner," *CQ*, 6 (1964),
       298-319.

In "The Ancient Mariner," Coleridge uses material
from the reports of the European maritime expansion to
express his disapproval of the Christian plan of redemption by suffering and to explore his own mental condition of "neurotic guilt." The Mariner feels burdened
with guilt, even though by his own principles he does
no wrong. After all, he kills the bird for food, the
storm having prevented revictualling; and it is the
mariners' invented superstition which causes them to
blame him. He does try to get help, but his heroic
effort results in their death and his continued penance--
fates determined by a game of dice. His suffering is
lessened when he surprises himself by admiring the creatures which earlier, when they had legs, he despised.

316. Enscoe, Gerald E. "Ambivalence in 'Kubla Khan': The
      Cavern and the Dome," *BuR*, 12 (1964), 29-36.

The speaker in "Kubla Khan" dreams of a beautifully
ordered garden, threatened with destruction by elements
which are both holy and enchanted, attractive and sus-
pect. In his final description, "A sunny pleasure-dome
with caves of ice!" (1. 36), he recognizes that hidden,
destructive forces are an integral part of the dome,
which possibly may not even exist on earth. In the last
section of the poem, having lost his vision of the dome,
he plans, if sufficiently inspired, to recreate it
through poetry.

317. Marcovitz, Eli. "Bemoaning the Lost Dream: Coleridge's
      'Kubla Khan' and Addiction," *IJP-A*, 45 (1964), 411-425.

One of the meanings of "Kubla Khan" concerns the loss
of the dream which was central to Coleridge's personality
and drug addiction. This fantasy--that he was a God-
poet-hero, nursed by a mother whose love and protection
would enable him to conquer his enemies and to win the
adoration of all witnesses--appears in several images.
The figure of Kubla Khan, for example, is a projection
of the self he wished to be, the Tartar turned creator;
and the pleasure-dome suggests his mother's breast.
Derived from the *Aeneid*, the three images of Alph, the
ancestral voices, and Mount Abora symbolize language or
the mouth, his oedipal struggle and failure to meet the
challenges of manhood, and the conflicts between the
mother and her children. The dreaded figure at the end
of the poem represents the typical revenge fantasy of
the child who has been shamed and humiliated.

318. McDonald, Daniel. "Too Much Reality: A Discussion of
      'The Rime of the Ancient Mariner,'" *SEL*, 4 (1964),
      543–554.

      Except for the Hermit, the characters in the poem
      struggle to avoid the reality which is suddenly forced
      upon them by the Mariner's experience of the physical
      mysteries of life, death, and the horrible grandeur of
      nature; the mental mysteries of primitive impulses,
      dreams, and guilt; and the spiritual mysteries of super-
      natural figures implementing a harsh moral law. In
      blessing the water-snakes the Mariner unconsciously
      accepts himself and his world, but he welcomes those
      events which bring his ship home. He does not choose
      to remind himself of the distressing facts of the human
      condition; nor do the Wedding-Guest, the Pilot, or his
      boy wish to hear them.

318a. Preston, Thomas R. "'Christabel' and Mystical Tradition,"
      in *Essays and Studies in Language and Literature*
      (Duquesne Studies, Philological Series, 5), ed.
      Herbert H. Petit (Pittsburgh: Duquesne University
      Press, 1964), pp. 138–157.

      An examination of the bedroom enchantment scene against
      a background of Crashaw's Theresan hymns and Boehme's
      mystical theology establishes the sexual embrace as a
      metaphor for Christabel's mystical union with the Divine.
      Within this metaphor, Geraldine seems to symbolize
      Christ and, like Boehme's Virgin Sophia, to be dual-
      sexed. Geraldine's embraces are good, though to the
      narrator they appear evil. Christabel does receive the
      embraces in pain, but her suffering, like St. Theresa's,
      is also pleasurable. Through her suffering she moves
      from physical to spiritual love; and, though she awakens
      with a sense of having sinned, she remains innocent and
      receives the protection of heaven. The embraces of
      Geraldine have personally illuminated her, as is sug-
      gested by the moon and light imagery. In contrast, Sir
      Leoline and Langdale Hall, both in need of salvation,
      are associated with shadows, death, and the drowsy cock.
      Sir Leoline's rejection of Christabel, as well as Cole-
      ridge's own statement, point to her eventual "desolation,"
      a mystic state following illumination and preceding the
      final mystic union.

319. Radley, Virginia L. "*Christabel*: Directions Old and
      New," *SEL*, 4 (1964), 531–541.

In the interest of a more valid criticism, studies of
"Christabel" should examine the notebooks and other relevant external evidence to find more information on the
date of composition, on Coleridge's knowledge of sexual
perversion, and on what he considered real. In addition
to support for the psychological interpretation of the
poem (see items 51, 65, 135), criticism needs a new
larger frame of reference which would combine the psychological with the logical approach (see item 30). One
possibility for such a reading is based on Coleridge's
intention of writing a series of poems reflective of all
aspects of love. It views the poem as a treatment of
ambivalence within four kinds of love--Christabel's for
Geraldine, Leoline's for Christabel, Leoline's for Lord
Roland, and Geraldine's for Christabel.

320. Raine, Kathleen. "Traditional Symbolism in 'Kubla Khan,'"
      SR, 72 (1964), 626-642.

      "Kubla Khan" treats the theme of the imaginative ex-
perience in the symbolic language of the Platonic and
Neoplatonic traditions. The river Alph, for example, is
reminiscent of the Cabalist symbol of the river of life
which flows from its unmanifested divine origin to the
lowest plane of manifestation, or matter. The image of
reflection (11. 31-32) suggests the Platonic concept of
the temporal world as a reflection of the eternal forms,
and the Abyssinian maid figures forth the recollection
necessary for the poet to re-create harmony in his poem.
The references to milk and honey (11. 53-54) echo
Plato's description of inspiration.

321. Rapin, René. "Coleridge's Dejection: An Ode, 76-95,"
      ES, 45 (1964), Supp., 220-222.

      The "viper thoughts" which constitute Coleridge's
"dark dream" (11. 94, 95) in stanza 7 of "Dejection"
are the "afflictions" (1. 82) of the previous stanza,
and "abstruse research" (1. 89) refers to his reading
and meditating on abstract books of science and philosophy. (Cf. item 151.)

322. Roppen, Georg. "Coleridge and the Mariner's Sea-Change,"
      in *Strangers and Pilgrims: An Essay on the Metaphor
      of Journey* (Norwegian Studies in English, XI), ed.
      Georg Roppen and Richard Sommer (New York: Humanities
      Press, 1964), pp. 172-208.

The dialectical structure of the objective voyage
dramatizes the Mariner's spiritual journey from crime to
expiation. A metaphoric dimension is established from
the outset by the vagueness of the ship's mission and
route. Instead of specific geographic terms, the ignorant but sensitive Mariner records his experience in the
imagery of climate and elements. The storm and the ice,
for example, reflect the fear, confusion, and desolation
which pervert his will and inhibit his awareness of the
divine living order represented by the albatross. Killing the bird of love and direction falls into the antithetical rhythm continued throughout the voyage by such
opposites as sunrise and sunset, the glorious and the
bloody sun, the wind and the calm, endless water and
nothing to drink, fixity and motion, day and night,
hideousness and beauty, life and death. The main points
of contrast, corresponding to the Mariner's crime and
expiation, are the land of ice and the tropical seas,
which are fused in his pastoral vision (ll. 367-372).

323.   Rudrum, A.W. "Coleridge's 'This Lime-Tree Bower My
       Prison,'" *SoRA*, 1 (1964), 30-42.

Although Coleridge scholars have given it little attention, "This Lime-Tree Bower" is a rich and complex poem.
Its convincing demonstration of the power of the imagination gives a satisfying sense of completeness which
derives partly from the order and harmony of its images.
In its revised form the images of the first paragraph
move down the scale of being from the poet's friends to
the individual, energetic ash and the nameless, relatively
passive file of weeds to the blue clay-stone. In contrast, the images of the second paragraph ascend from
man to God. The transfiguration of nature in which God
is revealed is prepared for by the vitality and dignity
of the ash, the sense of release in the sudden enlarge-
ment of perspective, and the bark whose sails "light up"
(l. 24) the blue sea. Like the final transfiguring
image of the black rook flying into the glorious sunlight, the bark brings together the two dark islands,
and the ash reconciles the opposite kinds of movement
within the dell.

324.   Schulz, Max F. "The Wry Vision of Coleridge's Love
       Poetry," *Person*, 45 (1964), 214-226.

After 1810 the joyful idealism of Coleridge's early
love poetry becomes a wry recognition that the idea must
be rooted in the actual, that unnourished love will die.

Poems like "The Happy Husband" and "Recollections of
Love" eulogize an immutable love-sense which in other
poems is associated with a permanent home. In "The
Eolian Harp" and "Reflections" the flowers surrounding
the honeymoon cottage help suggest love. But in "The
Improvisatore" and "Love's Apparition and Evanishment"
love is ephemeral--a "drooping plant" (1. 10), an "annual flower" that will never revive (1. 27). These
late poems as well as the earlier ones reflect Coleridge's
longing for domestic affection, both marital and maternal. His fixed response to the frustration of this need
partly accounts for his failure to write any great love
poetry.

325. Wasserman, Earl R. "The English Romantics: The Grounds
      of Knowledge," *SIR*, 4 (1964), 17-34.

      Coleridge's epistemology provides the dramatic form
      for his Conversation Poems. In "This Lime-Tree Bower,"
      for instance, the isolated speaker uses his imagination
      to accompany his friend Charles Lamb through the dell
      to the glowing plain.

326. Whalley, George. "'Late Autumn's Amaranth': Coleridge's
      Late Poems," *PTRSC*, 4th Ser., 2 (1964), 159-179.

      Contrary to the suggestion of a few lines in "Dejec-
      tion," Coleridge's late poems show that his poetic powers
      did not die in 1802 but continued to develop until his
      death in 1834. In the central, more productive years
      from 1797 to 1807, Coleridge had written poems in seve-
      ral different styles, including contemporary, rhetorical-
      political, conversational, and symbolic. After 1807 he
      modulated the conversational manner in the personal Asra
      poems and in the increasingly honest self-portraits, but
      in the later emblem and metaphysical poems he consciously
      turned from naturalistic imagery, logical sequences,
      smooth transitions, blank verse, and intricate stanzaic
      forms to a highly stylized, more literary, intellectual,
      and abstract imagery, allegory and dialogue, bold and
      abrupt collisions, couplets, and rough rhythms. Cole-
      ridge's attitude toward these changes is indicated by
      the inclusion of nearly all of the late poems in his
      last collected edition.

1965

327. Abrams, M.H. "Structure and Style in the Greater Roman-
      tic Lyric," in *From Sensibility to Romanticism: Essays*

Presented to Frederick A. Pottle, ed. Frederick W.
Hilles and Harold Bloom (New York: Oxford University
Press, 1965), pp. 527-560.

Displacing the neoclassical "greater ode" as the
favored form for the long lyric poem, the greater Romantic lyric evolved from the eighteenth-century local poem,
primarily through Bowles's sonnets, and has its closest
analogue in the seventeenth-century devotional poems.
Its structure and style were firmly established by the
interchange of mind and particularized nature in the
easy blank-verse paragraphs of Coleridge's "The Eolian
Harp." This intimate address to a silent auditor was
followed by his other Conversation Poems, including two
masterpieces of the greater lyric, "Frost at Midnight"
and "Dejection." The meditation in these poems expands
the unstated significance of the outer scene with which
the poems begin and end.

328. Boulger, James D. "Christian Skepticism in *The Rime of
the Ancient Mariner*," in *From Sensibility to Romanticism: Essays Presented to Frederick A. Pottle,* ed.
Frederick W. Hilles and Harold Bloom (New York: Oxford
University Press, 1965), pp. 439-452.

An analysis of the structure of "The Ancient Mariner"
shows that like the *Aeneid,* it presents a dream world
that is neither irrational nor sacramental. It is a
world of pure imagination, of effects whose causes are
spiritual but unknown. Normal logic cannot account for
the morality of shooting the albatross, the presence of
the various spirits, the appearance of sun and moon, the
speed of the voyages to and from the Pole, the Mariner's
trance, or for that matter his fall and redemption.
During the voyage he becomes skeptical of "reality" and
ordinary ways of knowing—hence the significance of his
perception of objects at sea mainly in terms of color
rather than form.

329. ————. "Imagination and Speculation in Coleridge's
Conversation Poems," *JEGP*, 64 (1965), 691-711.

In spite of the contradictions in the speculative sys-
tems upon which they are based, the Conversation Poems
achieve a precarious, temporary unity derived from the
power of the imagination to control the imagery. In
"The Eolian Harp," for example, the passive image of the
wind-harp helps express an idealistic view of the world
(11. 44-48) which assumes the projective theory of the

mind. And the passive impression of clouds "rich with light" (1. 4) leads to the light of the "one Life" (1. 26). The images of light and darkness in "This Lime-Tree Bower" come together in the dusk at the end of the poem when the speaker submerges his feelings of fear and uncertainty in the imaginative act of blessing the rook. In "Frost at Midnight" the image of light appears in the descriptions of the poet's active imaginative experience as well as the child's passive absorption of nature's good influences. Then at the end of the poem the child's education is accomplished by the cooperation of the passive redbreast, apple tree, and thatch under the sun with the active ministry of frost under the moon.

330. Braekman, W. "The Influence of William Collins on Poems Written by Coleridge in 1773," *Revue des Langues Vivantes*, 31 (1965), 228-239.

It was not in 1776 as has been thought but in the summer of 1773 that Coleridge first became interested in Collins' poetry. As he traveled from Cambridge to his home in Ottery St. Mary, he must have been reading a copy of Langhorne's edition of Collins, for on its fly-leaves he has penciled two poems, "The Rose" and "Kisses," which echo words and images from Collins' "Ode to Simplicity" and "Ode on the Poetical Character." Another poem linked with this period, "Absence: A Poem" ("Lines on an Autumnal Evening") sounds like Collins, though some canceled lines show specific reminders of Gray's ode "The Progress of Poesy."

331. Bryant, E.P. "'The Rime of the Ancient Mariner': A Coleridgean Reading," *Standpunte*, 18 (1965), 15-30.

Like Southey, modern rationalist critics find the supernatural world of "The Ancient Mariner" unintelligible and pointlessly mysterious. But to Coleridge, who believed in the possibility of knowing that which cannot be apprehended by the senses, the spirit world of Christianity was real. And he used it in the poem to give universality to the Mariner's experience of sin, punishment, and redemption. Although he did not require that a poem adhere to factual probability, in the process of rewriting he eliminated the marvelous details which were merely theatrical and irrelevant to his main purpose of conveying the Mariner's spiritual states. The incident of the spectre-ship, for example, is not meaningless horror but the Mariner's perception of the terror of alienation from God, of utter spiritual isolation.

The events of Part VI are not pointless supernaturalism
but a repetition of the pattern of alternate suffering
and relief that is the Mariner's penance. The interre-
lation of two narrative situations is not just a device
to avoid a sprawling structure but a means of pointing
to the contrast between past and present, between two
opposing spiritual states, between two different modes
of being. The supernatural manifestations help define
the Mariner's level of being.

332.   Campbell, Clare. "The Ancient Mariner," *CQ*, 7 (1965),
        93.

        Contrary to William Empson's view (see item 315), "The
        Ancient Mariner" is a Christian poem. The blessing of
        the water-snakes releases the Mariner from unwilled evil
        though not from his individual responsibility.

333.   Chandler, Alice. "Structure and Symbol in 'The Rime of
        the Ancient Mariner,'" *MLQ*, 26 (1965), 401-413.

        Drawing several images from the Book of Revelation,
        Coleridge interweaves structure and symbol in a central
        pattern of destruction and rebirth through the technique
        of repetition by inversion and modulation. The homeward
        journey reverses the departure and many of the events
        following it. The Mariner's joy in human companionship
        as he walks to church replaces his lonely sea journey
        away from the church, and his compulsive speech reverses
        his silence. Most of the inversions, however, belong to
        a series of modulations, such as the sequences of images
        built on the wind, on sound, on the color red, on feed-
        ing and drinking, on motion, and on circles and clefts.
        Thus by the time the Mariner blesses the water-snakes,
        they have become part of a chain which associates them
        with the albatross, the angelic troop, the seraph band,
        and the whirlpool in the bay. The rosy-red bride turns
        into the red-lipped Life-in-Death and finally into the
        Bride of the Lamb.

334.   Chayes, Irene H. "A Coleridgean Reading of 'The Ancient
        Mariner,'" *SIR*, 4 (1965), 81-103.

        The narrative point of view, the epigraph from Thomas
        Burnet, the parallels and allusions in chapter XII of
        Biographia Literaria and in the parable of the two kinds
        of mystics in *Aids to Reflection*--these pieces of evi-
        dence point to Coleridge's association of "The Ancient
        Mariner" with the problem of the limitation of human

knowledge. Epistemological error marks almost every
stage of the Mariner's adventure. The voyage itself,
unconsidered and unguided, would be, in Coleridge's
terms, a transgression of the "bounds and purposes of
our intellectual faculties." Normal human understanding
has not equipped the Mariner to comprehend the sea
world: in shooting the albatross he attempts to perceive
with the senses what Christian orthodoxy leaves without
sensible form. As a result, in the becalming episode,
he suffers from delusion and delirium, dramatized most
obviously in the appearance of the skeleton ship. Only
in his imaginative vision of the water-snakes and later
in the universal harmony of the dawn singing scene is
the mode of perception appropriate to the object. The
returned Mariner continues to make errors of judgment
and discrimination. By his literal answer to the Hermit's
question, the mechanical repetitions of his tale, and
the concluding moral aphorism, he demonstrates a mis-
understanding of the Hermit and of his own experience.
Ironically, it is not the Mariner but the Wedding-Guest
who has been made wiser.

335. Coburn, Kathleen. "Reflections in a Coleridge Mirror:
      Some Images in His Poems," in *From Sensibility to
      Romanticism: Essays Presented to Frederick A. Pottle*,
      ed. Frederick W. Hilles and Harold Bloom (New York:
      Oxford University Press, 1965), pp. 415-437.

      That Coleridge continued to think and feel like a poet
      is evidenced by his sensitive use of a cluster of images
      including the mirror, the babe at the mother's breast,
      the spring with the cone of sand at the bottom, the bee,
      the spider, and the sheltering tree. Found also in
      Quarles's twelfth emblem, Book I, and its accompanying
      illustration, these images arise from the search for
      the self and the related attempt to reconcile inner con-
      flicts expressed in the notebooks and in such late poems
      as "Work without Hope," "Inscription for a Fountain on
      a Heath," and "Youth and Age."

336. ———. "Who Killed Christabel?" *TLS*, May 20, 1965,
      p. 397.

      Supporting the evidence presented by T.F. Dibdin and
      Elisabeth Schneider (see items 173, 288), a notebook
      entry of September-October, 1829, indicates that Cole-
      ridge himself believed Tom Moore, not Hazlitt, wrote the
      notorious attack on "Christabel" in the *Edinburgh Review*.

337. Fleissner, Robert F. "The Mystical Meaning of Five: A
      Notelet on 'Kubla Khan,'" *ES*, 46 (1965), 45.

      Recognizing the presence of five in nature and religious
      ritual and its significance in pagan lore, architecture,
      painting, and nineteenth-century experimental psychology,
      Coleridge substituted it (1. 6) for the "six" of the
      Crewe MS. in order to suggest the idea of finiteness
      linked with infinity.

338. Gerber, Richard. "Cybele, Kubla Khan, and Keats: An
      Essay on Imaginative Transmutation," *ES*, 46 (1965),
      369–389.

      The imaginative center of "Kubla Khan" is the dream-
      alliance between Kubla and Cybele. (See item 298.)
      Submerged in the walls and towers and fertile ground of
      the first section, the chthonic goddess appears directly
      in the second section in such images as the green forested
      hill, the panting earth, and the wailing woman. The
      mighty fountain and the "cedarn cover" (1. 13) developed
      under the additional influences of descriptions in Pur-
      chas, Bartram, and Bruce. This association of Kubla
      and Cybele is echoed in Book II of *Endymion* when Cybele,
      with no narrative function, appears just a few lines
      after the "Kubla Khan" passage (11. 593–636).

339. Houston, Neal B. "Fletcher Christian and 'The Rime of
      the Ancient Mariner,'" *DR*, 45 (1965), 431–446.

      In addition to Coleridge's notebook entry, "Adventures
      of *Christian*, the MUTINEER," and his knowledge through
      Wordsworth of Christian's return, several pieces of in-
      ternal evidence point to Fletcher Christian as Coleridge's
      model for the Mariner: the identification of the imagina-
      tive ship of the Argument with the *Bounty*, the mutiny of
      which affected some two hundred men; the similarity of
      their guilt, their impetuous crime against God and na-
      ture, and their isolated life-in-death existence upon
      return; specific references to Christian such as the
      Scottish term "kirk," the albatross, the phrase "by him
      who died on cross," and the cross-bow; the authenticity
      given to the moral of guilt and redemption by Christian's
      experience.

340. Martin, C.G. "A Coleridge Reminiscence in Yeats's 'A
      Prayer for My Daughter,'" *N&QNS*, 12 (1965), 258–260.

      Although the description is less rich without visual
      and kinetic images, stanza 6 of Yeats's "A Prayer for

My Daughter" is similar to the scene in the second half
of Coleridge's "Ver Perpetuum" in its paradoxical use of
"perpetual," its metaphor of growing plants to suggest
spiritual harmony, and its religious treatment of a
secular issue, a parallel made apparent by the original
context of Coleridge's poem in an essay on the evils of
the slave trade.

341. Meier, Hans Heinrich. "Ancient Lights on Kubla's Lines,"
      ES, 46 (1965), 15-29.

      The imaginative center of "Kubla Khan" is not books of
      travel or the Cybele myth (see item 298) but the tradi-
      tional dream of the happy garden as exemplified in the
      descriptions of Paradise by Milton, Dante, and Vondel
      and of the Garden of Adonis by Spenser. These sources
      account for much of the imagery of lines 1-11; for the
      quality of eternal mutability, or union of the static
      and the dynamic, which dominates the landscape; and for
      the following elements in later lines: time and its de-
      structive action (11. 20-22), the Serpent and a witch,
      the tainted fountain and river (11. 16, 17, 21), the
      wound of Adonis and the realm of Chaos in which is lo-
      cated the womb of nature (11. 17-24), the Syrian damsels
      lamenting Adonis (1. 37), the eternal war and tumult
      caused by the ancestors Chaos and Old Night (11. 29-30),
      the good Genius as the poet of the last section, and
      Adonis as both Kubla and the river. The pervasive but
      subordinate erotic imagery points to a generalized pre-
      sence of Cybele-Attis or Venus-Adonis rather than to
      the identity of Cybele with anything in particular.

342. Ober, Warren U. *"Heart of Darkness*: 'The Ancient Mari-
      ner' a Hundred Years Later," *DR*, 45 (1965), 333-337.

      Conrad's view of the evil in man and nature is a re-
      versal of Coleridge's theme of spontaneous love as a
      means whereby alienated man can resume his place in an
      ultimately beneficent universe. Though more subtle,
      Conrad's handling of characterization and of the frame
      device is reminiscent of Coleridge's.

343. Pafford, Ward. "Samuel Taylor Coleridge," *Emory Univer-
      sity Quarterly*, 21 (1965), 3-14.

      Though Coleridge always believed in the vitality and
      oneness of reality, he was able only for a short time
      (1797-98) to maintain within his belief a place for his
      own creative experience. In "The Ancient Mariner" he
      dramatizes most completely the living unity of all

dimensions of reality. But in the second part of "Kubla
Khan" his imaginative achievement gives way to despair
over the possible decline of creative powers, and in
"Dejection" he is left with only an intellectual commitment to the idea of an organic universe.

344.   Richards, I.A. "Coleridge's Minor Poems," in *Critical
       Essays on English Literature*, ed. V.S. Seturaman
       (Madras: Orient Longmans, 1965), pp. 1-18.

       Although Coleridge's minor poems are self-contained
       and do not lend themselves to the application of infer-
       ences from biographical details, their meaning can be
       enriched by considering them in the context of other
       poems. "To William Wordsworth," for example, describes
       a light "reflected, as a light bestowed" (1. 19). This
       could be the "phantom light" (1. 10) of "Dejection,"
       the sunlight reflected from the earth onto the moon and
       back again to the earth. The "Helmsman on an ocean
       waste and wide" (1. 23) in "Constancy to an Ideal Object"
       recalls a phase of "The Ancient Mariner." "Self-Knowl-
       edge" is a commentary on the opening of Epistle Two of
       Pope's *Essay on Man*; and "Limbo," the companion piece
       of "Ne Plus Ultra," begins with facetious punning and
       rhyming about the hero of Donne's "The Flea."

345.   Scarfe, Francis. "Coleridge's Nightscapes," *Etudes
       Anglaises*, 18 (1965), 27-43.

       Beginning with "To the Autumnal Moon," Coleridge wrote
       a number of nightpieces, poems in which he specifically
       states that he is writing in the evening or at night.
       In most of these poems he associates the twilight with
       retreat to a state of peace and hypnotic well-being.
       The night suggests joy, and the moon represents hope,
       poetic inspiration, and imagination. But in "Christabel,"
       "Kubla Khan," and "Dejection" the moon has sinister,
       daemonic, and destructive connotations.

346.   Seturaman, V.S. "Coleridge's 'Dejection--An Ode': A
       Reconsideration," in *Critical Essays on English
       Literature*, ed. V.S. Seturaman (Madras: Orient Long-
       mans, 1965), pp. 31-39.

       In "Dejection" Coleridge mourns the loss not of his
       unified sensibility but of his imagination, the faculty
       which had enabled him to achieve an identity with nature
       that resulted in, among other things, a union of seeing
       and feeling. He often describes the transcendental ex-
       perience in images of light such as those in "Dejection,"
       "The Eolian Harp," and "This Lime-Tree Bower."

347. Smith, Raymond J., Jr. "Christabel and Geraldine: The
      Marriage of Life and Death," *BuR*, 13 (1965), 63-71.

      The association of love-life-death, which Coleridge
      probably found in Crashaw's poem on Saint Theresa, is
      one of the major themes in "Christabel." It appears in
      the central image of the symbolic and ironic marriage
      between Christabel and Geraldine, the dead child of Sir
      Roland. It is emphasized by the recurring mention of
      the death of Christabel's mother in childbirth; the para-
      site images such as the dormant oak tree on which are
      growing moss and mistletoe; the central image in Part II
      of the struggle between the snake and the dove; the color
      imagery which connects red with Christabel and life,
      and white with Geraldine and death; and the flux between
      love and hate seen in Leoline's rage, the sin for which
      Christabel is suffering in expiation.

348. Canceled.

349. Suther, Marshall. *Visions of Xanadu*. New York:
      Columbia University Press, 1965.

      Contrary to the arguments of Elisabeth Schneider
      (developed in item 155 and countered in the first chap-
      ter of this item and in item 204), a study of the
      images of "Kubla Khan" as they appear in a wide variety
      of Coleridge's other poems illuminates their symbolic
      meaning in "Kubla Khan." Kubla, for example, is not
      likely a villain. He is not associated mainly with evil
      or the artificial but with poetry and the absolute.
      Neither is his pleasure dome artificial in an unfavor-
      able sense; rather, it and the garden represent security
      and fulfillment, a refuge for vision and the resulting
      knowledge and delight. Thus, the paradise envisioned by
      the speaker is not false, though it is part of a contin-
      uing reality which includes the sinister as well.
      This combination of beauty and terror that exists in
      his natural-supernatural-artificial world is particu-
      larly suggested by the images in lines 12-36. The chasm
      is both beautiful and savage. The fountain, an emblem
      of the ambiguities in the creation of life and poetry,
      is both holy and savage. Afraid to follow her lover
      into such a world, the wailing woman provides a touch-
      stone from the ordinary world, as do the weavers of
      circles and the ancestral voices. In addition, the
      voices represent the threat of destruction characteristic
      of Coleridge's paradises. The image of the dome reflected
      in the river unites art and nature.

The significance of such a union becomes apparent in
the imagery of lines 37-54, which in tradition and in
Coleridge's other poems indicates a concern with the
poet and his experience, the poem and its creation, and
the world in which they exist. The Abyssinian maid in
a sense corresponds to the poet himself and, along with
the images of music and the mountain, suggests inspiration. Here and in the other poems the figure of the
poet and the image of honeydew are ambiguous.

1966

350. Anderson, Peter S., and John S. Stroupe. "Two Guests of
the Mariner," *EngR*, 17 (1966), 24-26.

Prepared for by the spiritual-temporal, night-day
polarity in the Burnet passage, the relationship between
the Mariner and the Wedding-Guest functions to establish
the Mariner's kinship with all beings, whether bird or
human guests.

351. Berkoben, L.D. "The Composition of Coleridge's 'Hymn
before Sunrise': Some Mitigating Circumstances," *ELN*,
4 (1966), 32-37.

Coleridge's accounts of his walking tours to Mount
Scafell suggest that he relied on his own experience
for the conception and execution of much of his "Hymn
before Sunrise." Although the last sixty lines of the
poem follow the structure of Brun's "Chamounix beym
Sonnenaufgange," the first section is an elaboration of
an entry in the 1799 notebook outlining a poem about the
spirit of a mountain. Other materials provided by the
letters and notebooks include the images of the wedge,
the goats, and the eagles, not found in the Brun poem;
the impression of terror and beauty; the idea of the
mountains as proof of God's creation; and the feeling of
ecstacy. (Cf. items 141, 142, 60.)

352. Carey, Glenn O. "Ethics in 'The Mariner,'" *EngR*, 17
(1966), 18-20.

According to Dorothy Waples' sane interpretation (see
item 13), "The Ancient Mariner" does have a moral purpose.
Not limited to lines 614-615, it occurs throughout the
poem as the Mariner progresses through the six stages of
Hartley's theory of associational psychology.

353. Chayes, Irene H. "'Kubla Khan' and the Creative Pro-
      cess," *SIR*, 6 (1966), 1-21.

      Confirmed by Coleridge's later critical principles and
      by the 1816 Preface, "Kubla Khan" is concerned with the
      process of poetic composition. In the first two stanzas
      the speaker describes a vision, passively received in a
      dream, which might furnish the materials for a poem. As
      his vision begins, it is mainly a paraphrase and elabora-
      tion by his fancy of the passage quoted from Purchas.
      But as it descends to the "deep romantic chasm" (1. 12),
      the details of the landscape are spontaneously created
      by his imagination. In the third stanza he purposely
      seeks to recreate his vision according to a preconceived
      plan. Because of the increased importance of the will
      and consciousness and the inclusion of an audience, this
      new creative process corrects the one at work in the
      dream-vision. The Abyssinian maid, for instance, re-
      places the "woman wailing for her demon-lover" (1. 16),
      and Mount Abora refers to a paradise on a higher level
      than Xanadu. Higher still is the paradise at the end of
      the poem which is inseparable from the poet's ecstasy,
      the fullest expression of poetic creativity.

354. Harrex, S.C. "Coleridge's Pleasure-Dome in 'Kubla Khan,'"
      N&QNS, 13 (1966), 172-173.

      The central image of the pleasure dome, as well as the
      chasm, might have been suggested by a passage in Gold-
      smith's *The Deserted Village* (11. 319-322, 342-344).

355. Harvey, W.J. "Help!" *EIC*, 16 (1966), 259-260.

      Why does the destiny of the Mariner, in contrast to
      that of the crew, depend on the random throw of dice?

356. Hoyle, James F. "'Kubla Khan' as an Elated Experience,"
      L&P, 16 (1966), 27-39.

      It is not the psychology of opium but the experience
      of elation that supports Coleridge's story of his effort-
      less composition of "Kubla Khan." That explains his
      writing such an energetic poem at a time when he had
      reason to be depressed; and that accounts for his fusion
      of diction and images from many sources, his symbolic
      method, his development of an obsessive landscape, and
      his reconciliation of opposite qualities.

357. Karrfalt, David H. "Another Note on 'Kubla Khan' and
      Coleridge's Retirement to Ash Farm," *N&QNS*, 13 (1966),
      171-172.

In addition to its location, within a fourth of a mile
of Culbone Church, its nearby stream and its enclosed
yard make Ash Farm, not Broomstreet, the likely place of
Coleridge's retirement. (Cf. items 177, 31.)

358. Kumar, Shiv K., ed. *British Romantic Poets: Recent
      Revaluations.* New York: New York University Press,
      1966.

      This book contains reprints from items 108 and 151
      abstracted above and from L.G. Salingar, "Coleridge:
      Poet and Philosopher," in *From Blake to Byron*, Vol. V
      of the Pelican Guide to English Literature (Harmonds-
      worth, Middlesex, 1957), pp. 186-206.

359. Little, Geoffrey. "'Lines Written at Shurton Bars ...':
      Coleridge's First Conversation Poem?" *SoRA*, 2 (1966),
      137-149.

      In spite of the absence of blank verse and a completely
      natural diction, "Lines Written at Shurton Bars" should
      be considered Coleridge's first Conversation Poem. A
      verse epistle to Sarah Fricker, it has the intimacy of
      tone and certain structural features admired in the later
      Conversation Poems. In a series of expansions and re-
      turns to the self the lonely speaker moves out of his
      lethargy, backward in time to a consideration of the
      possibility of self-destruction had he not been able to
      envision Sarah imaginatively, and forward in time to
      the realistic hope of their marriage. As in the other
      Conversation Poems his reverie is unified by a central
      image, an associative sequence of images suggesting a
      point of light in the darkness.

360. Martin, C.G. "Coleridge and Cudworth: A Source for 'The
      Eolian Harp,'" *N&QNS*, 13 (1966), 173-176.

      A philosophical source of Coleridge's image of the
      wind harp is Cudworth's *True Intellectual System of the
      Universe*, particularly his musical analogy illustrating
      the workings of plastic nature. His influence on the
      poem as a whole accounts for the shift from the sugges-
      tion of a passive (ll. 39-43) to an active mind (ll. 44-
      48) and for the rejection of the associationist implica-
      tions of the harp image in lines 39-43.

361. ————. "Coleridge, Edward Rushton, and the Cancelled
      Note to the 'Monody on the Death of Chatterton,'" *RES*,
      17 (1966), 391-402.

In his canceled note to the 1796 version of "Monody,"
Coleridge commends Edward Rushton's sympathetic elegy on
Chatterton and reflects its thought and phrases in a
verse fragment that might be the germ of a new poem. He
shows Rushton's influence again in "On Observing a Blossom on the First of February 1796" and in a late revision
of line 73 of "Monody."

362.   Maxwell, J.C.   "'The Ancient Mariner' and *The Squire's
       Tale*," *N&QNS*, 13 (1966), 224.

   The literary source of Coleridge's sun in "The Ancient
Mariner" (11. 174, 180) is Chaucer's "Squire's Tale"
(11. 393-394).

363.   Paris, Bernard J.   "Coleridge's 'The Eolian Harp,'"
       *Papers of the Michigan Academy of Sciences, Arts, and
       Letters*, 51 (1966), 571-582.

   Arising out of the tension between the first two move-
ments (11. 1-33, 34-48), the concluding movement of "The
Eolian Harp" (11. 49-64) returns to the beginning, re-
jecting introspection and speculation and affirming love,
imagination, and religious faith. These conflicting
approaches to God are both means of linking the human
consciousness, analogous to the harp, with the cosmos,
imaged by the breeze. But the "intellectual breeze"
(1. 47) is a God of metaphysics, unconcerned with
morality and religion and apprehended by an inert, solitary mind focusing on itself, whereas the "one Life"
(1. 26) is an indwelling spirit of love experienced by
an expanding consciousness whose freedom from self leads
to an imaginative perception of nature and the feeling
of universal benevolence.

364.   Radley, Virginia L.   *Samuel Taylor Coleridge*.   New York:
       Twayne Publishers, 1966.

   If there is unity in the body of Coleridge's poetry,
it is provided by the theme of the power of love.
Developed most fully in the poems of high imagination,
this theme, as well as other recurring motifs and stylistic innovations, is anticipated by a group of minor
poems including "Lines on an Autumnal Evening," "Sonnets
on Eminent Characters," the two versions of "Monody,"
"The Destiny of Nations," "Ode to the Departing Year,"
and "Religious Musings."
   In addition to theme the best minor poems are significant for their structural unity achieved through the

reconciliation of opposites. In "The Eolian Harp" tension develops from the juxtaposition of the beanfield
and the Edenic garden, of the harp indicated by the
title and the actual simple harp within the poem, of the
pensive Sarah and the coy maid. From the antithetical
personalities of the poet and Sarah arise two different
reactions to the environment and two opposite approaches
to God. The reconciliation of these opposites occurs in
the poet's reaffirmation of the value of faith. In "Reflections" the poet reconciles his conflicting desires
by recalling Clevedon while continuing to dedicate himself to humanitarian causes. In "This Lime-Tree Bower"
he finds joy in the midst of disappointment. With the
conclusion that the beauty in his bower is emblematic of
beauty everywhere, he reconciles the bower and the prison,
the beauty of the "wide landscape" with that of the bower.
In "Frost at Midnight" he brings together the frost and
the fire, nature and the city, the lonely city-cloistered
boy and the sleeping baby.

Structurally, "The Ancient Mariner" is also a poem of
opposites--the natural and the supernatural, heat and
cold, wet and dry, idleness and swift movement, silence
and roaring. Thematically, it concerns the ncessary
commitment to love if man is to rise above the ordinary
world of understanding. At the outset of the voyage the
Mariner is willful and selfish, insensitive and irresponsible. And at the beginning of the tale the Wedding-
Guest, like the crew, is a similar kind of man, concerned
only with externals.

In "Christabel" it is the ambivalence of earthly love
which is the main theme. (See also item 319.) Both
Geraldine and Christabel display a duality in their
natures, and as a result each has ambivalent feelings
toward the other. Such a love relationship is repeated
in Sir Leoline's ambivalent behavior toward Lord Roland
and Christabel. "The Conclusion to Part II" suggests
that in both cases intense love erupted in anger.

Like "Christabel," "Kubla Khan" is unfinished. But as
in other poems of high imagination, including "The
Ballad of the Dark Ladié" and "Lewti," Coleridge uses
antithetical images to demonstrate the proximity of the
known and the unknown, the world of the understanding
and the world of the imagination. The ideal world--
pictured in such terms as the pleasure dome, caverns,
Abyssinian maid, and honeydew--cannot be understood by
the distant ancestral voices and the commonsensical
listeners. Both "The Ballad of the Dark Ladié" and
"Lewti" concern unrequited love; it is only in the

projected ideal world that love is efficacious. These
poems, along with other poems of high imagination, have
a logical consistency not found in any of the post-
Lyrical Ballad poems except "Dejection," in which Coleridge realizes that his afflictions and his developing
interest in metaphysics have pushed aside imagination.

365.   Rothman, Richard M.   "A Re-examination of 'Kubla Khan,'"
       EJ, 55 (1966), 169-171.

       Coleridge carefully prepares for the poet's aspiration
       and disappointment in the final section of "Kubla Khan"
       by elaboration in the first two sections of contrasts of
       exultation and despair, of beauty and grim foreboding.

366.   Sastri, P.S.   *The Vision of Coleridge*.   Allahabad: Kithab
       Mahal, 1966.

       A survey of Coleridge's complete poetry points to the
       following conclusions.   The major themes and images were
       already present in the early poems, which had a consider-
       able influence on Wordsworth's poetry of 1798-1807.   A
       number of poems represent experiments with the sonnet
       form, and some of the greatest are the Conversation Poems
       with their typical contrast of the vast and the little.
       "The Ancient Mariner" has its emotional origins in the
       poet's own inner experience and in Shakespeare's tragic
       view of life; the imaginative pattern of sin, despair,
       and inertia becoming purity, freedom, and energy gives
       reality to the supernaturalism and to the unobtrusive
       moral.   "Kubla Khan" expresses the joy and sorrow that
       must accompany all mortal creation and the speaker's
       longing for the inspiration to create a permanent dome,
       or truth, of which the poet with the flashing eyes has
       only a visionary gleam.   "Christabel" suggests the help-
       lessness of man in a world where good and evil are
       united--where the evil Geraldine is introduced into a
       holy context, where Christabel's unspeakable experience
       is called a sweet vision, and where Bracy dreams of a
       dove coiled by a snake.   The Asra poems indicate a grow-
       ing despair which culminates in the loss of will expressed
       in "Dejection."   The later poems, however, reveal that
       his poetic powers never left him.
          Throughout his poetry Coleridge shows a childlike atti-
       tude toward the sensory world; he uses visual, tactile,
       kinetic, auditory, and kinesthetic images with precision
       and thematic intention; his similes picture what words
       cannot express.   Subdued shades fascinate him, and he
       attaches ambivalent significance to white, black and its

variations, red, yellow, green, and blue. The recurring
symbols of the moon, the mountain, the cave, the sea,
and the river refer to, among other things, the creative
process.

367. Schrickx, W. "Coleridge and the Cambridge Platonists,"
      REL, 7 (1966), 71-91.

      The influence upon Coleridge of Ralph Cudworth's *The
      True Intellectual System of the Universe* is seen in "The
      Eolian Harp" in the concept of a plastic power (11. 44-
      48) (see item 360) and in "Reflections" in the technical
      word "circumference" (1. 40) and in the associated words
      "God," "Temple," "World," and "imag'd" (11. 38-40).

368. Selander, Glenn E. "Coleridge and the Existential
      Imagination," *Proceedings of the Utah Academy of
      Science, Arts, & Letters*, 43 (1966), 13-23.

      Coleridge's poems show an existential concern with an
      understanding of himself and of the possibilities for
      man--including despair and alienation emphasized in
      "Dejection," a living death in the form of Geraldine,
      the restoration to authentic life represented directly
      in "The Ancient Mariner," and the pleasure of an exis-
      tence which embraces both life and death in "Kubla Khan."

369. Shelton, John. "The Autograph Manuscript of 'Kubla Khan'
      and an Interpretation," *REL*, 7 (1966), 32-42.

      The Crewe Manuscript should be seriously considered in
      any interpretation of "Kubla Khan." With no break be-
      tween lines 11 and 12, its format suggests that the
      "dome of pleasure" (1. 31) is the same one which Kubla
      decreed and that the violent birth of the river is re-
      lated to its meandering course through the gardens, the
      contrast implying the difference between the work of art
      and the original force of the vision which inspired it.
      The variant "Amara" (1. 41), one of the pseudo paradises
      in *Paradise Lost*, is an appropriate reference to Xanadu,
      which, as an impermanent product of man's creative poten-
      tiality, is an imitation of God's eternal creativity.

370. Starr, Nathan Comfort. "Coleridge's Sacred River," *PLL*,
      2 (1966), 117-125.

      Images of fountains and rivers appear frequently in
      Coleridge's prose and poetry. In "Kubla Khan," as well
      as other poems, the river suggests sensuous delight,
      power and energy, and the poet himself.

371. Watson, George. *Coleridge the Poet.* New York: Barnes
      & Noble, 1966.

      The most impressive feature of Coleridge's poetry is
its stylistic variety. The Conversation Poem, invented
by Coleridge, gives the illusion of being spoken in his
own voice because of its rich mixture of Miltonisms and
anti-Miltonisms, of the effusive tone of Gray as well as
the plainness of Cowper. This impression of naturalness
derives from the poet's addressing a friend or family
member, a fact that also determines the poem's shape and
direction. The blank verse alternates between calm and
passion as it moves to and fro between the particular
occasion and the general reflections to which that occasion gives rise, returning in the end to the starting
point. Such a pattern makes the verse letter to Sara
Hutchinson the most extended of the Conversation Poems,
even though it is not in blank verse.
      In "The Ancient Mariner," Coleridge more obviously
masks his own voice, at first by casting the whole poem
into medieval language and spelling and later, after
modernizing the style, by adding the gloss which is spoken
by some antiquary like Jeremy Taylor in seventeenth-
century Neoplatonic prose. The gloss and the ballad
form serve to intensify the historical, dramatic element
so that the stated moral clearly represents the view of
the Mariner, not Coleridge. Like many of the Wordsworthian characters in the *Lyrical Ballads*, the Mariner
is simple; through no will of his own, he passes from
the unthinking, animal felicity of youth to the intel-
lectualism and limited sensitivity of the grown man.
But for him and for the speaker of "Dejection," there is
no "abundant recompense" for the loss.
      The main interest in "Christabel" lies in the experi-
mental meter, which Coleridge accurately describes in
the Preface, and in the function of the supernatural.
As in Lewis' *Monk*, the supernatural in "Christabel" is
genuinely there, not a mere illusion to be exposed at
the end as in a Radcliffe novel. Another feature which
would have identified the poem to its readers as a Gothic
romance is the series of unanswerable questions used at
the beginning to heighten suspense.
      Unlike the language of "Christabel" and "The Ancient
Mariner," the language of "Kubla Khan" is strikingly
modern. (For a discussion of its precision and particularity, as well as the theme of the poem, see the earlier
article summarized in item 272.) Some of the last poems,
such as "Work without Hope" and "The Garden of Boccaccio,"

remind one of the conversational style. "The Delinquent
Travellers" is a brief Byronic satire against tourism
with rhyming four-footers which give a bouncing comic
vigor. Recurring themes in this notable group of poems
are unrequited love, as in "The Blossoming of the Solitary Date-Tree" and "The Improvisatore," and the human
paradox of creative despair, as in "Limbo."

372. Whalley, George. "Coleridge's Poetical Canon: Selection
      and Arrangement," *REL*, 7 (1966), 9-24.

      A survey of the editions of Coleridge's poetry shows
that none of them is satisfactory. Besides being incomplete, the lifetime collections have no consistent principles of selection and arrangement, and the two standard
editions of 1893 and 1912 are misleadingly monolithic
and distractingly diffuse. These problems could be over-
come by maintaining the chronological order observed by
Dykes Campbell and E.H. Coleridge but excluding from the
canon those poems not collected by Coleridge and those
printed only in the 1834 edition or in a periodical and
including tabulations of the exact constitution of the
lifetime editions, an index of titles and first lines,
and a system of classificatory marks to distinguish
canonical from the subcanonical materials.

373. Woodring, Carl. "Christabel of Cumberland," *REL*, 7
      (1966), 43-52.

      "Christabel" is a Lake poem in its use of Bracy's
dream as creative vision and especially in its setting
and characters. Although the specific Lake Country
names occur mainly in Part II, the scenic details of
both parts suggest the region of Cumberland. The de-
layed identification of the locale contributes to the
dreadfulness and the credence of the preternatural events.
The psychological complexity of Christabel and Geraldine
makes them seem contemporary. Not absolutely pure,
Christabel indicates her feelings of guilt and responsibility in her sleeplessness, her fearful dreams, and
her cry, "Sure I have sinn'd!" (1. 381). Her innocence
and receptivity to temptation help Geraldine work the
spell. Because Geraldine acts with reluctance and for
her own protection, she is not totally evil.

374. Woof, R.S. "A Coleridge-Wordsworth Manuscript and 'Sara
      Hutchinson's Poets,'" *SB*, 19 (1966), 226-231.

      Since the Dove Cottage manuscript contains versions of
Coleridge's "The Mad Moon" and Wordsworth's "Foresight"

and "The Tinker" which are earlier than those in "Sara
Hutchinson's Poets" and which must be dated in the spring
of 1802, George Whalley's dating of Sara's notebook
(1801) is too early; and his emphasis on its significance
in the early relationship of Coleridge and Sara is mis-
placed. (See item 174.)

375. Worthington, Mabel. "Comment on 'Kubla Khan as an
     Elated Experience,'" *L&P*, 16 (1966), 40-42.

     "Kubla Khan" probably does embody the psychological
     state of elation, or hypomania, especially since both
     parts show a strong upward movement. The date, however,
     is unimportant, and "holy dread" (1. 52) refers to the
     awe in face of the supernatural power of the poet.
     (See item 356.)

                              1967

376. Adair, Patricia M. *The Waking Dream: A Study of Cole-
     ridge's Poetry.* London: Butler & Tanner, 1967.

     In Coleridge's best poetry idea and image are fused in
     a waking dream, or what he called a "rationalized dream."
     Much of his earliest and latest poetry is too rational,
     but in "The Ancient Mariner" and "Kubla Khan" there is
     a mingling of the conscious with the unconscious, of
     shaping spirit with deeper impulse. In "Christabel"
     this balance is upset. In the early Asra poems the
     dream is beginning to fade, and by the time of "Dejec-
     tion" it is completely separate from the reason so that
     feeling can no longer attach itself to form.
     Though inferior in themselves, both the early poems
     and the late poems are worth studying because they throw
     light on the imagery and themes of the Conversation
     Poems, the three major poems, and the Asra poems. "To
     the River Otter" and "Song of Pixies," for example,
     anticipate certain images in "Kubla Khan," where in-
     stead of boyhood pictures they have become metaphors.
     Under the influence of Bowles, such personal poems as
     these show the beginning of the imaginative fusion of
     subject and object which became fully developed in "The
     Eolian Harp."
     In "Religious Musings" and "The Destiny of Nations,"
     Coleridge is concerned intellectually with the same theme
     which he presents imaginatively in "The Ancient Mariner"
     --the conflict between the natural and the supernatural
     explanations of the universe. His notebooks and letters

support the view that in "The Ancient Mariner" any connection between the moral and the natural world is doubtful. The elements of nature are capricious and remote
from man's moral experience, obeying their own rather
than any moral law. This explains the wind's unexpected
lack of sympathy with the death of the albatross, the
ironical verses in which the sailors change their judgment of the Mariner's act, the reduction of the polar
spirit to a possible hallucination in some of the sailor's minds, the determination of their fate by a dice
game, and their death by the light of the moon. Finally,
the Mariner's reconciliation with nature is only partial,
since he is not returned by natural forces and he is
never freed from guilt. The triteness of the moral verses make unconvincing God's relation to living creatures
and to nature. In time, the poem came to have a personal
meaning for Coleridge. The addition of the gloss and
the epigraph gives it a more spiritual, Christian coloring. And various textual changes, which parallel certain
entries in the Malta notebook, indicate that he had come
to associate the storm with his own guilt and fear, the
wind with spiritual and imaginative power, the polar
spirit with the subconscious, Life-in-Death and the
Mariner's fear with his own bitter experience, the death
of the sailors with the possibility of losing Sara
Hutchinson, the waning moon with evil, and the moon
gloss with his own loneliness as well as the predicament
of modern man. Even in the Conversation Poems, his
deeper conviction is man's estrangement from the natural
world, for when he tries to philosophize upon their
identity, the style becomes self-conscious and artificial.
   As in "The Ancient Mariner," again in "Kubla Khan"
the total meaning includes the associations that Coleridge had formed with the images. The Orphic legends
connected with many of the images enable him to suggest
the mingling of the conscious and the unconscious in
creative activity. The river Alph, for example, becomes
an image of the nourishment of the conscious by the unconscious through its association with legendary rivers
such as Alpheus and Helicon which flowed partly underground. The fountain, the caverns, and the sunless sea
add to the suggestion of the unconscious as an ancient
source of wisdom and power for emperors and divinely
inspired poets. The poet of the last lines deserves
the fear and respect of one who in Orphic ritual has
been initiated into divine mysteries; he is associated
with the Tartar priests who had the gift of prophecy and
with Orpheus and his followers who returned to life

burdened with the strange and terrible knowledge of the underworld.

In "Christabel" the unconscious is associated with evil. Geraldine exercises her influence, to some extent, while Christabel is asleep and her will is powerless. Through a gradual corruption of will, good and evil become indistinguishable; then follows the destruction of love and the consequent ineffectual suffering of the innocent. It was this vision of evil that Coleridge referred to when he said that "Christabel" developed more fully than "The Ancient Mariner" the truth of "our inward nature."

The pattern of the dove becoming the snake recurs again in the Asra poems. The feeling in these poems ranges from the sentimental unreality of the earliest poem "Love" to the somber bitterness of "Psyche." Only in the short poem "A Day-Dream" do the ideal and the real become one. Here, Coleridge uses the Platonic imagery characteristic of the Asra poems to suggest that through the perfection of the moment, life achieves a measure of eternity. But in the verse letter to Asra and in "Dejection" he recognizes this Platonic vision of perfect love as unattainable. The snake image, with its suggestion of a corrupt or debased love, reappears in his translation of Marini's sonnet "Alla Sua Amico," in the preface of "The Blossoming of the Solitary Date-Tree," and in "Psyche." "The Garden of Boccaccio" best overcomes the abstract, allegorical tendency of the last poems.

377. Coburn, Kathleen, ed. *Coleridge: A Collection of Critical Essays.* Englewood Cliffs: Prentice-Hall, 1967.

This book contains reprints from items 103, 299, 278, 240, 146, 155 abstracted above as well as an introduction to the history of Coleridge criticism, Yasunari Takahashi's synopsis of his "The Marriage of Night and Day: Notes on Coleridge and Romanticism" (in the Japanese *English Quarterly,* 1 [1964]), and other reprints which do not deal specifically with Coleridge's poetry.

378. Enscoe, Gerald E. "Coleridge's *Kubla Khan* and *Christabel:* Studies in Erotic Ambiguity," in *Eros and the Romantics: Sexual Love as a Theme in Coleridge, Shelley and Keats* (The Hague: Mouton, 1967), pp. 24-60.

Coleridge's attitude toward erotic, irrational forces is ambivalent: regrettably but inevitably, sexual forces destroy the secure, ordered, intellectualized concepts of human experience. In "The Ancient Mariner" and "Kubla Khan" the ambivalence is resolved within the poetic structure. The Mariner's diabolical appearance helps him accomplish his mission of moral enlightenment. (For Enscoe's analysis of "Kubla Khan," see his earlier article summarized in item 316.)

In "Christabel," however, Coleridge is unable to resolve his ambivalent feelings toward Geraldine and her sexual enchantment of Christabel and Leoline. The four brief incidents preceding the chamber scene use popular superstition to suggest Geraldine's association with evil, but they can also be interpreted as clues to her sexual, life-giving nature, which later in the chamber scene give significance to the mention of the mother's prophecy and to Geraldine's echo of Christabel's wish for the mother's presence. The evil of Geraldine's seduction is somewhat mitigated by her pity for her victim, her evident reluctance, her feeling of shame toward her sinister powers, and by the blurring in the final version of the specific image of physical horror. Christabel's loss of innocence is not lamented by the heavenly powers and, in fact, seems inevitable since Geraldine is identified with the only signs of life in the castle. But the final image of the awakened Christabel is unmistakably horrible, and the attitude toward her loss remains not only ambiguous but confusing.

379. Fields, Beverly. *Reality's Dark Dream: Dejection in Coleridge*. Kent, Ohio: Kent State University Press, 1967.

Coleridge's childhood witnessing of the primal scene, either actually or in fantasy, and identifying with both parents resulted in guilt, tension between fantasies of usurpation and passivity, uncertainty of his sexual identity, and eventually in explicitly stated dejection and the accompanying paralysis of feeling. This unconscious experience, the dark dream which he sensed was his reality, underlies the childhood runaway episode and the dream of October 3, 1802, and receives objective expression within the paradise-lost framework of the major poetry.

In "Christabel," for example, the dramatic personae are really projections of his own states of mind. The balance of five male and five female personae represents the presence of both male and female elements in his personality. (The fifth male is the tallest of the five kidnappers, a demon-lover who is the disguise for Christabel's absent lover; the fifth female is the baron's mastiff bitch, who is the disguise for Geraldine's mother.) Bracy, the "good" father, is the result of Coleridge's repression of agressiveness such as that represented collectively by the five kidnappers. Christabel and Geraldine are ambiguous in that neither one is completely good or bad, victim or victimizer. Christabel prays at the beginning under the oak tree and later after she has witnessed the primal scene between her father and Geraldine. On both occasions she adopts the pose of innocence to mask the feelings of aggression evidenced in such acts as carrying Geraldine across the threshold and offering her the elixir. Geraldine shows even more reluctance in the face of intimacy. Both she and Christabel have ambiguous sexual identities as seen in the horrifying description of Geraldine's undressing, in Christabel's identifying with both Leoline and Geraldine as she watches the primal scene, and in the suggestion of the mistletoe on the tree under which she prays.

In "The Ancient Mariner" Coleridge's sexual uncertainty appears in the image of the dead bird hanging at the Mariner's breast in a pendant position and in the serpentine, or phallic, imagery toward which he first feels animosity and later an unconscious homoeroticism. The blessing, like the stated moral, is an expression of passivity meant to disguise unacceptable aggression. The shooting of the bird is another indication of Coleridge's unconscious tension between the fantasies of usurpation and passivity. And as in "Christabel," punishment follows the witnessing of the primal scene (the pair on the deck of the phantom ship).

In the first section of "Kubla Khan" the narrator describes the primal scene in imagery which suggests the sexual harmony of male (river, towers) and female (dome, walls, caverns). But in the second section he presents an alternative point of view; the description has overtones of horror, as if he were imagining himself in the role of both the father and the mother. In the third section he becomes a poet-priest in an effort to deny his aggressions. The main theme which emerges from the two-part structure ("he can" but "I cannot") is the rivalry between Kubla Khan, who is mainly a father figure and who can decree his Eve and his Eden of sexuality, and the narrator, who because he has repressed the female element in his personality, cannot now revive it. In this context of rivalry the prophesied "war" refers to the endless war between generations of fathers and sons.

In the verse letter to Sara Hutchinson, the first draft of "Dejection," Coleridge's tensions and guilt resulted

in his most self-destructive mood. Having viewed the
primal scene represented by the image of the two moons,
he feels that he ought to be punished by death. He
wishes for the silencing of the lute and for the swelling gust and night showers. He is hesitant to express
his feelings and claims to have no verbal outlet because
they are feelings of aggression toward Sara as well as
himself. He attempts to disguise his animosity toward
her by speaking of her "wild Eyes" that pray and bless
after he has imagined her death ("sod-built Seat"), by
recalling the incident with her and Mary, by insisting
on his concern for her happiness, by extravagantly apologizing for having caused her pain, and by praying for
her sleep. But his hostile fantasies burst forth in
the catalogue of the wind's activities. He imagines the
pain and suffering simultaneously for Sara and for himself as punishment for such unacceptable impulses. He
shows sexual uncertainty by emphasizing, earlier in the
poem, the optical illusion of the moving stars and by
addressing the poem first to Sara and then to Wordsworth.
Uncertainty of his sexual identity and tension between
fantasies of punishment and passivity have resulted in a
general as well as sexual paralysis.

379a. Fleissner, Robert F. "Shakespeare in Xanadu," *Shake-
       speare Studies* (Japan), 6 (1967-68), 94-102.

       Parallels between "Kubla Khan" and *The Tempest* suggest
       that Coleridge was unconsciously inspired by the charac-
       ters, underlying meaning, and music of the play. Both
       the Khan and Prospero are superhuman and mysterious, and
       both Caliban and Coleridge's demon-lover combine savagery
       with enchantment. Primitivism is suggested by the "milk
       of Paradise" (1. 54) and by Caliban, who anticipates the
       noble savage. The song of the Abyssinian maid functions
       for relief, like the lyrics of Ariel; and the musical
       balance of the whole poem resembles the harmony at the
       end of the play.

380. Hassler, Donald M. "Coleridge, Darwin, and the Dome,"
       Serif, 4 (1967), 28-31.

       Coleridge consistently associated Darwin with ambition
       and may have connected his description in 1803 of the
       Temple of the Goddess Nature (*The Temple of Nature*, I, 89-
       92) with Kubla's pleasure dome.

381. Healey, George H. "A Sleeper in New Bond Street," *CLJ*,
       No. 2 (1967), 86-89.

The Cornell Library has recently discovered and pur-
chased a "sleeper," or unrecognized rarity, the third
copy of Coleridge's *Sonnets from Various Authors*. (Cf.
item 399.)

382. Martin, C.G. "Coleridge and William Crowe's 'Lewesdon
Hill,'" *MLR*, 62 (1967), 400-406.

Coleridge's "Reflections" resembles the experience,
the details, and the style of Crowe's "Lewesdon Hill,"
a poem which Coleridge probably read in March, 1795,
and which he later credited with helping him achieve a
natural diction. This relationship supports Humphry
House's derivation of the Conversation Poems from the
descriptive-meditative eighteenth-century local poem
(see item 151) and underlines the extent to which Coleridge gave structure and complexity to the genre.

383. ————. "Coleridge, Edward Rushton and the Cancelled
Note to the 'Monody on the Death of Chatterton,'" *RES*,
NS 18 (1967), 174.

The lines of verse in Coleridge's canceled note to
"Monody" are not Coleridge's reminiscence of some lines
in Rushton's elegy (see item 361) but are a quotation
from Gray's "Stanzas to Mr. Bentley."

384. ————. "Coleridge's 'Lines to Thelwall': A Corrected
Text and a First Version," *SB*, 20 (1967), 254-257.

The unpublished "Lines to Thelwall" was transcribed incorrectly by E.H. Coleridge in his 1912 edition of Coleridge's poems. It is printed correctly here, along with
the incomplete first draft.

385. Meier, Hans Heinrich. "Xanaduvian Residues," *ES*, 48
(1967), 145-155.

Although critical interpretations of "Kubla Khan" as a
finished poem are numerous, there remain several problems
for which the following solutions are suggested. Kubla
may be a Chinese emperor and, at the same time, a symbol
of the maker or guardian of a paradise because of the
presence of impressive elementary forces of nature. His
palace is called a "dome" (1. 2) because of its association with Pandemonium. The surrounding landscape is
"savage," "Holy," "enchanted" (1. 14), and "haunted"
(1. 15) because of its pervading taboo quality; it is
artificial in the favorable sense of artistic; and the
description of it proceeds swiftly and suddenly, recalling

Raphael's account of the creation and the Gardens of
Adonis of antiquity which symbolized the cycle of growth
and decay. The erotic imagery of the poem increases the
tension due to the suspense of ethical judgment, and the
images of the destructive hail and the productive grain
reinforce the reconciliation of opposites in lines 12-30.
Finally, the rich undertones of the visionary language
may be explained as a contribution of the imagery of the
Prophets Isaiah and Jeremiah.

386.   Ower, John.   "Another Analogue of Coleridge's 'Kubla
          Khan,'" *N&QNS*, 14 (1967), 294.

       Lines 1-12 of Gray's ode "The Progress of Poesy" de-
       scribe a stream analogous to the sacred river in "Kubla
       Khan."

387.   Canceled.

388.   Robertson, Jean.   "The Date of Coleridge's 'Kubla Khan,'"
          RES, NS 18 (1967), 438-439.

       The October 6, 1798, entry in Dorothy Wordsworth's
       journal does not invalidate Schneider's dating of "Kubla
       Khan" in 1799-1800 (see item 155) because Dorothy's use
       of "Kubla" for their drinking container refers to the
       German word *Kübel* or *Kublein*, a vat, tub, milking pail,
       or bucket.

389.   Røstvig, Maren-Sofie.   "'The Rime of the Ancient Mariner'
          and the Cosmic System of Robert Fludd," *Tennessee
          Studies in Literature*, 12 (1967), 69-81.

       The Mariner's crime is not disproportionate to its
       terrible consequences if the source of Coleridge's sym-
       bolism is seen as Renaissance syncretic Neoplatonism, a
       tradition which includes Hermetic and Cabalistic ideas.
       In light of the cosmology of Fludd's *Mosaicall Philosophy*
       (1659), an influential summary of the syncretic trend,
       the Mariner's thoughtless killing of the albatross is a
       willful breaking of the universal bond of love. It sig-
       nifies his ignorance of the spiritual powers governing
       all earthly phenomena. He comes to recognize these
       powers partly through God's action in the meterological
       occurrences.

390.   San Juan, E., Jr.   "Coleridge's 'The Eolian Harp' as
          Lyric Paradigm," *Person*, 48 (1967), 77-88.

In spite of its dramatic context, "The Eolian Harp" demonstrates a distinguishing feature of the lyric, the interaction of the scene and the isolated consciousness of the speaker. Although he addresses Sarah, he conveys a feeling of solitary exclusiveness in his possession of her and in his direction of her attention, as well as the reader's, to the external world of nature. He returns to the single self again with the word "Snatch'd" (1. 10), with the description of the spatial particularity of the harp (11. 12-13), with the introduction of another time and place (1. 34), and with the affirmation in the last verse paragraph of the reality of "this cot" and the "heart-honour'd Maid" (1. 64).

391.   Schulz, Max F. *"The Soother of Absence*: An Unwritten Work by S.T. Coleridge," *SoRA*, 2 (1967), 289-297.

Among the projected works attesting to Coleridge's efforts to revive his poetic imagination is a collection of at least fifteen poems concerned with his hopeless love for Sara Hutchinson. Originally conceived in 1802 as a long topographical poem in praise of the power of nature to calm distressed minds, by 1807 "The Soother of Absence" had grown to include such themes as the dependence of imaginative fruitfulness on domestic affections, the efficacy of love to give joy and peace, and the nature of love in very young children. These ideas reflect Coleridge's urge to find in love a spiritual meaning.

392.   Sharma, R.C., ed. *Coleridge: The Ancient Mariner*. New Delhi: Aarti Book Centre, 1967.

The editor's "Introduction" (pp. 1-44) discusses the thematic and structural aspects of "The Ancient Mariner" in order to suggest its richness and complexity, and a second essay by him, "'The Ancient Mariner': An Interpretation" (pp. 45-71), views the poem as a whole. A convincing interpretation of "The Ancient Mariner" must recognize its ballad form and meter, its refinement and modification of the supernatural tradition, its medieval atmosphere, the thematic and structural relevance of the Wedding-Guest, and Coleridge's stated interest in universal human emotions. The poem has all the qualities of the old ballads but surpasses them in realistic narration and description, in subtle delineation of mental experiences, and in metrical variety. In its treatment of supernatural events the emphasis lies not on the wonder

but on the Mariner's feelings of horror, pity, pain, and
joy under their impact. Unlike other literature in the
supernatural tradition, it concludes with a moral which
is both appropriate and adequate because it grows out of
the central event and carries the force of a revelation.
It uses the Wedding-Guest to show the interpenetration
of two levels of reality, to reinforce the Mariner's
experience, to highlight his various spiritual crises,
and to record the reader's emotional reactions to the
tale.

The subject of the poem is thus the humanizing experience whereby the Mariner and the Wedding-Guest acquire,
through suffering, an all-embracing pity and sympathy
and an appreciation of beauty which enable them to par-
ticipate in a wider fellowship. The tension between
companionship and isolation begins when the Wedding-
Guest is prevented from joining his friends and continues
when the merry spirit of camaraderie among the crew is
broken by the ship's isolation in the land of ice. Companionship is temporarily reestablished by the coming of
the albatross, the Mariner's blessing of the water-
snakes, his rescue by representatives of the human community, and his momentary contacts with those whom he
chooses to teach.

393.   Simmons, J.L. "Coleridge's 'Dejection: An Ode': A Poet's
       Regeneration," *UR*, 33 (1967), 212-218.

Contrary to the general critical opinion, the conclusion of "Dejection" is affirmative and poetically coherent. (See items 349, 306, 294, and, for contrast,
items 121, 134.) The poet's problem is a comprehensive,
moral one: having cut himself off from the external
world, he has lost not just his imagination but his
life--his "genial spirits" (1. 39), his joy, his ability
to feel, to love, and to communicate. This antithesis
between life and death is established at the beginning
of the poem, developed by the images of the wedding gar-
ment and shroud, and resolved in the last two strophes
by the poet's regeneration. Before his imagination begins to work, he responds to the moon and the storm like
the lute, mechanically remembering an old ballad and a
tale that Otway might have written. But thinking of the
lost child activates his love for the Lady, which so puri-
fies his heart that he can send his soul abroad in an
expression of that love.

394.   Stuart, J.A. "The Augustinian 'Cause of Action' in
       Coleridge's *Rime of the Ancient Mariner*," *HTR*, 60
       (1967), 177-211.

The theme, or "cause of action," in "The Ancient
Mariner," as well as various prose statements, indicates
Coleridge's interest in the Christian Platonism of Augustine, especially the doctrines centering on the concept
of original sin. The Mariner's shooting of the albatross
represents the latent evil in his will which determines
the self to sin. Alone, he is powerless to free himself:
even when he recognizes his sin, he repeats the wanton
act by envying the water-snakes for living. He must depend on the prevenient, irresistible grace, mediated by
his "kind saint" (1. 286), to free his will from its
corrupt state and to enable him to see that all being
is inherently good and ineffably beautiful. Such onto-
logical optimism, however, goes hand in hand with otherworldliness: as one of the elect of the Heavenly City,
the regenerated Mariner ensures his freedom from sin by
devotion to the mission of making others aware of original sin, by penitential prayer, and by the fellowship of
the church.

395. Sundell, Michael G. "The Theme of Self-Realization in
      'Frost at Midnight,'" *SIR*, 7 (1967), 34-39.

The theme of self-realization in "Frost at Midnight"
is expressed by the poet's musings and by his identification with his son, who, unlike the self-conscious
elder Coleridge and the city-bred child, will be able to
realize himself completely. In the external world the
self-reproductive process is suggested by the images of
frost, the owl's cry, the fluttering film, the breeze,
the clouds, the singing redbreast, and the shining
icicles.

396. Todd, Ruthven. "Coleridge and Paracelsus; Honeydew and
      LSD," *London Magazine*, 6 (1967), 52-62.

In its mystical connection with paradise, Coleridge's
use of "honey-dew" in line 53 of "Kubla Khan" conforms
to the descriptions in Paracelsus and alchemical tradition of the visionary attributes of honeydew of ergot,
or the psychedelic experience derived from LSD.

397. Walsh, William. "Coleridge and Poetry," in *Coleridge:*
      The Work and the Relevance (New York: Barnes & Noble,
      1967), pp. 91-136.

Except for the poems of magic, Coleridge's best poems
deal with private experience. In the very early poems,
especially the political and social sonnets, he shows an

amateurish gap between thought and expression, but in
1795 he began writing the more personal reflective-
descriptive and reflective-conversational poems. In
"The Eolian Harp" he manages to harmonize rhythm and
idea in order to suggest the conduct of consciousness in
its combination of activity and passivity, movement and
stillness, sound and silence. The speaker in "This Lime-
Tree Bower" moves from the primary human experience of
absence, expressed as an unfocused sense of loss, to
that of presence, expressed in creative observation
which includes past, present, and future. Of the more
traditional, impersonal poems, "Christabel" is marred by
its air of inexplicability, and "Kubla Khan" is not so
much a poem about the act of poetic imagination as it
is a suggestion about the energy of imagination as a
force which finds its release in images, images that in
this poem remain undeveloped. "The Ancient Mariner,"
however, is impressive for the suitability of its ballad
line and its direct, explicit similes, for the appropriate balance of the unmotivated fall and the unmerited
grace, and for the quietly implicit theme of man's dual
capacity for failure and recovery. After "The Ancient
Mariner," Coleridge returns to the descriptive-intro-
spective poem in which place is important both as the
setting and as an extension of the self. In "Frost at
Midnight" he responds to the universal motion of life
with deep feeling, which in "Dejection" has been replaced by listlessness and impotence caused by a break
in the direction of consciousness and by the separation
of awareness and feeling.

398.   Yarlott, Geoffrey. *Coleridge and the Abyssinian Maid.*
         London: Methuen, 1967.

   Biographical information can enrich the meaning of
Coleridge's poems. In the group of wedding poems the
conflicts between thought and feeling and between images
of confinement and freedom reflect the tension between
his duty to Sarah Fricker and his desire for Mary Evans.
Tension between thought and feeling appears, for example,
in "The Eolian Harp" in the resistance of the coy maid,
in the apologetic intrusion of lines 44-48, and finally
in his rejection of thought for faith that "inly *feels*"
(1. 60). In "Reflections" the dell is set in opposition
to the panoramic view from the mountaintop and the larger
concerns of public life.
   Even in the *annus mirabilis* poems, in which he appears
content with the dell and manages to blend thought and

feeling, the frequency of images associated with imprison-
ment suggest an unconscious fear that Sarah's type of
domesticity might stifle his creative powers. His visions
of his son's future in "Frost at Midnight" and "To the
Nightingale" convey a dimension of liberty greater than
he himself had enjoyed. And in "Kubla Khan" his parallel
usages and handling of Purchas support the conclusion
that he disapproved of Kubla's isolated paradise. In
opposition to its artificiality and sensuality stands
the cumulative force of the second section: the romantic
chasm, suggesting mysterious eternities scarcely perceived by Kubla; the struggling sacred river, symbolically
representing the processes of creativity; the wailing
woman; and the voices of tradition and morality. The
voices also point to a higher synthesis suggested by the
shadow-dome. It is this dome which the poet would create
if he could revive the inner psychological harmony given
him by the full and direct influence of the maid (Mary
Evans). But since he cannot, he describes only imagined
poetic fulfillment.

Like Kubla, the crew and the Mariner himself at first
act on the level of narrow understanding. Having no
sense of the wholeness of creation, he commits a crime
against universal love and consequently finds himself
imprisoned on a desolate waste of sea. Through a combination of the grace which he had repudiated and the
revitalizing of his imagination, he comes to appreciate
the beauty and energy of a universe that exists beyond
the reach of ordinary perception. His experience coincides with Coleridge's own recent rejection of religion,
his recognition of the importance of imaginative insight, and his feelings of loneliness and insecurity.
And after the Malta voyage, he saw the poem as an allegory of life.

In between the writing of Parts I and II of "Christabel," the personal identification became so weighty that
he could not finish it. The poetic representation of a
father's rejection of his child and his faithful retainer
had become a means of exploring his own altered feelings
toward Hartley (the "limber elf" of "The Conclusion to
Part II") and his involuntary wish for the death of
Derwent, his newborn son. The attachment between Sir
Leoline and Geraldine so resembled his own relationship
with Asra that Geraldine came to represent the guilt
feelings associated with Asra. This acquired personal
significance partly accounts for the characters' development of psychological complexity. In Part II, Christabel
loses some of her former self-assurance and innocence;

as her action is circumscribed by the spell, she becomes
increasingly isolated and helpless. Though she had deliberately chosen martyrdom, she did not expect suffering in the form of alienation from family ties. Geraldine develops more individualizing, sensual, and lamia-
like traits. Her presence activates the strong passions
that had lain dormant within Sir Leoline, causing him to
repeat his former mistake and thus destroy his only remaining personal relationships. Bard Bracy's dream
offers a symbolical explanation of the mysterious events
befalling them, but it is lost on his shallow self-
centered understanding.

  The guilt Coleridge associated with Asra and his children, as well as his dissatisfaction with Sarah's con-
fining dell, becomes explicit in "Dejection," where he
describes the resulting dissociation of personality which
was temporarily impairing his creative efforts and which
caused the poetic breakdown in 1802. Since he first
wrote the ode as a verse letter to Asra, it clarifies a
number of points on which the published ode is puzzling.
In the verse letter, for example, it is his strong feeling for Asra, not the wind, which frees his imagination
and provides the stimulus under which the deepest self-
analysis occurs. The wind represents the disorganized
unwholesomeness of his imaginative activity. The verse
letter also clarifies the outcome of his despair, the
reference to Asra's needing "healing" (1. 128), the hope
that the wind "be but a mountain-birth" (1. 129), and
the idea that joy is given only to the "pure" (1. 65).

399. Zall, Paul M. "Coleridge and *Sonnets from Various
      Authors*," *CLJ*, No. 2 (1967), 49-62.

  In the sixteen-page pamphlet *Sonnets from Various
Authors*, 1796, Coleridge displays his freedom as a young
editor, his preference for the loosely structured English
sonnet as a vehicle for propaganda, and his admiration
of Bowles's simple language and Christian philanthropy.
By the end of 1797, however, he had adopted Wordsworth
as his poetic model and a psychological, rather than
rhetorical, strategy for social reform. As a result,
he published three parodies of the earlier poems, the
"Sonnets Attempted in the Manner of Contemporary Writers."
(Cf. item 186.)

1968

400. Alley, Alvin D. "Coleridge and Existentialism," *Southern Humanities Review*, 2 (1968), 451-461.

Much of Coleridge's poetry, as well as his drama and prose, presents the central existential theme of man's estrangement and the resulting meaninglessness and despair. The Mariner's shooting of the albatross, for example, is meaningless and irrational, comparable to the murder in Camus' *The Stranger*. Cain wanders steadily onward but toward nothing in particular. Existential despair has caused the loss of imaginative powers for the speaker of "Dejection"; and after their encounter with the vampire Geraldine, Sir Leoline and Christabel are sure to live under the same despair. Like the existential man, all of these characters desire relief but realize their inability to achieve it; they fight for a life which is a Death-in-Life existence.

401. Ball, Patricia M. "Egotistical and Chameleon: Wordsworth and Coleridge," in *The Central Self: A Study in Romantic and Victorian Imagination* (New York: Oxford University Press, 1968), pp. 64-102.

In both the egotistical and the chameleon modes, Coleridge pursues the Romantic ideal of self-exploration. His desire to relate the particular moments of life to abstractions of thought and feeling appears in such early poems as "The Destiny of Nations," "To a Young Ass," "To an Infant," and "The Eolian Harp" and matures in the egotistical Conversation Poems. The presence of other people in these poems and in "Dejection" helps Coleridge to define himself and points to the dramatic potential more fully developed in the chameleon poems--"The Old Man of the Alps," "The Mad Monk," "The Ancient Mariner," and "Christabel." Neither egotistical nor chameleon, "Kubla Khan" describes the basic experience of self from which these methods of exploration arise.

402. Bate, Walter Jackson. *Coleridge*. New York: Macmillan, 1968.

At the time of the early poems Coleridge did not consider himself a professional poet, half-humorously apologizing that the best of them were merely "conversation" poems, midway between poetry and conversation.

This attitude freed him from the burden of self-demand
so that in the group of Conversation Poems he became
fluent and inventive, transmitting to Wordsworth and to
the nineteenth century generally an effective modification of the late Augustan reflective mode. For Coleridge
himself, however, the lack of a protective, superimposed
form had the disadvantage that it compelled him to defend
his personal good will. Thus in the Conversation Poems
he fell into his habitual role of usher, always surrender-
ing the blessing to another.

But in the three major poems the demands of a more
specialized form overrode his need to demonstrate personal benevolence. "The Ancient Mariner," for example,
is deliberately remote and symbolic. The Mariner's act
is ambiguous and, through his reaction to it, suggestive
of some form of evil for which he is thrown into the
nightmarelike experience of isolation and guilt. Though
he begins to recover from this paralysis when he extends
himself toward the moon, his redemption is never complete. He must tell his experience repeatedly, trying
but never able to understand it completely. He has
learned a profound and simple truth ("He prayeth best
...."), but he does not pretend to explicate the entire
mystery of human life and conscience.

The nature of evil continued to occupy Coleridge's
thoughts as he worked on "Christabel." The main interest
in the character of Geraldine is the ambiguity of evil
and its need for human cooperation. Though too limited
for much development, the actions of Christabel and her
father suggest the ambiguity of virtue, the open admission of evil by innocence, the betrayal of openheartedness and generosity. Such unpredictable contrasts within
the human heart are also the thought of the tacked-on
conclusion.

Unlike "Christabel," "Kubla Khan" only appears to be
a fragment. In the published account of its composition
Coleridge apologetically protects himself from the chal-
lenge within by stressing it as a "psychological curiosity," but its form and meaning suggest a self-sufficiency
not characteristic of his other fragments. Like many of
the later Romantic lyrics, the poem falls into two parts,
both of which suggest the hope and precarious achievement
of the human imagination. The "odal hymn" presents the
ideal in the form of Kubla's paradise which, despite
the monarch's efforts, is nevertheless threatened by the
ills of the past, the expectations of the future, and the
mysterious beginning and end of the river. The "credo"
then modestly and indirectly presents the poet's Amphion
claim to rival Kubla's architectural splendor with poetry.

In "Dejection" and "To William Wordsworth," Coleridge returns to the mode of the Conversation Poems. The thought of "Dejection," however, is far different, for now nature cannot be counted on to meet man halfway; harmony with it is wholly dependent upon man. And as Coleridge discovers in the powerful seventh stanza, if there is dejection instead of joy in his heart, the imagination may create images of horror. This discovery is not developed but almost denied in the coda, where he exits in the habitual usher-like gesture of the Conversation Poem.

The later poems, from 1817 on, are written in a style completely different from anything previous. Intensely personal and not meant for publication, they are characterized by a dense reflectiveness, an unusual, often reductive imagery (the comparison of the negative souls in "Limbo" to moles and live mandrakes), and philosophically sophisticated language. The religious poems--such as "Limbo," "Ne Plus Ultra," "To Nature," and "Self-Knowledge"--are especially impressive.

403. Dendinger, Lloyd N. "Stephen Crane's Inverted Use of Key Images of 'The Rime of the Ancient Mariner,'" *Studies in Short Fiction,* 5 (1968), 192-194.

Crane's gull, wind-tower, and shark contrast, especially in the responses provoked, with Coleridge's albatross, lighthouse, and water-snakes. This pattern of inverted parallelism is significant in illustrating the naturalist's rejection of the Romantic proposition that human experience may lead to moral certainty. Unlike the Mariner, the seamen in "The Open Boat" derive no definite moral from Crane's largely non-committal images.

404. Gérard, Albert S. *English Romantic Poetry: Ethos, Structure, and Symbol in Coleridge, Wordsworth, Shelley, and Keats.* Berkeley: University of California Press, 1968.

See items 240, 239, 263 for summaries of "The Discordant Harp: The Structure of Coleridge's Conversation Poems" (pp. 20-39) and "Counterfeit Infinity: Coleridge and the Symbol" (pp. 40-63). These two chapters are slightly expanded to include brief comments on "Religious Musings," "Ode to the Departing Year," and "The Destiny of Nations" and more lengthy comments on Coleridge's new definition of the word "symbol."

405. Huang, Roderick. "William Cowper and 'The Rime of the Ancient Mariner,'" *University of Windsor Review,* 3 (1968), 54-56.

Cowper's notion of "One Spirit" (*The Task*, VI, 238-240) probably suggested to Coleridge the Mariner's offense against the "one Life"; certainly the moral at the end echoes *The Task*, VI, 560-587.

406. Jeffrey, Lloyd N. "'Human Interest and a Semblance of Truth' in the Slaying of Coleridge's Albatross," *CEA Critic*, 30 (1968), 3-5.

The Mariner's irrational shooting of the albatross represents the kind of psychological truth which Coleridge required of supernatural characters. Unlike many modern readers who find the Mariner's act unmotivated, Coleridge recognized that without "original sensibility" man is selfish and cruel.

407. Littmann, Mark. "The Ancient Mariner and Initiation Rites," *PLL*, 4 (1968), 370-389.

In both its plot and subplot, "The Ancient Mariner" recapitulates the archetypal pattern of an initiation rite. Part I consists of the Mariner's separation from the community, his crossing of the first threshold (the equator), his seemingly immediate entrance into the Otherworld, and the appearance of the icebergs symbolizing the difficulties of the passage. Once in the Otherworld, the Mariner makes his first mistake: he shoots the guide to his initiation. Consequently, in Parts II and III the ordeals are intensified: abstinence, silence, the partaking of blood as a special food--these precede the Mariner's confrontation with the Goddess, who appears as Life-in-Death, the Moon, and the Virgin Mary. Having accepted this vision, the Mariner in Part IV becomes reconciled with a God who for him is the polar spirit, a tutelary divinity who resides in his unconscious mind. Part V contains his rebirth and return journey, magically accomplished by the polar spirit and the Moon. Upon reentering the community in Part VI, the Mariner in Part VII makes his second mistake: he fails to consider his new stature and enlightenment and entreats the Hermit to shrive him. For this violation of his role, the "penance of life" falls on him. Compelled to tell his experience to the Wedding-Guest, he guides the young man in an initiation which parallels his own, as well as the bride's.

408. Lupton, Mary Jane. "The Dark Dream of Dejection," *L&P*, 17 (1968), 39-47.

The verse letter to Sara Hutchinson indicates that the
emotional center of "Dejection" is Coleridge's inability
to maintain his regressive fantasies of Sara as the protective, gratifying mother. As she becomes seductive
and threatening, he reacts with unconscious hostility,
which, after the release of libidinal energy in stanza 7,
he tries to compensate for by the effusive prayer at the
end.

409.   Piper, Herbert W.   "'The Eolian Harp' Again," *N&QNS*, 15
        (1968), 23-25.

        Contrary to the argument of C.G. Martin (see item 360),
        the letter to Thelwall is not conclusive evidence for a
        connection between Cudworth and "The Eolian Harp"; a
        more satisfactory source for the harp image is Priestley's
        harpsichord animated by God; and there is no indication
        that Coleridge's later ideas were present in embryo.

410.   Robinson, Fred C.   "Coleridge, Personification, and the
        Personal Genitive," *Die Neueren Sprachen*, 17 (1968),
        564-566.

        In spite of Coleridge's emphatic strictures against
        neuter "whose," it sometimes occurs in his poetry with
        no intended personification.

411.   Schulz, Max F.   "Coleridge's 'Ode on the Departing Year'
        and *The Sacred Theory of Earth*: A Case for Analogical
        Criticism," *Concerning Poetry*, I (1968), 45-54.

        An underlying sense of original sin gives moral inten-
        sity and mythic dimension to the political theme of "Ode
        to the Departing Year." Thus the "scanty soil" of line
        156 refers not only to Romantic self-pity, to Coleridge's
        future move to the country and his past journalistic and
        present poetic efforts, and to his sympathy for the farm
        laborer and outrage against the privileged classes. It
        also refers to the degeneration of post-Edenic man and
        nature, a popular idea coherently set forth in scientific
        terms by Thomas Burnet in *The Sacred Theory of the Earth*.
        Coleridge knew the work and shows its specific influence
        in the oceanic action of stanza 8 and in the echo of the
        creation image in his description of the potential
        destruction of the world.

412.   Weathers, Winston.   "Coleridge and the Epic Experience,"
        in *The Archetype and the Psyche: Essays in World*

Literature (Tulsa: University of Tulsa Press, 1968),
pp. 63-75.

In various images, Coleridge's poetry describes the
epic experience of the First Eden, the Fall, the Hegira
(Descent, Sojourn in the Depths, Ascent), and the future
Paradise. The fact that Paradise is always a vision, a
dream, or a hope and that Hell receives such frequent
and extensive attention indicates that Coleridge's world
view is colored by a haunting despair. Most of the poems
simply identify the stages within the whole experience or
treat fully only one of them. "Christabel," for example,
discusses in some detail the inevitableness and the injustice of the Fall. "The Ancient Mariner" is perhaps
the most complete account, though it only hints at a
regained Paradise. "Kubla Khan" depicts both Paradise
and Hell, the two conditions of most interest to Coleridge, and concludes with the poet's wish to create the
epic experience in its wholeness.

413. Wendling, Ronald C. "Coleridge and the Consistency of
      'The Eolian Harp,'" *SIR*, 8 (1968), 26-42.

In returning to the actual world of faith in God and
love for Sarah, the conclusion of "The Eolian Harp"
does not contradict the earlier activities of the imagination and the reason. It does express their insuf-
ficiency, and in this way contributes to the major effort
of the poem to harmonize the speaker's aesthetic, philosophical, and human concerns. At first, he has separated
the actual from the imaginary, as indicated by his for-
getfulness of Sarah, the polarized imagery, and the shift
in tone. But as the poem proceeds, he discovers the
validity of the imagination. His daydreams and recollections lead to an objective insight which is expressed
through the reintroduction of the harp as symbol in the
passages of philosophical illumination (11. 26-33, 44-48).
The symbols suggest two intellectual analogies for the
mind's imaginative activity: human generation and divine
creation. In the conclusion the speaker finds that
neither of them adequately explains the fullness of his
own experience.

1969

414. Armstrong, John. "Coleridge: 'The Ancient Mariner' and
      'Kubla Khan,'" in *The Paradise Myth* (New York: Oxford
      University Press, 1969), pp. 124-147.

In contrast to Blake and to his own critical theory,
Coleridge's imagination shows an innate bias toward
passivity. In "The Ancient Mariner" his imaginative
torpor explains the Wedding-Guest's fear of the Mariner,
the atmosphere of nightmare, the shooting of the albatross, and his omission of crucial material from *The
Frogs*--the old sailor and the voyage to the underworld.
Coleridge probably recognized the imaginative drowsiness
in "Kubla Khan" and for that reason insisted that it was
a fragment.

415. Boulger, James D., ed. *Twentieth Century Interpretations
of "The Rime of the Ancient Mariner": A Collection of
Critical Essays.* Englewood Cliffs: Prentice-Hall, 1969.

The editor's introduction (pp. 1-20) is essentially a
revision of item 328. It omits most of the specific
parallels of "The Ancient Mariner" and the *Aeneid*, adds
discussions of Coleridge's biography and the early history of the poem, and expands the considerations of
modern criticism and philosophical context. In addition
to the introductory article, the book contains excerpts
from items 94a, 151, 103, 313.

416. Coburn, Kathleen. "Coleridge and Restraint," *UTQ*, 38
(1969), 233-247.

One way of finding consistency in Coleridge's writing
is to view it in the light of his personal struggle
against any kind of restraint. In the poetry his sense
of self-defeat appears in images of coercion and imprison-
ment. "The Dungeon," "The Foster Mother's Tale," and
"The Three Graves," for example, all deal with external
restraints; and "The Wanderings of Cain," "The Ancient
Mariner," and "Christabel" treat self-enclosure.

417. Dunn, John J. "Coleridge's Debt to Macpherson's Ossian,"
Studies in Scottish Literature, 7 (1969), 76-89.

Macpherson's *The Poems of Ossian* is a neglected source
of Coleridge's three major poems. Even before composing
them Coleridge admired Ossian and knew the poems intimately and thoroughly, as demonstrated by his casual
references in such varied contexts as the Preface to the
first edition of *Poems* and the political address "On the
Present War," by his plans for an opera based on *Carthon*
and for an essay on Ossian in his projected history of
English poetry, by his checking out of the Bristol library
the two volumes of Ossian, and by his eclectic borrowings

in the early sonnet "Anna and Harland" and in the two
avowed imitations, "Imitated from Ossian" and "The Complaint of Ninathóma." In "The Ancient Mariner" Coleridge
probably used Ossian as a source for the rapid, abrupt
narrative style, for the simple diction and such specific phrases as the description of the wedding celebration
(11. 7-8) and the use of "blast" (1. 49), and for the
dramatic narrator whose primitive view of the world
makes plausible such introductions of the supernatural
as the image of the "frightful fiend" (11. 446-451).
In "Christabel" Coleridge adopted two of Ossian's stylistic devices: the use of "roll" to describe the eyes of
Geraldine (11. 246, 595) and Leoline (11. 444, 648) at
times of emotional crisis and the combination of an abstract noun and a preposition in the phrase "in her
loveliness" (1. 237). Finally, Coleridge found the
"ancestral voices" (1. 30) of "Kubla Khan" among those
in Ossian, most likely in a passage from *The War of Caros*.

418.   Fulmer, O. Bryan. "The Ancient Mariner and the Wandering
       Jew," *SP*, 66 (1969), 797-815.

       The legend of the Wandering Jew best explains the in-
tended meaning of "The Ancient Mariner," particularly
its improbable events, its concluding moral, and the
Mariner's continual punishment. Coleridge said he had
in mind the Wandering Jew, eternally repeating his story,
and critics have noticed similarities to various literary
representations of the Jew as well as to others of the
type, such as Marmaduke in *The Borderers*, the Earl in
Scott's "The Wild Huntsman," and Coleridge's own Cain
(items 203 and 124; see also items 292 and 112a). Such
parallels mean that the supernatural incidents of the
Mariner's voyage really happened; they are not his hallucinations. In harmony with the legend, the concluding
moral is not the Mariner's summary of how he has attained
salvation but his explanation to the Wedding-Guest of
the attitude necessary for prayer. The Mariner himself,
like the Jew, remains unredeemed. Though he has re-
pented of his inhospitality, a sin reminiscent of the
Jew's repudiation of Christ, he may never receive forgiveness until the last judgment.

419.   Gaskins, Avery F. "Real and Imaginary Time in 'The Rime
       of the Ancient Mariner,'" *North Dakota Quarterly*, 37,
       No. 4 (1969), 43-47.

       Like other poets of the nineteenth century, Coleridge
understood time as both objective, or real, and subjective,

or imaginary. In "Time, Real and Imaginary" he represents
objective time as an endless race and subjective time as
the different perceptions of the two participants. Earlier, in "The Ancient Mariner" he makes the same distinc-
tion. The wedding in the frame story establishes the
real present time; the Mariner relives a past in which
the objective categories of time are blurred; and the
Wedding-Guest gradually turns his attention away from
the future as he experiences vicariously the Mariner's
continuous guilt and penance.

420. Gibbons, Edward E. "Point of View and Moral in 'The Rime
  of the Ancient Mariner,'" *UR*, 35 (1969), 257-261.

  Even though he objected to intrusive didacticism in
  poetry, Coleridge never removed the lines of explicit
  moralizing in "The Ancient Mariner" because they contribute to the structural unity of the poem. Like most
  of the poem, they are spoken by the Mariner, a passive,
  superstitious Catholic sailor. They represent his limited
  understanding of the significance of what has happened.

421. Gingerich, Solomon Francis. "Coleridge," in *Essays in
  the Romantic Poets* (New York: Octagon Books, 1969),
  pp. 17-87.

  Essentially a reprint of "From Necessity to Transcendentalism in Coleridge," *PMLA*, 35 (1920), 1-59, this
  essay gives a more compact treatment of "Religious
  Musings" and "The Destiny of Nations" and a fuller discussion of "The Ancient Mariner" and *The Friend*. But
  since the expansion consists mainly of fuller quotations
  and added comments which sometimes had originally appeared as footnotes, the only significant revision is
  the seven-page discussion of Coleridge's literary
  criticism.

422. Haven, Richard. *Patterns of Consciousness: An Essay on
  Coleridge*. Amherst: University of Massachusetts Press,
  1969.

  In "The Ancient Mariner," Coleridge most fully develops
  his concern with the figure of the mental traveler, the
  systolic rhythm of his experience, and, upon his return,
  the confrontation with commonplace reality. The Mariner's voyage takes him out of time and space, the world
  of ordinary consciousness, and into an extraordinary,
  inner world where he discovers the extremes of alienation
  and communion, of contraction and expansion of self.

Neither he nor the rational minds he encounters understand his experience, though he does *know* what has happened and witnesses to it with authority and persuasion.
In contrast to the Mariner, the returned travelers in
"Reflections" and "The Eolian Harp" dismiss their visions
of wholeness and revert to the public language of social
ethics and religious orthodoxy. In both poems the
speakers' participation in expanded consciousness is
prepared for by imagery which de-emphasizes the distinc-
tion between thing and thing. But in addition to such
careful preparation, [the reconciliation of inner and
public experience] in "This Lime-Tree Bower" makes it a
more satisfying treatment of the patterns of experience
in "The Ancient Mariner."

423.   Jacobus, Mary. "William Huntington's 'Spiritual Sea-
       Voyage': Another Source for 'The Ancient Mariner,'"
       N&QNS, 16 (1969), 409-412.

       Although William Huntington's "A Spiritual Sea-Voyage"
       is more reassuring and straightforward, it could have
       been a source for several events in "The Ancient Mari-
       ner"--the ship's becalming, the crew's doubt and conten-
       tiousness, the Mariner's being singled out as the cause
       of their trouble, his lack of harmony with the spiritual
       world, the ghostly ship's approach, the storm that re-
       animates the dead sailors, their angelic song and trans-
       figuration, and the ship's destruction.

424.   Mackenzie, Norman. "'Kubla Khan': A Poem of Creative
       Agony and Loss," *EM*, 20 (1969) 229-240.

       With continuity and completeness "Kubla Khan" develops
       the agonizing ambivalence and loss of poetic creativity.
       Ambivalence is suggested by Kubla's limited control over
       Xanadu's mysterious, violent forces as well as by the
       spasmodic nature of the fountain, the disappearance of
       the river after only a brief course, and the threat of
       war. The possibility of loss, inherent in these images,
       is clearly realized in the caves of ice, in the use of
       "once" (1. 38), and in the conditional tense with which
       the poet envisions his unappreciated poetic success.

425.   Margaret Immaculate, C.S.J., Sister. "Odes of Words-
       worth and Coleridge," *Horizontes*, 12, No. 24 (1969),
       63-67.

       Both Wordsworth and Coleridge faced the problem of a
       changed relationship with nature that resulted in

diminished poetic power. But, unlike Wordsworth, Coleridge could find no relief or consolation for his loss.

426. Rauber, D.R. "The Fragment as Literary Form," *MLQ*, 30 (1969), 212-221.

Coleridge's "Kubla Khan" exemplifies the suitability of the fragment to the romantic ideals of infinity in content and active imaginative response in the reader. The Preface convinces the reader of the reality of an unapprehensible whole and encourages him to continue the poem in his imagination.

427. Teichman, Milton. "The Marriage Metaphor in the *Rime of the Ancient Mariner*," *BNYPL*, 73 (1969), 40-48.

The wedding in the background of the Mariner's tale functions metaphorically to objectify his spiritual union with God and nature. Like the spiritual marriage in Revelation, the Mariner's wedding results in a fresh perception of the world; in contrast to his relationship with the Nightmare Life-in-Death, it is accompanied by images of music and dancing that parallel the loud bassoon and merry din. Its spiritual nature is emphasized by the Mariner's preference of communal worship over the wedding feast and by the sobering effect of his tale on his listener, who is, appropriately, a Wedding-Guest.

428. Visweswariah, H.S. "Motive-Finding in 'The Rime of the Ancient Mariner,'" *LC*, 8, No. 4 (1969), 27-38.

Coleridge intended the Mariner's crime to be purposeful and triumphant, not motiveless. As a young initiate, the Mariner kills the sailors' totem animal when the wind is failing them, in order to reestablish their bond with the father. The mariners regard the bird as a symbol of the wind, as a father who is both tyrannical and loveable. They worship it as their guardian and fatten it for the ritual killing. Afterward, they continue the ritual of totemism by first mourning and then rejoicing.

429. Werkmeister, Lucyle, and P.M. Zall. "Coleridge's 'The Complaint of Ninathóma,'" *N&QNS*, 16 (1969), 412-414.

Except for the omission of one stanza, Coleridge altered "The Complaint of Ninathóma" very little. His increasing regard for the poem may be explained by his eventual recognition of it as an "imitation" rather than a "copy."

430. ———. "Possible Additions to Coleridge's 'Sonnets on
      Eminent Characters,'" *SIR*, 8 (1969), 121-127.

      Coleridge was probably the author of three political
      sonnets published by the *Morning Chronicle*--"Sonnet To
      the Earl of Lauderdale" (February 7, 1793), "Sonnet. To
      the Right Honourable C.J. Fox" (October 2, 1793), and
      "To Lord Stanhope On Reading His Late Protest in the
      House of Lords" (January 31, 1795). Evidence of Cole-
      ridge's authorship includes the signature, "One of the
      People," for both the sonnet to Lauderdale and the one
      to Stanhope; the similarity of diction, rhetorical
      structure, and debt to *Cato* in the sonnets to Lauderdale
      and to Fox; the use in the first two sonnets of initial
      vocatives, diction, imagery, metaphor, and phrases,
      which also appear in other poems by Coleridge; and the
      publication of political sonnets, at this time, by no
      one except Coleridge.

                              1970

431. Bhattacharya, Biswanath. "Mismanaged Sensibility," *LC*,
      9, No. 3 (1970), 81-83.

      In the self-pitying lines about "abstruse research"
      ("Dejection," 11. 89-93) Coleridge attributes his poetic
      sterility to the loss of joy and to the exclusiveness
      of his concern with philosophy, not to intellectual acti-
      vity itself.

432. Bloom, Harold, ed. *Romanticism and Consciousness:
      Essays in Criticism.* New York: W.W. Norton, 1970.

      This collection contains item 327 and an excerpt from
      item 151.

433. D'Avanzo, Mario L. "Coleridge's 'This Lime-Tree Bower
      My Prison' and *The Tempest*," *Wordsworth Circle*, 1
      (1970), 66-68.

      In both "This Lime-Tree Bower" and *The Tempest* confine-
      ment to a lime grove results from a poverty of spirit--
      the poet's feelings of isolation and self-pity and
      Prospero's desire for revenge. Love for a friend brings
      release. And the imagination, working through the poet's
      joy and Prospero's Ariel, animates nature.

434. Duff, Gerald. "Speech as Theme in 'The Rime of the
      Ancient Mariner,'" *Humanities Association Bulletin*,
      21, No. 3 (1970), 26-31.

Indicating social unity and order, speech functions
thematically in both the frame story and the Mariner's
account of his crime, punishment, and partial redemption. When the Mariner shoots the bird that had responded to the men's calls, he violates the reason and
social order on which speech is based. His punishment
thus includes isolation, disorder, speechlessness, and
non-verbal communication--conditions which are heightened
by the Wedding-Guest's interruptions and by the reference at the beginning of the poem to the exchange of
marriage vows. In a world of silence and irrationality
his redemption begins with his instinctive blessing of
the water-snakes. Afterward the albatross falls from
his neck, he can pray aloud, and he hears the celestial
sounds of the mariners in the mast scene, the supernatural
voices speaking of his further penance, and the human
voices of his rescuers. Although he reenters the human
community, his strangely powerful speech sets him apart.
Like the Wedding-Guest left speechless at the end of the
tale, his insight into the social and spiritual dimensions of marriage distances him from the merry din of
the wedding party.

435. Emslie, MacDonald, and Paul Edwards. "The Limitations
of Langdale: A Reading of *Christabel*," *EIC*, 20 (1970),
57-70.

Like the other inhabitants of Langdale, Christabel and
Leoline view the world in oversimplified terms that prevent their recognizing the mixture of good and evil
which characterizes Coleridge's and Blake's world of
experience. (See item 255.) Christabel's limitations
are suggested not only by her actions but also by the
qualified description at the beginning of the poem, by
images such as the lifeless oak and its vulnerable leaf,
and by the use of repetition to point out the contrast
between reality and Christabel's perception of it. Her
initiation at the end of Part I results in dreaming
"With open eyes" of that "which is" (11. 292, 295).
Leoline, on the other hand, continues to respond to the
surface of life, seeing only Geraldine's beauty and mis-
interpreting Bracy's dream.

435a. Gilpin, George H. "Coleridge: The Pleasure of Truth,"
South Central Bulletin, 30 (1970), 191-194.

Through their ascending structure and musical qualities the Conversation Poems illustrate Coleridge's idea
that the purpose of a poem is the pleasure which comes
from imaginative perception of metaphysical truth.

436. Heath, William. *Wordsworth and Coleridge: A Study of
      Their Literary Relations in 1801-1802*. Oxford:
      Clarendon Press, 1970.

      The spring of 1802 marked a turning point in the liter-
      ary careers of both Wordsworth and Coleridge. Until
      then they had written for each other, Dorothy, and the
      Hutchinson sisters; afterward this intimate, responsive
      audience was replaced by a less critical public. In
      "Resolution and Independence" Wordsworth freed himself
      from the counsel of Dorothy and Coleridge, addressing
      his later poems to the people. And in the verse letter
      to Sara Hutchinson and "Dejection" Coleridge expressed
      his sense of exclusion from the Wordsworth household
      and later directed most of his attention to literary
      criticism.
          Coleridge's mood, concerns, and language in the verse
      letter were anticipated by the letters and notebook en-
      tries of the preceding year. In them he shows despon-
      dency, envy of the Wordsworth household, frustration
      over his inability to reconcile his affection for Sara
      Hutchinson and his love for his children, interest in
      Davy's recommendation of chemical study as a means of
      self-control, and conviction that for him poetry was
      necessary but impossible. He began imposing a literary
      form onto his unhappiness when he projected a series of
      love poems, the first of which could be a précis for the
      verse letter, and when he published in the *Morning Post*
      the "Ode to Tranquillity," containing the image of Sara's
      mossy seat.
          Bringing together his concerns partly in response to
      Wordsworth's reading of the first four stanzas of the
      "Intimations" ode, Coleridge read the verse letter on
      April 21, revised it during the summer, and published
      it as "Dejection" on October 4, Wordsworth's wedding
      day. In neither form, however, was Coleridge's attempt
      to transform experience into art as successful as Words-
      worth's in "Resolution and Independence." The verse
      letter lacks control and consistency, although the image
      of Sara as the conjugal mother dove perfectly conveys
      the integrity and harmony from which the speaker is
      excluded. In the first version of "Dejection" Sara is
      replaced by Edmund, the personal lines about Coleridge's
      unhappy marriage are omitted, and the poem becomes a
      statement to a fellow poet about the experience of having
      composed the verse letter and then realizing, after hear-
      ing "Resolution and Independence," how convincingly a
      better poet could overcome despair. But, although the

revised poem avoids the formlessness and self-pitying
tone of the verse letter, it has other problems. The
lines about the giving and receiving of life come, not
as a conclusion based on preceding explanation, but as
an assertion. Statements about the past are made within
this general proposition rather than in the process of
discovery, with the result that "Reality's dark dream"
(1. 95) has no clear referent. And the concept of joy
is introduced in stanza five in its most significant
sense rather than acquiring meaning gradually and then
providing a resolution.

437.   Leitz, Robert C., III. "Fletcher Christian and the
       Ancient Mariner: A Refutation," *DR*, 50 (1970), 62-70.

   Neal B. Houston's argument that Coleridge modeled the
Mariner on Fletcher Christian (item 339) is unconvincing
because it is based on speculation and analogy rather
than facts and because it reduces the poem to an anagram.
The rumor that Christian returned to England conflicts
with the numerous accounts of seamen who visited Pitcairn
Island and talked with Alexander Smith, the one survivor
among the *Bounty* settlers. All the seamen's reports
ʳgree that Christian died on the island. If the Mariner
ᴜust be identified with an actual person, a more credible
choice would be that of George Whalley, who sees the
Mariner's experience as Coleridge's own (item 103).

438.   Lupton, Mary Jane. "'The Rime of the Ancient Mariner':
       The Agony of Thirst," *AI*, 27 (1970), 140-159.

   The dominant impression in "The Ancient Mariner" is
not the regeneration, which is unconvincing and occurs
late in the poem, but the loneliness and stagnation.
The love and acceptance of genital sexuality which
prompts the Mariner's blessing of the water-snakes, the
rain which quenches his thirst and fills the empty
buckets, the sleep which rests his body—these signs of
life renewal are temporary, and the moral at the end of
the poem is a cover-up for his hostility. The Mariner
leads his Death-in-Life existence because in shooting
the albatross he has acted against a supernatural totem
animal who represents the polar spirit and the unknown
forces of the universe. On a psychological level he has
repeated the oedipal crime, and he and the crew who share
his ambivalent feelings toward the father-bird are guilty
of patricide. By repudiating the wedding feast he is
reacting against the sexual desires which made him kill
the father-bird.

439.   Parker, A. Reeve. "Wordsworth's Whelming Tide: Coleridge
       and the Art of Analogy," in *Forms of Lyric: Selected
       Papers from the English Institute*, ed. Reuben A. Brower
       (New York: Columbia University Press, 1970), pp. 75-
       102.

       Coleridge's response to Wordsworth's reading of *The
       Prelude* is not primarily a cry of despair; it is a
       triumphant expression of release. By means of the
       "Lycidas" analogy, which Wordsworth had used in the long
       apostrophe at the end of Book Ten, "To William Words-
       worth" moves from a limited view of self, overwhelmed by
       unfulfilled potential, to a larger awareness of the con-
       tinuousness of self as part of the one Life. The summary
       of *The Prelude* (ll. 11-47), for example, echoes the
       language of "Lycidas" and thus associates the calm, self-
       assured Wordsworth and Milton's angel, self-knowledge
       and knowledge of God. The "forlorn" (l. 61) confession
       in the fourth verse paragraph parallels the lament in
       "Lycidas"; Coleridge becomes the drowned poet, but the
       pathos is mitigated by the elegiac structure of the poem
       as a whole. The next verse paragraph continues the pas-
       toral analogy as Coleridge dismisses his personal anxie-
       ties and the unbecoming grief of his mourning friend.
       Similarly, the last section is more than a return to
       Coleorton; it is an assertion of the one Life--with
       Coleorton analogous to Heaven, the silence when Words-
       worth had finished comparable to the pause in *Paradise
       Lost* after Raphael's account of the creation, and Cole-
       ridge's resurrection of spirit reminiscent of the final
       gesture of Milton's uncouth swain.

440.   Pirie, David. "A Letter to [Asra]," in *Bicentenary
       Wordsworth Studies in Memory of John Alban Finch*, ed.
       Jonathan Wordsworth (Ithaca, New York: Cornell Univer-
       sity Press, 1970), pp. 294-339.

       One of his best poems, Coleridge's verse letter to Sara
       Hutchinson is both personal and universal, moving and
       impressive, seemingly spontaneous and highly unified.
       But in its various revisions, without the personal pas-
       sages and original contexts, it loses much of its power
       and subtlety. In the spring of 1802 Coleridge regarded
       the failure of perception not as a philosophical issue
       but as part of a single spreading disease, a personal
       disability inseparable from his other problems. As a
       result, the imagery of "A Letter" is multidimensional
       and subtly interrelated. The wedding image, for example,
       suggests not only the combination of activity and

passivity in perception but also the impossibility of
Coleridge's marrying Sara Hutchinson and his increasing
isolation from his wife, his friends, and nature. Re-
minding us that the poem itself is a letter, the phrase
"Ill Tidings" (1. 238) reinforces the association of his
loss of imaginative power with his feeling of distance
between himself and those he loves. The image of the
doves contains and resolves the loneliness implied earlier by the vainly wooing thrush, the nightingale struggling to sing a love song, the lost child in the storm
sequence, and his own children. In the revisions, however, the wedding image functions on a philosophical
level only, and vague "afflictions" (1. 82) have caused
the loss of imaginative power. Even in "Dejection: An
Ode" (1817) the transition to the storm passage is incongruous and awkward. The image of the lost child can no
longer look forward to Coleridge's references to himself
and to his own children; its ambivalence is less useful
without the return to the protection offered by Sara as
the mother dove. And the vocatives are used only as a
device.

441.   Pollin, Burton R.   "John Thelwall's Marginalia in a Copy
       of Coleridge's *Biographia Literaria*," BNYPL, 74 (1970),
       73-94.

       Among Thelwall's marginal comments in his copy of
       Biographia Literaria is a variant version of the first
       seven lines and the closing couplet of Coleridge's son-
       net "To John Thelwall."

442.   Prickett, Stephen. *Coleridge and Wordsworth: The Poetry
       of Growth*. Cambridge: Cambridge University Press,
       1970.

       Coleridge conceived of mental growth as the product of
       continual modification of perception. In "Dejection,"
       for example, ambiguities surround "Fancy," "abstruse
       research," "patient," "natural man," "infects," and
       "haply"--not to mention the combination of defeat and
       cautious hope in the imagery of stanza 7. The effect
       of such ambiguity is to suggest that he is not sure whe-
       ther to regard his loss as a development or a disaster.
       A similar ambiguity in the Mariner's experience allows
       his final state to be interpreted as either a new depth
       of insight or irreparable damage. The ambiguity in
       "Constancy to an Ideal Object" is suggested by the image
       of the Brocken-Spectre and indicated by the sudden shift
       of tone from fear and despair to acceptance and

exultation. In "Frost at Midnight" the word "toy" suggests an ambiguous attitude toward the irrational associations of boyhood. This ambiguity, which for Coleridge
was a fundamental characteristic of perception, is present even in "Limbo," where everything exists in a world
of "seems."

443.   Schwartz, Lewis M.   "A New Review of Coleridge's
       Christabel," *SIR*, 9 (1970), 114-124.

       The most perceptive of the few favorable contemporary
reviews of "Christabel" is the unsigned article, reprinted
here, in the London *Times* of May 20, 1816. (See also
item 209.) Its author was probably Charles Lamb. Since
the review appeared five days before the poem, it must
have been written by a friend who wanted to offer en-
couragement. Lamb had been interested in "Christabel"
for a long time and regarded it highly. In a letter
thirteen years earlier he had mentioned details about
Chaucer's Squire's Tale that are the same as those chosen
by the reviewer. Like the reviewer's, Lamb's style is
characterized by digressions and allusions; and in his
review of Keats's *Lamia* volume he, like the reviewer,
associates "Christabel" and Chaucer, selects descriptive
passages for quotation, and calls special attention to
the poet's picture of the heroine in prayer. Even more
convincing is Lamb's letter to Wordsworth of April 26,
1816, in which he praises Wordsworth's *Letter to a Friend
of Burns* and cites one particular phrase as especially
apt. The reviewer quotes from the same pamphlet and
includes the same phrase.

444.   Warner, Oliver.   "Coleridge's 'Naval Poetry' and Southey's
       'Life of Nelson,'" *N&QNS*, 17 (1970), 169-170.

       Under the title "Naval Poetry," the first volume of
the *Naval Chronicle* printed a favorable review of
Lyrical Ballads, quoting two lengthy passages from "The
Ancient Mariner." Later Southey maintained the Romantics'
link with the *Chronicle* by publishing a scathing review
of the editors' biography of Nelson and then writing one
of his own.

445.   Woof, Robert.   "Wordsworth and Coleridge: Some Early
       Matters," in *Bicentenary Wordsworth Studies in Memory
       of John Alban Finch*, ed. Jonathan Wordsworth (Ithaca,
       New York: Cornell University Press, 1970), pp. 76-91.

Before actually meeting Wordsworth in August or
September of 1795, Coleridge knew and appreciated Wordsworth's first published work.   In two early versions of
"Lines on an Autumnal Evening" Coleridge borrows a
couplet from the Errata to the 1793 text of *An Evening
Walk*, and later in "Lines Written at Shurton Bars" he
uses the phrase "green radiance."   Contrary to his marginal comment, it was after meeting Wordsworth, probably
in March of 1796, that he added the note acknowledging
An Evening Walk as his source.   The longer manuscript
version of the note clearly indicates his personal
acquaintance with Wordsworth as well as his knowledge of
Descriptive Sketches, its unfavorable reception, and,
probably, the yet unpublished *Salisbury Plain*.

Indexes

INDEX OF AUTHORS

239

INDEX OF POEMS DISCUSSED